Help Mom with the Dishes

TINA —

THANKS FOR
HELPING MOM WITH
THE DISHES!

TREASURE THE MOMENTS
SAVOR THE MEMORIES

Al

Tina —

Thanks for helping Mum with the dishes!

Treasure the moments
Share the memories ♥

Help Mom with the Dishes

✦

Lessons from Life's Classroom

Albert R. Koch

iUniverse, Inc.
New York Lincoln Shanghai

Help Mom with the Dishes
Lessons from Life's Classroom

Copyright © 2006 by Albert R. Koch

iUniverse books may be ordered through booksellers or by contacting:

iUniverse
2021 Pine Lake Road, Suite 100
Lincoln, NE 68512
www.iuniverse.com
1-800-Authors (1-800-288-4677)

ISBN-13: 978-0-595-39788-4 (pbk)
ISBN-13: 978-0-595-84196-7 (ebk)
ISBN-10: 0-595-39788-3 (pbk)
ISBN-10: 0-595-84196-1 (ebk)

Printed in the United States of America

For Suzanne
  Who taught me how to see with my heart,
  And adds magic to all my days
And for Christine, Kevin, John, and Daniel
  Four of the very best,
  With love.

Contents

Adolescence to "Adultville"

Life Lessons: Passages

Family

Working: Pay for Play

Parenting

Teaching: Chalk Dust and Classrooms

Calendar Contemplations

Seasonal Snacks

Koch's Choice

Preface

In 1990, given an opportunity to pen a weekly newspaper column, I began writing from my perspective as a parent, high school teacher, and resident of a small industrial Midwestern city. Sharing lessons learned in life's classroom, I've sought to convey the joy and innocence of childhood, the expectation and apprehension of adolescence, the poignancy of family, the challenge of parenthood, and the exultation of teaching.

Many of those essays are collected here in *Help Mom with the Dishes*. They celebrate the resonance of life—change, passage, seasons, events, and adventure. These accumulated experiences have become treasures of the heart. Enjoy the resonance.

—A.R. Koch

Introduction

Preoccupied with busy schedules from sunrise to sunset, we seldom pause long enough to give thanks or acknowledge appreciation for life's good moments. Only on a few special occasions do we celebrate and remember with loved ones and friends. We can do better. Every day should be a day of thanksgiving.

That's why for nearly 40 years, I've given my students the same homework assignment each day: "Help Mom with the dishes." It's more than a request for them to volunteer for chores around the house; it's a gentle reminder to tangibly express thoughtfulness, kindness, and decency toward others.

But beyond my high school classroom, "Help Mom with the dishes" has universal application. It serves as a personal invitation for all of us to make our own sunshine and share it with others.

The essays in *Help Mom with the Dishes* are my thank-you notes to those who touched my life and helped me become who I am. Together these stories form the mosaic of a life. They capture significant events, portraits of family and friends, meaningful places, and insightful reflection on ordinary days that became extraordinary moments to remember.

Help Mom with the Dishes is a tapestry of triumph; it is also a journey of commitment. Most of all, *Help Mom with the Dishes* is about promises and love made visible. I believe we should use the gift of each day to enrich, brighten, and enhance the lives we touch with laughter and love. I hope these stories inspire you to do the same.

The Wonder Years

Home

Home is one of my favorite words. Encased within the sound of those four letters are the feelings, emotions, images, and events that give shape and substance to life. "Home," in the words of poet Robert Frost, "is the place where, when you have to go there, they have to take you in." Home, however, is much more. More than a compilation of mortar and brick, plaster and wood, home is a state of mind, a reference of who, where, and what we are. Home is where the heart is. Home is tranquility base, the oasis used to renew one's spirit and refresh one's soul. Home is our safe harbor, a secure anchorage to weather life's storms. Home is family, filled with the laughter and delight of children.

Home is where we bear personal sorrow and shed private tears. Home is sanctuary, our refuge in time of despair and sadness. Home is barefooted breakfast, freshly brewed coffee, and the morning paper. Home is the sight and sound of loved ones. Home is raking a leafy lawn, shoveling midwinter's snow, and sweeping the porch. Home is oven-baked bread, Mom's homemade noodles and chicken soup. Home is washing windows, dishes, laundry, and cars. Home is budgets, grocery bills, house payments, and taxes. Home is stability. Home is change. Home is marks on the wall measuring a child's height. Home is responsibility assessing growth. Home is trust and tolerance, patience and kind words. Home is the main office for "Give me another chance, Mom?" Home is sharing, caring—belonging.

Home is privacy to be alone with one's thoughts. Home is the wish factory for kids big and small, young and old. Home is comfortable sofas and overstuffed chairs. Home is familiar; stairs and floors that creak "hello" with each step—a wall-to-wall welcome mat!

Home is celebration station for holidays; trimming the Christmas tree and decorating inside and out. Home is a house of cards: Thank You, Birthday, Anniversary, Retirement, Thinking of You, Christmas, Valentine, and Report Cards. Home is an alphabet of letters, business and personal. Home is a coin-free Laundromat for college kids home for the weekend. Home is lazy afternoon naps, listening to the radio, or pensive reading. Home is falling asleep in front of the TV late at night. Home is listening to a child's nighttime prayers by the side of the bed.

Home is the joyful noise of children growing up. Home is a service station for teenagers: food, fuel, restroom, and phone. Home is hugs and encouraging words. Home is touch and tenderness. Home is not-enough-hot-water, piles of laundry, and occupied bathrooms. Home is forgiveness and forgetting one's mistakes. Home is the dream factory. Home is "my" room. Home is peace. Home is sleepless nights caring for a sick child. Home is anxiety when adolescents are late. Home is the best diner anywhere. Home is chores and cherished moments.

Home is the hardware store's Promised Land. Home is the bank's best friend: mortgage, insurance, and mortgage again! Home is ground zero for "Because I said so!" Home is "Honey-do" land: "Honey, do this," "Honey, do that." Home is pre-school and playground, *Sesame Street* and *Mister Rogers' Neighborhood.* Home is *Oprah* and daytime soaps. Home is where Mom teaches the Golden Rule. Home is Mom and Dad.

Home is stopped-up drains, bad-tempered gadgets, and overworked appliances that go on strike. Home is writing letters to lifelong friends. Home is cookies and milk before bedtime. Home is reminiscing about "The Good Ol' Days." Home is going to bed early, dog-tired. Home is knowing your way in complete darkness. Home is the keeping place for treasured times. Home is permission to stay out later. Home is rules for using the car. Home is holidays and vacation from work. Home is where skinned knees and scraped elbows are taken for repair. Home is the place you want to be when you're cold or hungry, lonely or afraid. Home is what you carry with you no matter where you go or what you do. Home is protection from scary things.

Home is an attitude, a goal to attain. Home is a Full-Service, Open 24 Hours, No Waiting, Easy Credit, Appointment Not Necessary, Your Satisfaction Guaranteed or Your Money Back—a place of the heart. Home is what I wish everyone had. Home is what every child needs. Home is better than homeless. Home is what really mattered to E.T. Home is where we landscape our character. Home is where the quality goes in, before the person comes out.

And when it's time to leave, home is where we all want to go. Privately, we hope the poet is right; that "Home is the place where, when you have to go there, they have to take you in." Home is remembering the times of our life. Home is love.

Radio Daze

I was raised on radio. Born in 1941 B.T., "Before Television," the radio was always on in our house. We kept the Crosley percolating from morning to night. From early on, I awoke to the morning news broadcast, dressed while listening to *Happy Hank* (featuring his dog Squeaky), and started the day with *Don McNeil's Breakfast Club*. We visited each morning with *Arthur Godfrey Time* and followed the radio soap opera adventures of *Backstage Wife, Our Gal Sunday, The Romance of Helen Trent*, and *Just Plain Bill*. *The Bob and Ray Show* brightened our afternoons along with a variety of network musical shows.

All of these broadcasts served as appetizers for the late afternoon and evening banquet when a kid could tune in his favorite adventure or mystery program and turn loose his imagination. After more than 50 years, the names still invoke fond memories of time well spent. *Jack Armstrong, The All-American Boy; The Tom Mix Ralston Straightshooters; Bobby Benson and the B Bar B Riders; Sergeant Preston of the Yukon; The Lone Ranger; The Adventures of Superman; The Green Hornet; Captain Midnight; Straight Arrow;* and *Dick Tracy*.

We faithfully followed their adventures, and pleaded with Mom to buy the sponsor's product. We needed an ample supply of coveted box tops in order to send for the special offers and premiums. Each hero had their own special diet to fight the bad guys. Jack Armstrong ate Wheaties; Straight Arrow thrived on Nabisco Shredded Wheat; Superman loaded himself with Kellogg's Pep to go up, up, and away; Tom Mix was fueled by Hot Ralston; Sergeant Preston and his wonder dog, Yukon King, fortified themselves with Quaker Puffed Rice; The Lone Ranger and Tonto fought for justice nourished with Cheerios; and Captain Midnight washed it all down with gallons of Ovaltine.

For a dime and a box top or two, a kid became an official member of Tom Mix's Straightshooters. Hot Ralston always gave me constipation, but I shoveled it in until I had enough box tops for a Sheriff Mike Whistling Badge, a rocket parachute, and, an official Straightshooter photo album. While my box tops and dimes went to a magical place named Checkerboard Square in St. Louis, Missouri, I went to the bathroom to diffuse a potential lethal explosion. The radio announcer always urged us to hurry, because the offer was limited. Tell me about it.

Hooked on radio meant hooked on premiums. I ate Wheaties by the bucketful, just so I could send in for my authentic Jack Armstrong pedometer. (I passed up on the replica of Betty's luminous bracelet. I couldn't handle any more Wheaties—I was starting to germinate!)

As a kid, I never thought about a conspiracy when I discovered that *The Lone Ranger* was sponsored by the company that made Wheaties. Instead of wheat, however, the Masked Man, Tonto, Dan Reid, and presumably all the horses, chowed down on Cheerios ("Those tasty little O's"). Because I was wary about ticking off the Lone Ranger (although I didn't sweat Tonto), I ate tons of Cheerios. During one period of my premium frenzy, I needed four box tops and a dollar to buy the complete layout of The Lone Ranger Frontier Town. A kid could buy each section separately for one Cheerios box top and twenty-five cents ("No stamps, please") or send for the whole town—four box tops and a dollar.

I sucked down Cheerios like a starved vacuum cleaner. I wanted the whole town, and I wanted it *now*! I scrounged trashcans all over town looking for deposit bottles until I had four quarters. Excitedly, I sent the box tops and coins to General Mills, the headquarters of Jack Armstrong and The Lone Ranger, in Minneapolis, Minnesota. By this time, the postman and I were on a first-name basis.

Superman faked me out. He wasn't big on premiums, but I went ahead and ate cases of Kellogg's Pep just in case. Every so often, I'd get a chance to send my dime and box top to Superman's branch office in Battle Creek, Michigan, but between you and me, I got snookered into eating all that Pep. Superman was too busy messing with Lois Lane to worry about box tops. He had his own special offer.

I fell into the same trap listening to Straight Arrow. These were the adventures of a rancher named Steve Adams who would change into a Comanche Indian and fight for law and order. Here was a guy with a severe identity crisis, who dressed up every night like it was Halloween. I was thoroughly duped, and never gave it a second thought. Clearly, the guy had a problem. Maybe Straight Arrow overdosed on Nabisco's Shredded Wheat; Lord knows, I almost did. To this day, I can't stand to see a box of those straw-like biscuits. Even seeing a bird's nest makes me queasy. From a nutrition point of view, those pillows of shredded wheat were loaded with fiber; by the end of the season, Straight Arrow fans were passing wicker furniture.

I didn't have any such problem with Quaker Puffed Wheat and Quaker Puffed Rice. These were the staples of Sergeant Preston of the Yukon and his wonder dog, Yukon King. (King probably wondered why all Preston fed him was air-puffed grain while he froze his bazooka off in the frozen tundra.) When Sergeant Preston offered his secret signal ring for two box tops and thirty-five cents, I was so excited, I puffed my own rice! As soon as my ring arrived from Preston's summer home in Chicago, I took it to school to secretly signal the guys. Unfortunately, Sister Bruiser, who was not a fan of the Sergeant, didn't like dogs, hated cold weather, and wasn't too thrilled with anything having to do with Quakers, intercepted my signal and took the ring. It disappeared down the bottomless pit of her nun's garb, never to be seen again.

Sister Bruiser (named after the patron saint of black-and-blue marks) thought I would be devastated after losing my ring. No chance. To me it was just a minor setback. I had plenty of reserve in my parochial survival kit. Sister didn't know that I was also a card-carrying member of Captain Midnight's Secret Squadron, with an SS2 decoder badge. She had no idea what a waxed Ovaltine seal and a dime could do for a kid. There were moments though, when I envisioned Sister Bruiser in a certain cereal factory being "shot from guns!"

Today's kids don't know what they've missed. Television came along and numbed their imagination. They'll never know the adventures that were purchased with box tops and a few coins. Nor will they experience the exciting, spine-tingling episodes of *The Shadow, Lights Out, Inner Sanctum,* or *Suspense.* Those of us raised on radio will never forget. We're veterans of Radio Daze.

By the way, does anyone know where I can get a Sergeant Preston Secret Signal Ring?

Grapes of Wrath

What follows is a true story—well, sort of. Information has been altered in order that my bingo privileges are not jeopardized. Although this happened many years ago, traumatic feelings still return every so often, reminding me of my personal encounter with the grapes of wrath.

The events depicted took place in Sacred Heart School, Room 1. As a first-grader, I liked school—at least in the beginning. To get to school, my two older brothers and I would cross the alley, cut through a neighbor's yard, hike down Sheridan Avenue, hang a left at 118th, walk to LaPorte Avenue, and run the short distance left to Sacred Heart. Never having attended kindergarten, everything was new and exciting. I especially like the stuff that went with first grade: books with book covers that advertised banks and funeral homes, letter cards, recess, small bottles of milk, cigar boxes, crayons, clay, oil cloths, pencils, and yellow writing paper with superwide lines. I liked reading and learning new words. As a left-hander, my handwriting was nearly illegible, so I took extra care with printing my letters and drawing pictures. I liked art, too.

Back in those ancient times, first and second grades were combined due to limited space, so students shared a single classroom. In charge of these future saints was Sister Perpetua. An overpowering figure in yards of black robe and flowing habit, it served to amplify her stature and authority. Fastened to her waist by a braided sash of black nylon, hung a huge rosary. This heavenly anchor of salvation jingled and jangled with her every step. Even after all these years, just thinking about the sound of those celestial chimes, brings on an attack of the cold sweats.

Sister Perpetua was one nun you didn't mess with. She had massive hands that kids more-or-less knew could put your lights out. Without a whole lot of discomfort, Sister could've worn her wristwatch on her thumb. By the second day of school, the guys knew the score: Misbehave in Sister Perpetua's class, and you'd never see third grade!

As I said, I liked art. Every Friday afternoon was art time. Once a month, as a special treat, we worked with clay. As part of the art supplies, each kid purchased two square sticks of gray modeling clay. When not in use, the clay was kept in a

8

cigar box. Students had to procure the cigar box along with a piece of oilcloth large enough to cover the desktop. When clay time came, oilcloths would be spread to protect the surface of the then 40-year-old, battle-scarred desks.

All work in parochial school is tied to religious lessons; art was no exception. After reading the Wedding Feast at Cana to us, Sister instructed us to make something with our clay that related to the beautiful story of Jesus' First Miracle. Sister intended for us to make replicas of the water-filled earthen jars, described in the Scriptures. I, however, full of innocence and eager to impress my new teacher, decided to expand on her idea by making a model of the wine-bearing grapes.

Before anyone was allowed to work with their clay, Sister gave the class two Cardinal Rules, which, if broken, would incur her wrath:

Rule 1: Do not roll your clay into the shape of a snake.
Rule 2: Do not roll your clay into the shape of a hot dog or sausage.

From my seat near the back of the room, over by the windows, I set up for clay work. Unfortunately, as a first-grader, I wasn't too sure how grapes grew. Bushes? Vines? Trees? Arbitrarily, I selected trees. With arduous fervor, I set to work. From one stick of clay, I rolled about a dozen good sized spheres—grapes grew in bunches—that much I knew. With the remaining clay stick, I formed the trunk of my grape tree. Even in its horizontal position, I could tell it was a fine trunk of a tree. I definitely had an artist's eye. Things were shaping up nicely. The other first-graders had made clay jars; I was the only one with a grape tree!

Soon it was time for Sister to check our work. Desk after desk was adorned with clay urns fit for a royal wedding. I listened to her words of praise as she made her way toward my desk. I heard the sound of her rosary and swishing robe. Somewhere deep inside my brain, an alarm went off, and an inexplicable feeling of foreboding filled every pore of my body.

When Sister caught sight of my desk, she hit the brakes hard! Before her eyes, like an alien protrusion, my grape tree stood proud and erect, surrounded by the cluster of gray grapes. Her eyes widened and took the shape of saucers. In a voice the triggered seismographs in three states, she bellowed: "You were supposed to make a jar—a clay jar! And LOOK WHAT YOU'VE DONE!"

Using a doubled fist and one powerful steroid-like swing of her sledgehammer arm, Sister brought the wrath of righteousness—with bull's-eye accuracy—down upon my work of art. In an instant, she crushed my trunk and smashed my grapes! I, myself, came within an eyelash of being martyred. Miraculously, she came to her senses and realized that my artistic expression was not the work of the

Devil, but blissful ignorance. Even so, as not to give temptation a second chance, she took away my clay, taped my cigar box shut, and locked it in her storage cabinet. All in all, it was a very traumatic experience.

Of course, I continued to go to school. Even considering an occasional setback, I did quite well. I even graduated from college. And that's not too shabby for a kid who had his grapes smashed in the first grade.

Lent: God's Diet Plan

This is another of my "true" stories. The names have been changed to protect the Korean orphan babies we adopted in the sixth grade.

Each year, Americans spend billions on diet plans and weight-loss programs. We have this thing about not being fat. We are obsessed with keeping thin, having a slim figure, and getting regular exercise. Health clubs make a fortune as millions of our fellow citizens run, swim, cycle, and sweat on a daily basis in order to attain an image of good health and physical fitness.

Specialized companies sell equipment engineered to exercise every known part of the human body. The garment industry designs, manufactures, advertises, and markets official workout clothes to look good until one is victorious over the "battle of the bulge."

Grown men and women, some educated in our most revered institutions of higher learning, actually *pay* money in order to reduce the unwanted undulations of their bovine bodies. They believe that by running, smacking a ball in a glass-walled room, or going against a machine with the same name as a tropical mollusk, they'll lose weight. There may be some merit in that approach, but there is an easier way, a less expensive plan, and a more efficient method to get the job done. It's been around for a long time, and a great number of people follow it religiously. It's called Lent: God's Diet Plan.

Lent is the period of time preceding Easter for people to practice self-denial. For six weeks, beginning on Ash Wednesday, Catholics are encouraged to give up some delight or pleasure, as penance for living an imperfect life.

The training for this ecclesiastical weight-loss program began in parochial grade school. Lent became the ultimate challenge of will and self-discipline. It was the Church's annual tournament of fasting. Throughout the school, the Sister in charge of the particular class would have each child state what they were going to give up. It was a classic contest of boys vs. girls. Then, she'd set up a chart to keep track of the individual's progress toward their Lenten goal.

Back when I was in grade school, kids would give up candy, cookies, and similar sweet-tooth snacks. (Luxuries like television, videos, and computer games were not yet available to corrupt young minds.) The nun in charge of the sixth grade had been carefully selected for her teaching expertise and because she was expert at handling human units of this age. She did not believe in taking prisoners! She also believed in accountability.

With our commitment inked on the chart, Sister brought a scale to class, and on Ash Wednesday, following Mass, conducted a voluntary weigh-in. Each day during Lent, Sister asked for a show of hands of those students who were being faithful to their Lenten pledge. Everyone with his or her hand up received a gold star for the day.

By the time a kid gets to the sixth grade in Catholic school, he's pretty much figured things out. To a prepubescent male, Lenten "give-ups" are nothing more than a minor detour along the highway of Twinkies and Moon Pies! He also learns how to manipulate the system.

On the morning of the Ash Wednesday weigh-in, several of the boys who volunteered met on the playground and loaded up their pants pockets with gravel to weigh them down. One kid brought in a substantial supply of Red Ryder B-Bs and filled his socks and shoes until he could barely lift his feet. When he stepped on the scale, Sister recorded the weight and chortled: "Giving up sweets will do you a world of good, Matthew." Matthew kept his eyes lowered. (This was standard body language in Catholic school for indicating humility.)

Only boys volunteered for the scale. Sixth-grade girls usually made Lenten commitments like: "I gave up fighting with my brother," "I'm helping my mom every day," "I'm offering ten aspirations for poor people," or "I'm putting all my extra pennies in my miter box." Big deal! The guys were doing big league penance. Going without a Twinkie or Hostess Cupcake for six weeks was torture. But when you are in the sixth grade, you want to impress everybody—so you make the big sacrifice!

The boys who volunteered for the weigh-in were recorded on the chart. Flesh, bones, gravel, and B-Bs all blended together in a graph of pre-Lenten overindulgence. Sister smiled to herself: "Giving up sweets will *indeed* do these boys a world of good. God will be pleased." The boys, however, weren't so pleased. They couldn't wait until recess. Sitting in class with your clothes full of pebbles and B-Bs was *very* uncomfortable!

Sister eagerly awaited each days report on her student's battle with self-control. Religiously, when asked if they were keeping their Lenten promises, the boys and girls would collectively raise their hands and chorus: "Yes, Sister."

Most of the girls, and a few of the boys, actually gave up gum and candy for Lent. But the guys who dummied-up their weight with playground ballast continued to indulge themselves with their usual inventory of frosting-covered car-bohydrates; they were enjoying the best of both worlds.

As Lent drew to a close, it was obvious, judging by the quantity of gold stars on the chart, that the majority of the sixth grade class had taken another solid step toward salvation. And when the loss of unwanted pounds was verified, Sister presented several boys with ribbons of merit to further acknowledge their achievement. The girls, unaware of the boys' shenanigans, were *very* impressed. You boys should thank your Guardian Angel for helping you win this award," suggested Sister.

Actually, the boys were grateful. So grateful, in fact, that they presented the parish Monsignor with a gift box of Twinkies and thanked him for not paving over the playground's gravel!

As the years go by, one draws heavily upon the experiences of one's childhood. The older one gets, the more important those lessons become. So it is with Lent. At middle age, when one's anatomy draws additional expanses of unneeded flesh, like a magnet going to metal, the Lenten diet plan affords a person the opportunity to purge the unwanted ballast and tone up one's sagging landscape.

Now, there are all kinds of Lenten meal recipes to encourage the conscientious soul to cut back on their intake of food during the season of self-denial. The Church helps, too, by designating several meatless Fast Days. But it's not like it use to be. Today, everything is run on the honor system. How strongly one adheres to one's Lenten commitment is no longer monitored by a discipline-minded nun. Nor do we have to publicly account for our resolve by raising our hand.

Perhaps that's why we tend to increase our girth as we get on in years. Maybe we need a no-nonsense, habit-wearing, keeper-of-the-chart to make certain we don't stray from our goal. I, for one, would like to give it a try. Especially now, since I have an old pair of trousers with huge pockets!

Parochial Penance

Some may find this hard to believe, but as a youngster, there were occasions when my proclivity for mischief earned a considerable amount of disciplinary action. As a result of my behavioral creativity, various classroom penalties were assigned for assassinating the rules.

Back then, school authorities (especially nuns) and parents were not bashful about dispensing discipline. Anything short of capital punishment was acceptable. Sentencing was rendered by the classroom monarch. In many instances, the arresting officer, judge, jury, and warden were one and the same person. For the most part, my run-ins with righteousness centered on my reluctance to curb inappropriate behavior, unsolicited wisecracks, and sarcastic quips. Not only did Sister Bruiser not have a sense of humor, she rarely appreciated my editorial comments. Verbal creativity was not welcomed in the highly regimented, structured parochial environment. As a result of my clever remarks, many recess periods were spent lathering the blackboards with chalked penance. Time and again I wrote the same refrain: "I will not talk in class. I will not talk in class. I will not talk in class…" But I did.

The fault for these youthful transgressions was not entirely mine. My guardian angel, whose primary assignment was to keep me out of trouble, was occasionally faked-out by the opposition. With these periodic lapses in goodness, things naturally went awry. Like the time Sister asked where the Declaration of Independence was signed, and I blurted out: "At the bottom." In spite of my classmates' laughter, another penance was issued. Sister was not amused.

With each infraction, my penance escalated. Usually, punishment involved writing "X" number of times, whatever Sister dictated. As in algebra, the value of "X" changed. And in my case, "X" always increased exponentially. Sister encouraged me to go to confession and ask God's forgiveness. She didn't know of course, but I had a standing appointment in the confessional every Saturday afternoon.

Sixth grade is not the easiest year for a kid. For my buddy Hubie Tucker, sixth grade was the toughest three years of his life! All sorts of changes take place, and it's tough to adapt without losing your place in life.

One particular morning, Sister began with a pop quiz based on questions from our *Baltimore Catechism*. As the rapid-fire questioning began, rote-memory answers filled the classroom as called-upon students eagerly responded. I had been daydreaming about one of the early maturing girls in class when Sister called my name.

"Albert?"

"Yes, Sister?"

"Name the Sacraments."

I did okay at first, knowing Sister wanted quick, tip-of-your-tongue answers. The instant I hesitated, she challenged me. "Come on, one more. Quickly!"

Out of the corner of my eye, one of the guys tried to cue me by making a kicking motion, obviously trying to get me to remember Confirmation. Rattled by Sister's insistence, I misspoke and said: "The Sacrament of Punt Formation!" Sister was livid, assuming my answer was a premeditated wisecrack—mocking the Sacraments. "OK, Mr. Smart Aleck," Sister boomed. "For punishment you are to begin with the number one, and write out every number in succession until you use the letter "A"!

Initially, I thought I'd caught a break. Only later did I realize I had to write out numbers up to one thousand before using the letter "A." Had I'd known about Lawrence Welk's method of counting, I would have been home free. Sister would have gotten a single number: A-one.

Determined not to let this happen again, I kept out of trouble, stopped thinking about Mary Ellen's bosom, and stayed out of Sister's way. Never sure when my guardian angel was on duty, I wasn't taking any chances. Things went quite well until one day several weeks later. We were studying World War II. The lesson focused on The Battle of the Bulge. One of the guys patted the full-figured girl across from me saying in a low voice: "Looks like you lost *your* Battle of the Bulge!"

Shamelessly, I laughed out loud. The humor once again escaped Sister Bruiser and she awarded me a major league punishment: "You are to write a 1,000-word report on the Battle of the Bulge. It's due the day after tomorrow—or else!" The "or else" made chills run down my spine. Sister wasn't kidding. Not wanting to be a martyr, I knew I had to think of something—and fast!

That evening, I figured out a solution while listening to *The Lone Ranger*. The morning my report was due, I came to class confident. Sister wanted an accurate, 1,000-word report of the battle, and that's what I gave her.

My report began: "The American army was on one side, the German army on the other." The report ended with: "And, the battle was over." In between, I filled the lines with: "Bang, bang, bang, bang, bang, bang. Both sides reloaded. Bang, band, bang, bang…" Sister was literally shell-shocked! When I finished my narrative, the entire class cheered the victorious American army. We stood up, said the Pledge of Allegiance, and then went out for recess. I waited for the wrath of righteousness to come thundering down upon me, but all was quiet on the Western Front. Obviously, my guardian angel was on duty—working overtime protecting me.

Not only did I survive sixth grade, I was promoted to grade seven. Yes, there would be more unauthorized laughing, followed by more punishments as the value of "X" skyrocketed. But, as always, I did what I had to do. I survived—thoroughly enjoying the magic, mischief, and laughter of the Wonder Years.

Sandlot Baseball in Sticker Stadium

As 12-year-old seventh-graders, we loved baseball. For us, baseball season started the week after the last snow melted from the sandlot across Atchison Avenue. As soon as the sun had enough courage to defy the March winds, we'd be choosing up sides during school in our classroom and arguing baseball, instead of trying to figure out what products came from Peru, or what killed the Dead Sea.

At Sacred Heart School, Catholic boys were expected to keep their minds on their lessons—not baseball. And, when they didn't, Sister Attila would swoop down like an angry penguin, squawking about how the Devil was working to see us fail. Actually, the Devil had nothing to do with it; most of the time we were trying to decide who would take Hubert Tucker on their side.

Hubert Tucker was the reason baseball has a right field. It was the only position you felt secure putting him. Oh, Hubie could catch all right, but he was totally uncoordinated. Once, when he tried to sing in the shower, he almost drowned. He just couldn't convince his body parts to work as a team. He was normal in every other way, but when it came to athletic ability, it was disaster city. It seemed as though Hubie's control center went on automatic klutz the instant he picked up his baseball glove. He was a little slow running the bases, so the team that chose him on their side was allowed to let him have a head start running toward first base.

Along with these minor limitations, Hubie was also allergic—to everything! Throughout spring, summer, and fall, Hubie's nose ran. In the winter, when his nose was too cold to run, it skated. Whatever microscopic particles of dust or pollen that would happen to float by the front of his face, Hubie would instinctively snuff them up his nose, activating his sinus waterfall. To his credit, Hubie always produced the most attractive nose bubbles during the height of hay fever season.

Consequently, he was never without a huge white handkerchief. So often did he have to haul out his hankie that he appeared to be under a constant flag of surrender. Still, we needed him to even out the numbers for two teams, so Hubert always played.

Choosing sides while in class allowed for more playing time after school. For until daylight-saving time kicked in, we were always playing under the threat of

17

darkness. That was the major reason why we were all such rabid Cubs fans; we understood what it was like to play America's pastime without lights.

We played on land owned by the railroads. In between the Pennsylvania and New York Central railroad tracks was a parcel of land several acres wide and an acre deep. Wild with sticker-weeds, small boulders, and countless pieces of broken glass, the field had been cleared, raked, and even mowed by seventh-graders whose mothers couldn't get them to mow their own yard. Granted, the place wasn't glamorous, but it was our ball field. We named it Sticker Stadium.

Playing sandlot baseball is different from playing regular baseball. Usually, in sandlot baseball, right field is out. This is because there is a shortage of players, and a majority of right-handed batters. The few kids who are left-handed can't pull the ball, so who needs right field?

There are special rules and conditions for leading off and stealing. And, since there is not a first baseman—pitcher's hands are out. The equipment isn't the same either. The sandlot pro swings a bat that has been cracked at least twice, and mended with an assortment of wood screws and nails. The coverless baseball used in Sticker Stadium games was held together with a dozen yards of electrical friction tape, and weighed in at about six pounds!

Later on, when I played baseball in an organized league, I had problems adjusting. All those years I played at smacking that midget-sized bowling ball triggered an impulse that has been tough to suppress. The first time they threw an official baseball to me to pitch with, my first thought was to run into the dugout, rip off the cover, and wrap it in black tape. Old habits die hard!

Once the game started, I assumed the role of manager and strategist. I knew where each kid on the opposing team would hit the ball. As pitcher, I would lay the ball in the strike zone and let him hit it right to one of my perfectly positioned defensive players for an easy out. It was a tight game. After eight innings, we were winning 1 to 0. In the top of the ninth it was three up and three down. We couldn't hit a watermelon with a two-by-four. The score remained one to nothing. The entire game, I had pitched so cleverly that all the opposing batters had to hit to left field. I wasn't taking any chances.

Since right field was out, I had no choice but to position Hubert in center field. To make matters more interesting, he had forgotten his glove and I had to loan him my first baseman's mitt. This is the glove that looks like the oversized claw of a lobster. So there was Hubert, standing in center field, with a first baseman's mitt on the wrong hand. (I neglected to mention that I am left-handed and Hubie is a righty.)

Jim Harmon, the next batter, hit a sharp single over short. Man on first. The next two guys were easy outs. Leroy Girman struck out. And Jim Tallion popped out to the third baseman. One more out and the game was ours. Dusk had begun to move daylight off to one side. The darker it became, the better I pitched. The next batter was Jack Wisemiller. I was thoroughly confident. Jack was a right-handed batter who always swung late but rarely struck out. When he hit the ball, he would usually send a lazy fly ball to center field. End of game. Even slow-as-a-slug Hubert could catch a fly ball. No problem. I stepped off the pitching rubber, and motioned Hubie to move toward right center. Just in case Jack hit my money pitch, I wanted to be ready. "Stay awake out there," I yelled over my shoulder to Hubie. "Play ball," Hubie chattered back. "Let him hit it!" He was really into the game.

I had two strikes on Jack. He stepped out of the batter's box, tapped his shoes with the bat, spit, wiped his hands on his jeans, and stepped back in the box. I wound up and fired a waist-high fastball right over the plate. I saw Jack grit his teeth, narrow his eyes, and begin to crank the bat around. I didn't see anything happen, but I heard it. Crack! I jerked my head out of the way just in time to see a blur of black tape whiz over my head. Jack had smacked a screaming line drive out toward center field, directly in line with Hubert. I turned fully toward the outfield, and saw Hubert standing still as a statue. The ball was sizzling right at him. He just stood there smiling, admiring a dandelion he had just picked. "Hubie," I screamed, "the ball!"

Hubert came to conscious awareness in slow motion. I watched him blink and shift his head to one side and then the other, as he tried to get on track with the ball. His eyes couldn't pick it up. He was bobbing his head like a prizefighter, a look of panic beginning to take over his face.

He dropped his dandelion. The first baseman's glove was dangling limply from his left wrist like a shell-shocked crustacean. I heard his feeble cry: "I-I can't see the ball! I-I-I'm going to sneeze!" Both of his hands were now in front of his face holding his hankie.

"ACHHOOOOOOO!" Hubert's sneeze exploded and echoed across Sticker Stadium at the same instant that Jack's line drive collided with his head. The ball ricocheted off his noggin like a pinball and landed softly in the glove of our second baseman, Denny Bryerton, who was backing up the play. Hubie was flat on his back, knocked out cold by the impact of the ball. As he regained consciousness, surrounded by his teammates, we all asked in unison: "Hubie, are you all right?" Hubert blinked his eyes and kept saying: "I went to sleep. I went to sleep."

As I mentioned earlier, there are different rules for playing sandlot baseball. We added one more: Whenever Hubert is on our team, he gets to play center field wearing a hard hat!

Field Trip

As each school year begins, it's only a matter of time before students begin bringing permission slips home for parents to sign. Like a famous celebrity, kids pursue mom for her autograph on the dotted line, sanctioning their foray to the outside world. Along with reading, writing, and arithmetic, there is another curriculum known as the Field Trip. For many, the field trip is viewed as an extension of the classroom, an added opportunity to broaden the educational horizons of energetic curious youngsters with inquiring minds.

As a seasoned parent-chaperone, I've logged hundreds of field trip miles, visiting museums, parks, galleries, and zoos. If buses offered frequent rider coupons, I'd have a roomful. During our kids' grade school years, I rode education limousines to places near and far, enjoying the sights and sounds while feasting on brown bag lunches featuring gourmet cold-cuts and warm canned soda.

Spending the day with exuberant, high-spirited youngsters as they encounter new experiences and make fresh discoveries about their world is enjoyable to watch and delightful to share. But as any chaperone knows, a field trip can take on a life of its own. Regardless of how well planned or how carefully thought out they are, there's always the potential for unforeseen circumstances to take over. Let me tell you about the mother of all field trips. It took place in the spring of 1952.

What brought this topic to mind was a recent reunion of my grade school class from Sacred Heart School in Whiting, Indiana. Back then, field trips were big deals. In an age of hand-me-downs and scarce resources, many families had limited mobility. The family car had not become the necessity it is today. Luckily for the kids at Sacred Heart, there was an active PTA. Though both parents were members, it was the moms who organized and planned field trips. Because of their efforts, many of us went to zoos, museums, and art galleries for the first time. Once we visited Chicago's Tribune Tower and watched as the "World's Greatest Newspaper" was printed. Kindly pressmen fashioned paper hats for each kid as a souvenir. After that outing, everyone wanted to be a newspaperman.

But the most memorable field trip in the history of Sacred Heart School was the one to Chicago's Stockyards. Well-planned and thoroughly organized, the

PTA moms thought this would be a rich educational oasis. Enthralled with their selection, they invited the lower grades as well as the sixth-, seventh-, and eighth-graders. Several buses were lined up and filled with enthusiastic youngsters. A trip to Chicago was big time, and this was going to be the biggest!

We smelled the stockyards before we saw them. A pungent order slammed into our young nostrils causing eyes to water and throats to gag. Once inside, we climbed stairs to a balcony overlooking the slaughterhouse's main floor. Lined up along the railing, we couldn't believe our eyes and ears. Animals were being assassinated with hammer, mallet, and knife. Carcasses swung from chains as they were being processed. Workers sloshed about, their work galoshes splashing animal fluids with every step. Hoses washed away wastes just in time for the next batch to arrive. It didn't take long for sight, sound, and smell to affect us young observers.

Some kids got sick. Others cracked jokes and made weird animal noises. Younger kids started to cry, then got sick, too. On the floor, livestock was being dispatched with blows and blade, while on the balcony, kids were crying, retching, and laughing.

As quickly as possible, chaperones and stockyard employees moved us away from the sights on the main floor. Adult guides herded us (no pun intended) into the cafeteria and tried to calm us down. PTA moms cleaned up dozens of kids baptized by eruptions of internal fluids. Order was slowly being restored when the cafeteria staff began serving us lunch. Unaware of the trauma, they served hot dogs and hamburgers. One look at the meat and we flashed back to brown-eyed steers being knocked senseless a few doors away. One of the older kids shouted: "MOOO-MOOO-Ouch!" Another boy spoke to his hamburger: "Didn't I just see you in the other room getting smacked in the head?" That was all it took—another round of upchuck and tears commenced, as field trip moms tried to restore order.

The field trip ended early. On the way back to school, it was pretty quiet on the bus considering our age. Unlike our trip to Tribune Tower, no one expressed a desire to work in the stockyards. It was a long time before any of us could look at a hamburger without feeling queasy.

More than 50 years later, when reminiscing with classmates, we laughed about that field trip until tears came. We all agree, in spite of what happened, our trip to the stockyards was wonderful! It was a "moo-ving" experience. So to all those super moms who made our field trips possible: Thanks for the memories.

Summertime

Summertime. The word is almost magic! It evokes thousands of images, spread across a lifetime. Summertime was always the beginning of the annual parole from school. For three glorious months, a kid could forget about clean clothes, brushed teeth, combed hair, homework, and school. As soon as the final bell had rung, kids scrambled out of the schoolhouse, with visions of baseball and playgrounds, bathing suits and beach parties ricocheting inside their heads like a game of pinball!

Summertime meant fun time! We couldn't wait to start consuming another allotment of daylight-saving time. Nor could we wait for summer to become part of us, soaking up rays from the playboy of the seasons, sporting fashionable sunglasses, playing baseball under bright blue cloudless skies, and feeling the coolness of the waves washing over sand-coated feet as we played out parts and acted out youthful scenes. Nourishing friendships by sharing the abundant flow of carefree hours, we enriched the times of our lives.

There was just one slight problem with the above scenario: Mom didn't buy it. She never subscribed to such an idyllic summer. Her concept of three months without school did not include the word "vacation."

Somewhere in the Mommy Training Manual, there's a chapter entitled "Summertime Is Chore Time!" It used to amaze me how one lady could consistently come up with so much work. It was even rumored that she had received an exemption from child labor laws. Within 24 hours following the end of the school year, Mom would declare war on dirt!

While I thought about baseball and the beach, Mom thought about me mowing the lawn, helping with laundry, scrubbing floors, going to the grocery store, dusting, cleaning the garage, washing windows, and vacuuming every surface in the house—twice. I was the only guy to return to school in the fall with detergent burn and dishpan hands. I dealt with more dirt than a Hollywood gossip columnist.

So fast was I in becoming an expert on laundry that I could have written advertising copy for Procter & Gamble. I rarely went to the beach, yet I saw more Tide than a merchant marine. Name a laundry problem, and I'll tell you how to solve it by sorting the clothes for cold, warm, or hot water. To bleach or not to bleach, that was the question. The manipulative skills gained using clothespins to hang laundry in the backyard far exceeded anything I later learned as a machinist. By the time I was a senior in high school, I was a blue-ribbon domestic. As Mr. Mom, I was way ahead of my time. Martha Stewart could have taken lessons from me! Even so, I had my limitations.

Every Tuesday, I'd stand before the ironing board of education and assassinate wrinkles. If there is a black hole of housework, it's ironing; and in our house, we ironed everything. As I plied the hot iron over freshly laundered clothes, I would daydream, drifting in and out of awareness as I thought about parties at the beach, swimming in the cool, refreshing lake, and roasting marshmallows over a cozy fire on the sand at night. I could almost smell the roasting marshmallows. Suddenly, I realized I was roasting my shorts! At summer's end, a number of garments from the family laundry bore numerous iron-scorched tattoos.

By September, most kids wore the spoils of summer with considerable pride. Suntanned faces were tangible evidence of vacations well spent. Stories about homeruns and sandlot victories were matched against beach time at the lake, memories of drive-in movies, prizes won at a July carnival, lakefront fireworks, quiet moments of a summer romance, and time spent horsing around—all filling summertime pages in life's yearbook. I had vacation stories, too. Granted, it was no Disneyland, but it wasn't all drudgery either; doing daily chores taught me valuable lessons.

I learned that work is love made visible, and that in a family, there is no free lunch; everyone needs to do his or her share. I still enjoyed my vacation. After the work was done, I was free to pursue the fruits of summer. The lessons learned in Mom's Summer Work Camp have become more valuable as the years go by. All in all, moms are pretty smart.

Now another summer is at hand. Those youthful, verdant years passed too quickly. We enjoyed the magic for only a short time. Today, those images are like faraway stars, twinkling in the summer night. We savor their loveliness, but are no long warmed by their flame. That warmth must come from within each of us—we must supply the magic.

The days of summer are filled with voices and events, woven among the friends and faces that make up a lifetime. We dream of an endless summer that we know in our hearts cannot be. Still, summer is the essence of youth, the perfume that carries its fragrance and makes those of us who are ancient believe once again in that magical time of the young.

With the advent of another summer, perhaps we should think about the little kid in each of us who excitedly awaits this season. Remembering, too, that by nourishing friendship, and doing our chores, we enrich the times of our life.

Penguinaphobia

Most of us are afraid of something. In fact, we come from the kid factory equipped with two fears: the sound of loud noises and falling. All other fears are learned. Because of the incredible human brain, the vast majority of us are able to control and manage our fearfulness without adversely affecting the way we live.

Sometimes, though, fear gets the upper hand and becomes a dominant force. What starts out as timidity evolves through anxiety, worry, apprehension, alarm, dread, panic, and terror until it becomes a life-controlling phobia. Phobias are, in many cases, persistent abnormal, illogical, intense fears of specific things or situations. Millions of people suffer from thousands of phobias. Scientifically, over 700 specific phobias have been labeled, with new phobias still being identified in clinics throughout the world.

Many phobias are well-known: acrophobia—fear of heights, claustrophobia—fear of enclosed spaces, hydrophobia—fear of water, and triskaidekaphobia—fear of the number 13. Other phobias are more obscure. However, to the one afflicted, they are just as terrifying.

Consider for example, arachibutyrophobia—fear of peanut butter sticking to the roof of the mouth. A little-known fact is that one of the fastest growing phobias in modern America is ballistophobia—fear of bullets. Especially when they are fired directly at you! That fear is right up there with sophophobia—fear of learning. Today, a considerable number of school-age kids suffer terribly from this phobia.

As I said, most of us are afraid of something. Once identified, it often takes years to overcome and conquer our fears. They're not something we talk about freely—especially while trying to get them under control. But, afterwards, when a particular fear has been vanquished and no longer has dominion over us, we become more open and willing to discuss our inner triumph. That's why it's time to tell you about the fear of fears—penguinaphobia!

I was personally afflicted by penguinaphobia for eight years. Rampant in the '40s and '50s, today this phobia has all but vanished. Some of us suffer occasional flashbacks when look-alike images trigger the mind, but such incidents now rarely cause a flinch. Gone, too, are cold sweats, full-body tremors, uncontrolla-

26

ble bladder, gooseflesh, palpitations, jitters, chattering teeth, and stuttered speech.

Penguinaphobia was the fear of choice for thousands of kids who attended Catholic school when nuns ruled. Wearing yards of black cloth with white-linen habits, these ecclesiastical soul-savers were intimidating and imposing figures. Their floor-length religious garb, coupled with white frontal covering, gave them an easily identifiable image. They subscribed to a no-nonsense approach to education. Many Sisters earned reputation for taking no prisoners. Their forte was discipline through fear. If anyone fooled around in school, they paid the price—immediately!

Recalcitrant lads wound up on the wrong end of Sister's guided muscle as she served up an effective knuckle sandwich. By third grade, most parochial school boys knew how to bob-and-weave like pro boxers. The slower, less-coordinated kids had to keep their dentist on 24-hour call. But in spite of such foreboding consequences, free-spirited guys with a terminal proclivity for mischief regularly tested Sister's pugilistic prowess.

On rare occasions, Sister would leave the classroom for a few minutes. Instinctively, we'd post a lookout. During her absence, freedom would break out and we would recklessly act normal, relaxing our false rigid demeanor. As soon as the lookout spotted Sister coming back, he would voice the warning: "The penguin is coming! The penguin is coming!" Immediately, smiles evaporated, freedom was revoked, and we resumed our stoic, silent behavior. Sister returned to her throne and reclaimed her academic domain, totally in control.

One day, however, when Sister was out of the room, our strategy failed. Someone said something funny and everybody started laughing. While our lookout was rolling on the floor, doubled up with laughter, Sister returned. From three rows away I could see her crimson face and threatening "How-Dare-You-Laugh-Without-Permission" look. As if using a tracking device, she swiftly swooped down on the instigators. With more than her rosary swinging, Sister delivered a substantial lesson in discipline. When she finished, she scanned the rest of the class. Without saying a word, her ice-cold stare conveyed her message: Joy was not part of the curriculum. That night, and until I graduated, I had a recurring nightmare of being chased and attacked by a giant penguin.

It took years to get over my penguinaphobia. For a long time, I couldn't even look at a tuxedo without becoming emotional; and I stayed away from the zoo's Antarctica exhibit for obvious reasons. Then one day, I read that nuns were modifying their traditional dress to more modern attire. Miraculously, the intimidating image of no-nonsense, take-no-prisoners nuns faded from my mind.

I must confess though; every now and then I still dream of a giant penguin, but these episodes are a little different. As soon as I'm about to be attacked, Batman shows up and saves the day. Although I appreciate his efforts—where was he when I was in grade school? We sure could have used a lookout who didn't laugh!

Sister Hawkeye and the World Series

It's World Series time again. Once more, the boys of summer turn into men of October as the best two teams in baseball battle it out for the title of world champion. Many Americans view this final week of baseball matter-of-factly, showing only a passing interest. There are others who project an "I could care less" attitude. But to the true fan, the connoisseurs of baseball, the die-hard horsehide addicts, and kids of all ages who keep the field-of-dreams flame forever burning in their hearts, the World Series is the pinnacle, the Mecca, the emotional climax of the baseball season.

Rabid fans will go to extreme measures, meet every challenge, and overcome any obstacle in order to listen and watch the World Series. This is the story of how one particular group of kids in 1952 climbed the technological and ecclesiastical mountain to do just that.

The contenders for baseball's top prize were the American League's Yankees and the National League's Dodgers. During the regular 154-game season, New York's win-loss record was 95-59. Brooklyn's was one victory better at 96-58. These were the best of the Majors. To give one an idea of how tough these teams were, they were the only two teams who even had a *chance* of beating the Whiting Little League All-Stars in 1952.

Throughout the seventh grade, students challenged one another with mock wagers as to which team was better: Dodgers! Yankees! Dodgers! Yankees! Evenly divided, we decided to wire the classroom and listen to the Series on the radio.

As seventh-graders, we knew we'd have to be extra clever if we intended to tune in the Fall Classic while in school. We would have to solve two major problems: This was 1952, BBTR (Before Battery Transistor Radios), which meant radios were bulky and needed electricity for their thirsty vacuum tubes. Problem two was our teacher. The Sisters of Providence taught students at Sacred Heart School.

Seventh grade was the domain of Sister "I-Never-Miss-A-Thing" Bernard. Sister Bernard was one of those legendary nuns who had superhuman senses. She was the prototype for GPS; her whole body was a tracking device. Nothing got by this lady. She had the eyesight of an eagle, the hearing of a deer, the scent of a bloodhound, and the strength of a grizzly bear. In other words, Sister Bernard was well equipped to handle seventh-graders!

We nicknamed her Sister Hawkeye. No matter what shenanigans we tried, we were never successful at putting one over on the Hawk. Even so, we decided the Series was too important not to try one more time. Jack Wisemiller volunteered the radio. Jim Tallion, Dennis Bryerton, Jim Harmon, and I provided the extension cords. The nearest wall outlet was in the cloakroom, more than 20 feet from the bookcase where we planned to hide the radio. Leroy Girman brought the tape, and by the morning of Game 1, we were ready to put our plan into action.

By the time parochial kids get to seventh grade, they've bonded. They stick together like heavy-duty epoxy, fused into a single-minded unit of pre-adolescent mischief. It's all for one, and one for all. Translation: It was us against Hawkeye!

The logistics involved were mind-boggling. At the precise opportune moment, we had to sneak in the radio, stash it in the bookcase, and run the extension cords to the outlet. The plan called for making a false front from cardboard to hide the radio. A couple of artistically talented seventh grade girls took care of that by drawing backs of books and coloring them with crayons. After adding a hole for the volume control, it was ready to tape in place. The wiring would be a little more difficult.

Seventh-graders know how to pick their spot. We planned our work, now it was time to work our plan. When Sister Hawkeye went out to monitor the class on the playground during recess, the baseball conspirators snuck back inside and began preparing Room 7 for the autumn classic. We carefully threaded the extension cords along the outside wall. At selected intervals, we taped it to the baseboard, blending it with the dark oak wood.

Outside, our classmates kept the Hawk occupied so Sister Never-Miss-A-Thing wouldn't notice our absence. Luckily, the girls in our class were masters at decoying nuns. Normally, they would ask questions about their studies or something to do with school. But today, realizing the magnitude of our escapade, they went for her cognitive jugular by inquiring about how one becomes a nun. Sister Hawk took the bait like a starving shark.

We worked feverishly to complete our task. The start of Game 1 was but a few hours away. We taped the camouflaged cover in front of the old Silvertone, plugged in the extension cords, and waited while the tubes warmed up. It worked fine. Jack set the station and adjusted the volume. We unplugged the radio and snuck back to the playground just before Sister Hawk called an end to recess. Like they say in broadcasting, timing is everything.

Every afternoon while the Series was in progress, one of the guys would saunter up to the pencil sharpener by the cloakroom door and pretend he was sharpening a pencil. At the same time, one of the girls would to Sister Hawk's desk on the opposite side and ask a question, giving the phony pencil-grinder time to plug in the radio. We'd sit in our seats, books in front of our faces to smother our snickers, listening intently as Dressen's boys battled Stengel's men.

During Gillette commercials, we put on a coughing jag to help cover the chimes in the tagline: "To look sharp, feel sharp, and be sharp, use Gillette Blue Blades today!" We were awash in our own cleverness, intoxicated with success as we operated our clandestine radio caper throughout the Series. It went the full seven games. Snider, Robinson, Reese and company took Games 1, 3, and 5. Mantle, Rizzuto, Bauer, and friends won Games 2, 4, and 6.

The seventh and final game was played on Tuesday afternoon, October 7, at Ebbets Field in Brooklyn. Because of Billy Martin's last-second, knee-level catch of an infield popup lost in the sun by first baseman Joe Collins, the Yankees won the game and the World Series. As I was about to exit the classroom for the day, Hawkeye's voice stopped me cold in my tracks. Hawkeye had a way with words. Using my full name, she ordered me to stay. Blood pressure: up. Beads of sweat formed on my forehead. My stomach tied itself in several Navy-type knots. Goosebumps were fighting it out for a place on my body.

When we were alone, she placed her hand lightly on my shoulder, looked me in the eye and said, "I'm glad the Yankees won." Not only was I stunned by her words, realizing that she *knew* all along about the radio, but *I could swear I saw her smile!* Imagine, granite-faced Hawkeye smiling—*and a baseball fan!*

Looking back on this event, it was my first encounter with a near-miracle experience. All those prayerful aspirations and J.M.J.'s finally paid off! As she lifted her knock-you-upside-the-head Size 10 meat hook from my shoulder, she said, "Just between you and me, the boys did a nice job with the radio." I was so dumbfounded and shocked by her remarks, I never told the guys that she knew. It's too bad there isn't a special section in baseball's Hall of Fame for nuns. Sister Hawkeye would be a charter member!

My House

This is about buildings. Now, there are all kinds of buildings—skyscrapers, factories, churches, schools, and of course, houses. And buildings come in all shapes and sizes. Most of us spend the better part of our lives in buildings of one type or another. In buildings we are born, grow up, play, work, eat, learn, pray, and sleep. And, for the vast majority of us, a building is where we'll end our days, hopefully surrounded by loved ones and dear friends.

It doesn't take long for certain buildings to become familiar, comfortable structures we use as reference to identify who, and what, we are. In no time at all, we become quite attached to these life spaces. From a young age, we associate both ordinary and extraordinary events with the places where they occurred. It is the accumulation of these events that add to the sum total of our life. I want to tell you about a few of the important buildings in my life. I'll leave the factories, churches, and schools for another time. This is about houses—the ones that made the greatest impression on my life while growing up. Ordinary houses that became home.

Studies show that the average American moves seven times in a lifetime. Based on my stack of U-Haul receipts, I've moved more often than a delegate to a prune convention. Since those early job-searching migratory treks, however, I haven't had to add to U-Haul's annual revenues. The changes of address experienced as a boy were due to a growing family's need for larger accommodations. There were three.

The first house that became home was not even a house. It was a garage on Lincoln Avenue that someone had built living quarters above. We lived there until I was six. Included were two bedrooms, a parlor, bath, and kitchen. It also had a pantry where I noisily played with pots and pans while Mom prepared dinner. I shared the smaller of the bedrooms with an older brother.

I recall stuffy humid summer nights, when Dad cooled us with a cardboard fan, while softly singing lullabies. In winter, books replaced fans. Mom and Dad took turns reading the nightly bedtime story. To an imaginative six-year-old, the garage flat was a palace. In the small adjacent yard, we played tag, shot marbles, and built castles in a sandbox under the stairs leading to the back porch. This was the same backyard where we raised the turkey that became Thanksgiving dinner. The following year, our family moved into my late grandmother's house on Oliver Street.

Granny's house was huge. The high ceilings added to the spacious feeling of the nine rooms. Victorian in design, complete with steeple and attic cupola, the house had been built by my grandfather in the late 1890s. It was the birthplace of my father in November 1903. Now, in 1947, our family of six called it home.

I can still hear the creaky "voice" of the dark oak stairway, protesting young feet on their way to the upstairs bedroom. In wintertime, snuggled warmly under a down comforter, I'd listen to the lonely sound of a steam locomotive's whistle as it rolled on through the night. Images, like random color slides, beckon the mind to look once more at childhood scenes. The carousel of pictures flash by: the homemade tree swing, fastened by heavy rope to the giant back yard oak tree; Easter chicks and ducklings raised to adults; Saturday-night baths in a claw-footed cast-iron tub big enough for the Pacific fleet; warm spring evenings sitting on the stoop watching fireflies advertise their skill; snow forts and snowmen; walking to first grade at Sacred Heart School. Picture after picture waiting their turn on the screen.

We lived in Grandma's house for less than two years. In early 1949, we moved again. This would be our last move as a family. Now, when classmates asked where I lived, I answered: "Cleveland Avenue. My house is on Cleveland." We didn't need house numbers, we used geographic markers along with the street names: "Dennis lives by Southside." "Joe lives by Sacred Heart." "Mary lives by the Community Center." I lived by the White Castle.

The house at 1814 Cleveland is where I grew up. The better part of grade school, all of high school, apprentice school, even my freshman year at college, took place while living there. Most of my boyhood memories are identified with this house. Oh, the stories that house could tell. This was the home when I played Little League, bought my first bike, had my paper route, played Pony League Baseball, became a teenager, worked as a pin boy, had my heart stolen by a dog named Sam, attended the prom, earned my diploma, worked in the mill, bought my first car, and spent several thousand days experiencing life. This was indeed home.

Now, four decades later, youthful scenes of those times flash strobe-like through the mind. Snippets from a lifetime tantalize and tease the senses with once-upon-a-time images. Like some cognitive comet, pictures race by, leaving in their wake a gossamer trail of stardust-like crystals, aglow with the stuff of living.

Today the houses I lived in as a boy have other families to enjoy them. Like old friends, I think about the places we shared as a family and treasure those moments more than ever. Like I said, there are all kinds of houses, every style and size. My favorite houses, the ones I remember, are the ones I called home.

Verbs of Life

One of the early English lessons we learned was identifying the eight parts of speech. Once understood, the arrangement of these parts gives substance to our thoughts and ideas. For those who have been away from the classroom for a while, the eight parts of speech are as follows: noun, pronoun, adverb, adjective, preposition, conjunction, interjection, and verb. Within these classifications are divisions, which expand versatility and usage, providing one with an almost unlimited range of communication.

In the course of our daily interaction with fellow human beings, we select various parts to convey our written and spoken messages automatically. Rarely in the course of conversation do we consciously consider choosing particular nouns, adjectives, and the like before speaking. After years of absorbing language, responding, and listening, we react without forethought. On occasion, we may be at a loss for words, or at times be speechless, but once verbalization begins, word choice is not contingent upon part-of-speech selection.

How a person uses language skills provides a good indication of intellectual ability. One's competency is demonstrated when spoken words are combined with actions and behavior. Together, words and deeds form an unbreakable partnership, which in turn showcases one's character.

As one grows from child to adult, we become acutely aware how important the words are we write and speak, for there is no more powerful force than the written or spoken word. From early on, we're taught to always "keep our word," to be one whose "word is their bond," and to honor the ultimate sanction between two people: "I give you my word." What we say, and what we do, determines the quality of one's character. In ways not fully understood, the parts of speech add to the sum total of who we are.

Many years ago, a class of soon-to-be-graduates listened intently as a learned scholar made a profound statement. Looking at their young faces, he told them that every human being is born with the potential for greatness. He talked to them about their importance and value. He cautioned them to choose worldly pleasures carefully. He suggested unselfishness, and proposed they consider sharing the gift of their life with others. He advised them to forego self-indulgence

35

and pursue a life of thoughtful service. He closed his remarks by presenting the students with the "Verbs of Life," explaining how action words could ignite an action life.

The list contained twelve words. Like twelve apostles, these verbs would serve as foundation for their character. If they willingly adopted the "Verbs of Life," he promised their lives would be embellished and enriched beyond their dreams.

Every student received a small white card with the "Verbs of Life" neatly typed in a single column. He waited a moment, and then read them aloud:

I am
I think
I can
I care
I know
I see
I hear
I ought
I will
I promise
I serve
I love

When he finished, the only sound was the sound of silence. He politely thanked his audience and quietly left the room.

That was a long time ago. I've long since forgotten the speaker's name, but I kept the Verbs of Life. Over the years, I've added others, making them part of who I am. Wherever that gentleman is, I'd like him to know that he was right. The Verbs of Life made a difference—beyond all dreams.

Hometown:
"The Little City by the Lake"

Trust Fund

Trust is a prized human quality. It's a trait we admire in good friends; an attribute each of us strives to make part of our personal resumé. Because trust is a learned behavior, it can be acquired in many ways. From an early age, through family and friendship, opportunities are presented for building trust. Sometimes these personal trust funds start unnoticed, with an ordinary, think-nothing-of-it encounter, and grow into personal treasures of incalculable wealth. What follows is a story about a hometown trust fund. It does not involve big money or banks. Rather, it concerns a bottle of soda pop, a kind neighborhood grocer, and a young lad.

In the days before supermarkets, warehouse clubs, and food chain stores, shoppers were served by neighborhood grocery stores. These food shops were owned and operated by individual families who lived behind, over, or next door to the family business. My hometown was no different; at one time, dozens of these neighborhood canteens dotted the residential landscape of Whiting-Robertsdale. These mom-and-pop operations played an important role in the life of the community.

Grown-ups viewed these food shops as survival stations, depending on them for safety and sustenance. Initially, when a neighborhood was new, these local markets often offered the only telephone available for residents. Patrons of a particular grocery would keep a running tab and pay according to an agreed-upon arrangement with the proprietor, a one-to-one personal relationship between neighbors. Countless times, familiar faces would rush in to make last-minute stops for Borden milk, Silvercup bread, or cold-cuts for a working man's lunch, thereby avoiding domestic chaos. Kids, on the other hand, focused on the penny candy counter and snack rack. Like starving ants at a picnic, street urchins would queue up with pennies and nickels in hand, scan the glass-enclosed confectionary inventory, and then load up jaw and pocket.

Ribbons of dot-sized candy on white paper tape sold for two cents per foot. These multi-colored sugarcoated spots were arranged in easy-to-eat rows. Kids of all ages ate candy and paper together—adding much needed roughage to their glucose-rich diet. In one year, several tons of Moon Pies, Twinkies, candy, and assorted snacks disappeared down pre-pubescent gullets, sloshed clear by gallons of Kayo, Nehi, Pepsi, and Coke. As usual, the cast-iron lining of these young stomachs never flinched.

By the time we were in sixth grade, our favorite oasis for snacks and soft drinks was Brozovich's. Successful businesses have three things in common: location, location, location. Brozovich's had the formula down pat. Not only did this store carry a full menu of penny candy, snacks, and sodas, it was also strategically located just north of the corner of 117th Street and Central Avenue—one block away from Sacred Heart School.

To a Catholic kid required to attend Mass every school day, this sugar bank was an ideal sanctuary to stay out of Sister Bruiser's sight. Even if you had served the 6:30 AM Mass, Sister expected you to go to Mass again at 8:00 AM and sit with your class. Fortunately, our guardian angel allowed us to drift over to Brozovich's to savor a Twinkie or Moon Pie, rather than have us in church for a double shot of salvation. Mr. Brozovich was a terrific guy and understood our plight. He let several of us sit on the front window bench, and enjoy our morning snack. He sold groceries but dealt in common sense. You could tell he genuinely liked us, and took an interest in our activities. Like a surrogate parent, he was never bashful when it came to scolding us for horsing around or getting too noisy. Nor did he hesitate to give us advice and counsel about our conduct, emphasizing the importance of values and responsible behavior.

As a high school student, I continued to make pit stops at Brozovich's. It was a welcome refreshment stand on the way home after a summer's afternoon of baseball at Whiting Park. In those days, a twelve-ounce Pepsi cost a dime. If you took the bottle out of the store, an additional two cents was charged to cover the deposit. Some stores even charged extra if the pop was cold. As a rule, storeowners did not allow self-serve customers. No one went behind the counter—especially kids. Mr. Brozovich, however, handled things differently.

One summer afternoon, on my way home after a ball game, I stopped in for a cold Pepsi. Tired and thirsty, I looked forward to a cool, refreshing drink. By now, Brozovich's was like an extension of our family's pantry. Mr. Brozovich and I always talked and shared stories. He was busy doing something in the back when I entered the store.

"Hi, Mr. Brozovich, how ya doin'?"

Hearing my voice, he responded, "Hiya, Cookie, what'll it be today?"

I stood in front of the cooler. "Just a Pepsi—a cold Pepsi to go."

Without coming from the back of the store, he said: "Help yourself, Cookie, I trust you."

I opened the cooler and brought out the ice-cold bottle. As I fished through my pockets, I realized I didn't have any money. I went back behind the counter, and replaced the bottle in the cooler. By this time, Mr. Brozovich came out of the back room into the store and saw me return the soda.

"I thought you wanted a Pepsi?"

"I did, but I forgot my money."

Mr. Brozovich opened the cooler and brought out the chilled bottle of soda.

"Here, Cookie, you look like you could use this."

Before I could speak, he said: "Pay me the next time you come in. I said I trust you."

With those few words, Mr. Brozovich opened a trust fund for me and enriched my self-worth. A few days later, I stopped in, paid him the twelve cents, and thanked him. Mr. Brozovich handed back the coins: "Thank you, Cookie, for keeping your word. You keep this, for when you get thirsty. This one's on me."

Like I said, some personal trust funds begin with an ordinary, think-nothing-of-it encounter and grow into personal treasures of incalculable wealth. At various times, heaven provides each of us with opportunities to enrich others, by word and deed. When presented, these servings of human kindness nourish and strengthen the spirit. They become trust funds of the heart.

Whiting Is My Mayberry

It didn't take long for America to fall in love with Mayberry, the fictional town in rural North Carolina where Sheriff Andy Taylor, his high-strung deputy Barney Fife, and the other fine citizens called home. Perhaps it was the gentle, low-key manner of Sheriff Andy, or the matronly guidance provided Opie by Aunt Bee that so endeared television viewers. Maybe it was the homespun flavor of the show, where a crime wave amounted to an abandoned car in front of Floyd's Barber Shop. Whatever the reasons, since October 1960, millions have watched and re-watched this idyllic portrayal of hometown America. And although I've never been to North Carolina, or visited a mythical city named Mayberry, I grew up in a similar town: Whiting, Indiana.

We've all heard the saying, "The right place at the right time." No one ever fulfilled those requirements better than I. I was blessed to be a child of the '50s, and it has made all the difference in my life. Like Mayberry, Whiting and its neighboring community Robertsdale came furnished with a sense of belonging. Somehow, This industrial, refinery-dominated "Little City by the Lake" captured the spirit and dedication of its founders and transferred them to succeeding generations.

The town's character was reflective of its citizens' work ethic, solid family values, social and civic responsibility, and religious reverence. These few square miles of hometown mid-America became a haven for family-centered living. Supported by an excellent educational system, bolstered by churches and parish schools, and anchored by a variety of businesses, Mayberry Midwest flourished, prospered, and thrived. Long before a television program would adopt this phrase as part of its theme, Whiting led the way as the place "where everybody knows your name."

Like make-believe Mayberry, the proprietors of Whiting's businesses projected images of stability, assurance, and friendliness. How neat it was for a kid to be recognized by various storeowners and receive their friendly greetings. Whether auditioning the latest hit record in Neal Price's Firestone Store, or on a family errand to the A & P, these personal relationships immeasurably enriched those formative, youthful years.

Frequenting establishments like Dave's Drugstore, Salmon's Barber Shop, Burton's Clothing, Ande's Pizza, Woolworth's 5 and 10, Central Drugs, Hot Dog Louie's, Newberry's 5 & 10, Walgreens, Nick's Snooker and Pinball Emporium, the Victory Restaurant, and The Community Center ("Kid Headquarters") added to the richness of Whiting's lore. Remembering the generosity, kindness, and decency of countless citizens solidified hometown allegiance. The merchants made you feel like a celebrity when they "donated" an extra scoop of ice cream to your root beer float, tossed in a free pair of socks with your clothing purchase, or "treated" you to an order of your favorite french fries. Things like that rarely happen in other cities; in Whiting, these perks were as regular as clockwork.

Attending public school in the Oil City made you an Oiler. I went a step further, adopting a brand from Standard Oil, and called myself the Permalube Kid! Life was sweeter than berries in May.

From little on, Whiting-Robertsdale was our Learning Center. The community became our most important classroom. We imitated older brothers and sisters, and drew heavily upon the experience of our elders. We had an abundance of positive role models who guided and challenged us to be better. We were taught to be accountable for our actions and responsible for our lives.

It was a kinder, gentler, romantic time. We felt safe and secure in those days. We could walk the streets, use the park, or just hang around without fright or fear. Back then, townspeople looked out for one another—they always managed to find a little neighborly time, exchanged greetings, and gave one a sense of belonging. A hallmark of the community was the efficient manner in which our police officers and firemen faithfully protected person and property. Although I can't recall any major crime wave when I was a kid, I'm pretty certain the residents slept and snoozed peacefully, as if knowing that legendary crime fighter, one-bullet Barney Fife, was on patrol. All in all, it was a neat place to grow up.

I'd like to convey my appreciation for all the good moments and memories. So to all the Aunt Bees, Sheriff Andys, and Barney Fifes; to all the Floyds, Gomers, Howard Spragues, Goobers, and Thelma Lous; and to everyone else who made this industrial Mayberry into a place of the heart: Thanks. And from all the Opies: Thanks, too, for being there when it mattered most.

The Most Important Building in Town

Over my 38 years as a high school teacher, I've often asked my students this question: What is the most important in town? If some disaster befell their hometown, and only one building with all its contents could be saved, what building would they choose to save? Responses vary from churches to banks, schools to businesses, with a majority voting for their house. As important as these places are, they would not be my choice. Although the buildings named are valuable, and even though I treasure my home, none of those qualify as the most important building in town. The title of "most important" is bestowed on the Library.

The library houses all that we are, have been, and plan to be. It is our community storeroom for yesterday, our access to today, and holds the promise of tomorrow. A library is the banquet hall for the mind. It exercises the imagination, encourages ideas, fosters the excitement of learning, expands cognizance, and offers unlimited adventure for the spirit.

The library serves as database for our conscience, memory, and legacy. It stands as the nucleus of civilization—providing an accurate, multi-perspective diverse record of human history. It is an equal opportunity provider of information. The library is the primary source whenever we choose to enrich or enhance our intellect. Each time we review, question, consider, or hypothesize, we directly (or indirectly) draw upon library sources.

The library is our warehouse for knowledge. It is a place where one can pursue the magic and mystery of the printed word, savor illustrative works, or listen to a symphony of sound. The library is a place for all seasons. It houses our thoughts, hopes, dreams, successes, failures, and our attempts to do better. The library is a place for all ages and all stations of life. It is a place to expand one's horizons, tease the emotions, or add to expertise. The library is sustenance for the soul—inspiring, nourishing, refreshing.

Libraries have been an important part of my life since I was a young child. And though I've been fortunate to make use of libraries at several major universities and within large metropolitan cities, there is one particular library I hold in high esteem with considerable affection: Whiting Public Library in Whiting, Indiana. Long before Disneyland existed, this majestic castle-like building became my magic kingdom. Built just after the turn of the twentieth century in 1905 by the Carnegie Foundation, the Whiting Library has served the Whiting-Robertsdale community for over 100 years!

When I was a youngster, our family lived on Oliver Street just south of the library, across the street from Whiting's McGregor School. As a first-grader, it was the first place I was permitted to go by myself. Countless times I walked across the street, climbed the stairs to the main entrance, went downstairs to the children's section and sat at one of the small oak tables reading beginner books.

At 10 o'clock each Saturday morning, kids would gather downstairs for story time. The librarian arranged the chairs in a half circle and, after we were seated, read us a story. She would hold the book up after each passage so we could see the pictures that went with the words. To a first-grader, these story hours were magic! Over the weeks, we enjoyed stories about animals, farms, and families. My favorite was the story of a little helicopter that has trouble learning to fly. Against today's topics, a story about a struggling helicopter may seem quaint, but in 1948, it was pretty heady stuff!

I remember my very first library card. Printed in black bold letters across the top of the blue-colored index card were the words: WHITING PUBLIC LIBRARY. In one corner was my card number: K76A. There was a place for one's name, along with spaces to record the due date of books checked out. When both sides were filled, a new card was issued. To help the novice library patron, the card was kept on file at the checkout desk. I liked watching the librarian as she checked out books. She had this special pencil with a date stamp attached by the eraser end. The card always looked so neat the way she'd stamp the due date inside the little box. It looked very official.

By the time I was a second-grader, having a library card was a big deal. It was the equivalent to the teenager's driver's license. Having a library card meant I could check out books and take them home. It signaled responsibility—you were growing up. It was a privilege to have your own library card; it made a kid feel special. It didn't take long before reading became a favorite activity. Nor did it take too many years before you were old enough to check out books from upstairs. That meant you were an eighth-grader. Next to your first library card, having upstairs privileges signified adolescence, and things didn't get much better than that!

Over the years, libraries have become the municipal report card. This single building contains the community's permanent record. The library reflects the strength of public commitment in moving forward, adapting to change, and refining techniques for information retrieval. In modern terms, the library has become a full-service institution. More than a collection of books, the library is the link, the continuity that affords new generations an opportunity to touch base with their heritage and history, forming a partnership with knowledge, and encouraging young and old alike to journey far beyond the threshold of their mind.

Today the modern library is the Grand Central Station of Information. Computerized and connected nationally and globally via the Internet, library services are technologically keyed to the ever-expanding needs of its patrons. Whiting-Robertsdale residents are fortunate to have a hometown library that reflects the vitality of their community. Within this building one may gain access to the past, present, and future: a comprehensive record of the people, places, and events that defines who and what we are. Next time you're in the area, stop by our local mind cafeteria and treat yourself. Come inside the castle-like "Magic Kingdom" on Oliver Street, the most important building in town.

Reflection on a Fall Day

Yesterday was one of those delicious autumn days. A warm Indian summer breeze, bright sunshine, and an avalanche of falling leaves wrapped around anyone who was lucky enough to be outdoors. I just couldn't resist. I went to Whiting Park to savor the late sunlit hours of the day.

Leaving the parking lot adjacent to the gun club, I walk across the road near where the swings wait for the next child, up the hill where the little stone and glass houses used to sit on their concrete terraces. I find a spot near the top of the hill and sit down on the grass. What an incredible sight! At the bottom of the hill, a couple of gray squirrels play tag among the fallen leaves, stirring them up in sprays of elm and oak and maple cornflakes. Out on Lake Michigan, the outline of a tanker makes its way toward Port Chicago. Kids bicycle on the path that winds its way through the park, and teenage sweethearts hold hands while leaning against the trunk of an old willow tree, oblivious to anyone else. The scene makes music for my eyes.

This is one of those rare golden moments in autumn when the sights and sounds and smell come together and trigger memories of younger days. Somewhere in the park a small fire burns; from this fire comes the perfume of burning leaves. This natural incense releases images from a melancholy closet somewhere in the mind. How many years has it been since this now aging adult sat on this hill in this park and, as a young boy, dreamed about future times?

Leaves rustle from a pocket of wind trying to be November. A small shiver chills and warms me at the same time. I watch falling leaves spinning, floating, sailing through their autumnal aerobatics. I follow a single leaf from its branch all the way to its landing place further down the hill. Random order, a universe in motion, noticed and unnoticed, senses touched and bypassed—such is the magic of autumn. It's not as light now. Evening is on its way. Cooler. I adjust my jacket. It is almost time to go. In less than an hour from now, the park will be awash in the light from the yellow-gold October moon, and be bathed in its harvested sunlight. Then, almost laughing, I decide what to do. The people in the park must think it odd that a guy would go to his car in the lot, only to return with a plastic lawn bag.

They watch him on his hands and knees, shuffling and scooping, using his hands like a rake to fill the bag full of leaves. I want to share and keep part of this autumn day, so I gather up a small portion of God's leafy cornflakes to take with me and send to friends. There is a need to savor these moments. I think about former classmates and friends who laughed and lived and shared the good times when we were young. I can sense their presence. They are a part of my life, and I am reluctant to let these thoughts fade. I feel a gentle sadness knowing that more than 17,000 days of a lifetime are already spent, and that my supply of these moments is limited.

Wistfully, I gather my collection of autumn leaves. They are elm and birch and oak and maple and willow. I feel them and crunch. I grab a random handful and playfully toss them skyward into the early evening's twilight. These leaves are part of my life's scrapbook. They are a part of all of us. Enjoy the autumn.

Community Center

"Where ya goin'?" When you're a kid, that's the question of choice asked by concerned parents. For those of us who grew up in Whiting, Indiana, the answer was always the same. With few exceptions, our primary destination became both response and location: "The Community Center." Later as we acquired youthful sophistication, our answer was condensed to a single word—"Center."

Center. Just the sound of the word opens a floodgate of images. More than a building, it *was* the center of our life. Within the friendly confines of this architecturally majestic building, generations of youngsters learned to swim, play basketball, checkers, table tennis, billiards, 8-ball, bowl, and—as a bonus—grow up. Under the watchful eyes of director Andy Yanas and the Center's staff, kids of all ages were welcomed and encouraged to participate in programs. Both boys and girls were given an opportunity to develop athletic ability, social skills, good manners, and proper behavior. Truly a place for all seasons, the Whiting Community Center sponsored outings, organized field trips, designed activities, and held events which enriched summer, enhanced autumn, enlivened winter, and embellished spring.

Built in the early 1920s by funds donated by the Standard Oil Company and John D. Rockefeller and his son, John D. Rockefeller, Jr., the Whiting Memorial Community House was a gift to the people of Whiting to be used as a social and recreational headquarters. Periodically, the Community Center hosted meetings of Standard Oil Company stockholders. This majestic building was erected in memory of those who served our country in World War I, and dedicated to the perpetuation of the principles for which they fought. And as intended, it did indeed become the community's center.

The Community Center was a home away from home. And like home, there were rules to obey. Before going swimming, a kid had to shower and pass inspection. Lifeguards would search for dirt. When found, it was back to the showers for another scrubbing. If you came to play basketball, you made sure you didn't bounce the ball in the lobby on the way to the gym—ever! Any kid foolish enough to engage in wanton dribbling earned a loud rebuke from Andy, Catherine, and a dozen retirees trying to watch the lobby TV. In order to play checkers, chess, ping-pong, or shoot pool, you had to go to the front desk and ask Andy or Catherine for the particular item. If your behavior was questionable, you always received a sermon along with the checkers, or whatever it was you wanted to play.

When I first started going to the Center, girls were not allowed in the pool-room. It was strictly a male sanctuary. Guys would congregate around the tables shooting a game of 8-ball, while girls stood by the doorway and watched. In the 1950s, shooting pool was not considered proper activity for young ladies. But the number one rule, the infraction that incurred the wrath of management, was wearing a hat inside the building. Pity the poor kid who absentmindedly came in wearing a hat. As soon as they were spotted, Andy would deliver a vocal reminder in stereophonic terms. He wasn't called "Chief" for nothing. Dressed in a vested suit with his trademark white shirt and bowtie, and standing about 5 feet 6 inches tall, Andy's presence and stature amplified his authority. I only forgot once. After hearing Andy's authoritative intonations, I was so intimidated, I went home and buried every hat I owned. I went to the Center often, and I wasn't about to take a chance on forgetting, so it was goodbye hats. I didn't even *own* another hat until I was 35. I figured by then the statute of limitations had run out.

The neatest place of all in the entire Community Center was the bowling alley. One could watch the pinsetters working in the pits, listen to the sounds of bowlers wreaking havoc on arrogant wooden pins, and learn interesting vocabulary when their bowling ball missed a desired target. Sitting in the spectators' section watching bowlers perform alley aerobics was a sight to behold.

Usually the air was thick with cigarette and cigar smoke as league teams battled each other for top honors. And on a good night, considerable folding money changed wallets because of stubborn pins that wouldn't fall or elusive spares not converted. Years later, as a teenager, I set pins at the Community Center. Hardy Keilman managed the bowling alley during the week, with my Dad taking over those duties on weekends. I know this sounds a little strange, but I loved setting pins. It was a real character-builder. Pin boys were paid ten cents a line, and on league nights, a single shift earned three dollars.

Aside from bumps and bruises, it was the best job around for a teenage boy. Setting pins required considerable skill: hand-eye coordination, spatial discrimination, and physical dexterity. I found out early that wood can hurt you, especially a bowling pin propelled by some maniac throwing a 16-pound bowling ball at 2000 miles an hour! You could always tell the pinsetters who weren't agile and quick. They had hickeys that read "Brunswick," and looked as if they'd been kissed by an air-hammer.

Over the more than 80 years since the Community Center opened, it has served the cultural, business, recreation, and leisure-time needs of the Whiting-Robertsdale area. More importantly, this building exemplifies and defines the essence of small blue-collar, industrial towns in America, and earned a special place in the hearts of those who made this place the center of community life.

Today, a new generation continues to enjoy the facilities and resources of this marvelous building. Although technology and other changes have taken place within this facility, hopefully years from now they, too, will fondly recall the good times spent at the Whiting Community Center. I offer a word of caution, however. As they take advantage of the opportunities available to them, I suggest they remember, once inside, to take off their hat. Somewhere, Andy Yanas is still watching!

Hot Dog Louie's Purr-fect Chili

Recently, I read a story about a new medical breakthrough concerning a cure for the common cold. Some high-tech genetic engineering outfit has come up with a new cellular recipe to fight the common cold. According to the article, this latest weapon against the sneeze and sniffles will be available to sinus sufferers of America within the next couple of years. So this is news?

Those of us who grew up around Whiting, Indiana, in the 1950s have known about a cold-cure for many years. It was inexpensive, formulated for both child and adult, and did not require a doctor's prescription; it was sold over the counter. Not available at any drugstore, this germ-killing, body-cleansing elixir was dispensed exclusively by Hot Dog Louie under his generic label: Chili.

Hot Dog Louie's was a cubbyhole of a business located on 119th near Oliver Street. It resembled an elongated telephone booth laid on its side. There was enough space for a grill, counter, stools, and room for customers changing direction to pivot—and that's all. Louie himself appeared to have been designed to fit within the establishment. A diminutive man, small in stature, Louie made up for his lack of physical size by the loudness of his voice. When irritated, Louie's vociferations would send shockwaves throughout the diner, causing a variety of multi-legged creatures to lose their footing on the apple slices in the pie case.

Louie didn't bother with an extensive menu: hamburgers, hot dogs, coffee, soda pop, and his special chili. For patrons with sufficient courage, Louie also sold pie by the slice.

Hot Dog Louie's had an atmosphere and ambiance all its own. The décor was Early American Grease. Should a customer look up—none were brave enough—they would see an array of stalactite dust bunnies hanging like gray, fuzzy icicles from the stamped metal ceiling. The flatiron gas-fired grill by the front window provided a tantalizing, mouth-watering view of scorching ground beef as Louie seared the prepared patties into hamburgers. At a right angle to the grill, against the back wall, was a well-used range top with several burners.

It was on one of these burners that Louie kept an ample supply of his ready-to-eat, cure-all chili. No one knew for certain the ingredients used to make the chili (and secretly, no one *wanted* to know). A customer would just order up a bowl, toss in a few crackers, and begin chowin' down. Louie was light-years ahead of his time. He guarded the formula of his chili long before Colonel Sanders came along with his secret herbs and spices. Given the therapeutic nature of his spicy bean stew, Louie could've built a cold-curing empire—a chili HMO!

For company when business was slow, and to control a problem of uninvited mice, Louie kept a cat in residence. Walking by the closed diner late on a winter's night, one would see the feline mice-marshal peacefully snoozing on top of the still-warm grill. Sometimes Louie would cover the grill with a towel for his purring sentry to lie on, but more often than not, the cat could be seen stretched out on the cozy iron bed, with its eyes closed, soaking up the remnants of the evening's grill grease with its fur coat. Because of this slovenly habit, Louie's customers nicknamed his cat "The Crisco Kid."

Mysteriously, the diner's patrol cat would disappear from time to time, never to be seen again. Oddly, this didn't seem to perturb Louie whatsoever, as he soon found another cat to assume the responsibility of rodent warden.

Although Louie's place was christened for hot dogs, it was the chili that became the customer's favorite, from pin boy to stock boy, oilman to steelworker, white-collar, blue-collar, or no collar at all. Word got around that if you felt a cold coming on, or had a cold already, the way to get rid of it was to eat Louie's chili. Usually a single bowl was sufficient. But, should you be troubled with chronically stuffed sinuses, a prescription of three bowls per week eliminated congestion and kept you breathing like a mating moose!

That's how it was in the good ol' days when you didn't have to worry about being sidetracked by a cold. Germs knew better than to try and take up residence in a Hot Dog Louie chili-eatin' he-man, but not any more.

Today when I get a cold, I long for a bowl of that fire-hot, flavorful boyhood remedy. Modern cold medicines aren't even close to the healing power of that amazing chili. Although pharmaceutical recipes boast of quick relief and pleasant taste, they are woefully inadequate when compared to Louie's peppered chili con carne. Take it from someone who knows: Louie's chili acted quicker. It purged the sludge of cold-causing germs from the system in a gigantic whoosh like Draino.

As for its taste, Louie's chili had a unique, hard-to-identify, unfamiliar meaty flavor. Nevertheless, I liked it. I thought it tasted PURR-FECT!

The Front Porch

Change is a part of life. Usually, most changes are subtle and take place over a period of time, affording intervals of adjustment and transition. Some call this progress. At times, I'm not too sure "progress" is the correct label. Take front porches, for instance. Before cul-de-sacs, subdivisions, and planned communities, most houses had them. Take a moment and recall.

Years ago, neighborhoods were neighborhoods. They were an extension of who we were. They identified a community's diversity, embellished character, and emphasized one's uniqueness. People not only knew who lived on their block, they actually *spoke* to one another. Today such neighborliness has been scaled back to reflect our more modern, hurried life style.

Remember when front porches were open? Many had a swing waiting for sweethearts to share romantic moments. Side-by-side, holding hands while swinging gently to night sounds of an early spring symphony—an invitation to anyone young-at-heart. Sitting on the home front's main observation deck, residents and passersby would exchange pleasantries and friendly small talk about this and that. These brief snacks of conversation were savored like after-dinner desserts enhancing early summer evenings, as homemakers relaxed on well-worn porch gliders.

Porches also served as the family dock for shipping and receiving. Packages and people began their quest or ended their journey via the porch. Drivers from Sears, Montgomery Ward, and UPS stopped by with C.O.D.'s—treasures in cardboard boxes and brown wrapping paper. Residents would "just happen to be on the porch" to greet the postman. And in the early, not-quite-light hours of the morning, the milkman would signal his delivery as he replaced empty bottles with full quarts of cold milk topped with cream. Just the sound of glass milk bottles caressing the metal carry basket awakens images of youthful mornings, bowls brimming with the "Breakfast of Champions" or "Those tasty little O's"—peaceful and unhurried moments providing ample opportunity to read the special offer on the cereal box.

Porches became prime targets and preferred landing zones for newspapers delivered on the fly by energetic newsboys as they bicycled through the neighborhood along their route. Sometimes their aim lacked precision, and an errant *Tribune, Times,* and *Daily News* reduced the number of empty milk bottles or shortened the life of an unsuspecting geranium. The front porch was a place for all seasons, for all occasions. To a young man coming to meet, for the first time, the parents of the young lady he wants to take to the dance, the front porch is terror. Later on, that same front porch became a favorite place to end a romantic evening when an understanding parent "forgot" to turn on the exterior light. The porch was the place the eventually led to happily ever after.

When you have kids of your own, the porch is training ground for behavior. "You can play outside, but stay on the porch!" Little by little, you expand their world and they increase their independence. The porch was used for compromise when adolescent and adult wishes seemed at odds:

> Mom and Dad: "We want you home by 10:00 PM."
> Teenager: "Can we sit out on the porch until 10:30? It's like being home, OK?
> Mom and Dad, remembering youthful times and another front porch: "OK."
> Teenager: "Will you leave the light off? It's brighter than the street light and gives me arc flash."
> Dad: "I'll change it to 40 watts. Wear your sunglasses!"

Somewhere along the road to progress, the front porch lost favor. The majority of new houses built today don't have old-fashioned porches—they have entrances! And older homes have been remodeled to enclose the front porch, making it a year-round living space. The porch swing is almost extinct. Most of us knew that whole-house air-conditioning and television would bring an end to the open front porch. It was inevitable. Television may have opened our window to the world, but it closed the one to our neighborhood. Nowadays, people prefer cool, air-conditioned comfort to outside swings and bothersome insects. Kids today grow up in front of electronic screens, rather than porch screens. Maybe that's why so many seem troubled. Those of us who've been around a while know from experience that porch screens are more user-friendly.

Even so, we enclosed our front porch several years ago. Now it has windows that open to screens to let in the best seasons have to offer. And there are no pesky insects to deal with. The swing was taken down and replaced with a couch. At my age, I'm not much of a swinger. But now that I own the place, I can stay out on the porch for as long as I want. The couch is comfortable, the breeze is delightful, and, when the lady of the house shares these moments, we keep the light off.

The front porch. It may not be the best place in the house, but it's close to the front.

Visit to a Castle

Some kids grow up in the shadow of famous landmarks like Yankee Stadium, Comiskey Park, or Wrigley Field. Such proximity to these hallowed structures has a profound impact on their lives. I, too, experienced this propinquity of greatness. Let me tell you about it.

I grew up in the shadow of the White Castle. Our house was less than a half-block from Whiting's porcelain palace. Everything and everyone on the 1800 block of Cleveland Avenue wore with pride the perfume of grilled beef and onions. Neighborhood wildlife and residents alike served as aromatic sponsors for America's favorite "Belly-Bombers." When meeting friends or conducting business around town, homeowners from this part of the city never had to mention their address. A couple of discreet sniffs by the other party was all that was needed. It didn't take a rocket scientist to figure out that you lived on White Castle Street!

That exalted recognition is one of the major reasons I continue to be so faithful to this hamburger fortress. Another is that one meets some of the most unforgettable characters there, especially in the wee small hours of the morning.

Years ago, long before the advent of the drive-thru window, customers could come into White Castle at any hour of the day or night. This 24-hour oasis of carbohydrates and caffeine was the final pit stop before heading home after an evening's adventures. Allow me to share with you a vintage episode from the movie called life.

It was just a few minutes this side of 3:00 AM when I entered the stainless steel and glass home of these beefy cholesterol cookies, taking my place in line. Ahead of me were two customers. Actually, there were three, because the two guys directly in front of me were together. As I waited my turn, the customer first in line made his move to where the counter-girl waited to take his order. It was at that moment that the unseen director of life's "movie" yelled: "Roll 'em, this is a take. ACTION!"

The man, obviously on the downside of his prime, was barely able to maintain a vertical position. He exuded the fragrance of distilled spirits commonly referred to as the "working man's plasma." It was evident he was a card-carrying charter member of the "Six-Pack Chug-A-Lug Club." Wearing a food-stained, cigarette-burned, tattered pink bowling shirt with the name of a grocery that has been out of business more than ten years, he spoke to the counter-girl with more sound than syllable. But being a seasoned, trained professional and veteran of the midnight shift, she was able to decode his utterances and proceeded to fill his order: two White Castles and a large black coffee—to eat here. The guy fumbled a wrinkled twenty to the top of the counter. The cashier totaled the order, and placed the man's change on the counter. He made a stab at his change, missed, and began to lose his balance. The counter-girl had turned to fill the coffee and didn't see him collapsing like a deflating rubber doll, sliding toward the floor.

The man's lips and nose mimicked the sound of airplane tires massaging the runway during a high-speed landing as they squeaked and chattered their way down the face of the grill counter, leaving saliva-streaked burnish marks on the stainless steel. Mercifully, he met the floor. There he stayed, motionless, oblivious to his surroundings.

Blinking his glazed eyes, he worked his fingers frantically as if trying to grasp the run on a ladder. Instead, he found the feet of the next customer, clamped his hands around both ankles, and held on for dear life.

With his order on a tray, the counter-girl approached the spot where she had last seen the customer. She looked over toward the booths—no sign of him. Peering over the counter's edge, she saw the pile of clothes that enclosed her customer, and she also saw the vise-like grip he had on the stranger's ankles. She looked pleadingly at the two guys and said: "Help me out." The two "recruits" were already in action. After brief negotiations with the pink-shirted man, convincing him that he was not going to fall down an elevator shaft, the man released his grip on the ankles. Carefully they lifted the folded man from the floor, helped him to a booth, and placed him in position so he could eat his hamburgers.

The counter-girl, following the two Samaritans, set the man's order on the table, and went back to work behind the counter. The two "draftees" were thanked and dismissed from duty. They returned to their place in line, picked up their now-ready order, glanced one last time at the pink shirt weaving in the booth, and headed out the door to the parking lot.

I had just finished giving my order to the grill girl when we heard a strange sound. Gurgling? Similar, but different. Then the answer jumped into my mind. It was the sound that we used to make in grade school when we blew through the straw to make bubbles in our milk. The only difference here was that this sound was more rhythmic, a definite cadence. Looking around for the source, all eyes zeroed in on it simultaneously.

The guy who had been put in the booth had tipped forward. As his head completed the arc toward the table, his nose had somehow lined up precisely with his cup of coffee. In what must rank as a classic dunk shot, his schnozzle was now submerged in his cup of black coffee. With the rim of the coffee cup supporting his face, he was now perfectly positioned to snorkel his coffee in between gulps of air. Mindless of his plight, he continued to serenade us with his nasal bubbling, with the two square hamburgers serving as sentries. Unconsciously, the waiting customers kept time to his proboscis percussions by tapping their feet on the floor. I stuck around for one more toe-tapping chorus, then picked up my order and went home.

Some people, when they cannot sleep, stay up all night and watch TV. Not me. I'd rather go to the White Castle for a sack full of Slyders and check out the clientele. One never knows when they'll see an Academy Award-worthy performance!

Capitol Visit

As kids growing up in the '50s we couldn't wait to visit the Capitol. No, not the one in Washington, D.C., but the one on 119th Street in Whiting, Indiana. Adorned with an elegant rectangular marquee, the Capitol Theater became the movie mecca for hometown kids. Every week, as if on cue, youngsters would begin their pilgrimage from their homes to the Saturday matinee. An hour before the 1:30 PM showtime, kids would queue in front of the ticket booth, hoping to commandeer a coveted front-row seat. Boisterous, energy-filled boys and girls made their presence known while waiting their turn at the glass-enclosed ticket window. For the price of a 14-cent ticket, these young film patrons would be feted to double-feature action, cartoons, adventure serials, "News of the Day," and "Coming Attractions."

At the time, Whiting boasted two movie houses, the Hoosier Theater and the Capitol Theater. Both were located on the city's main thoroughfare, 119th Street, almost directly across from one another. The Hoosier was for the more refined, sophisticated, mature moviegoer, while the Capitol welcomed younger film buffs who frequently reeked of Jujyfruits, Good and Plenty, Black Crows, and Dots. This confectionary smorgasbord served to cover up popcorn breath and carbonated soda burps.

Hoosier patrons came to watch screen idols such as Joan Crawford, Tyrone Power, Gene Tierney, Joan Bennett, and Charles Boyer. The Hoosier's balcony was an ideal place for romantically inclined couples to hold hands while onscreen melodramas unfolded. Capitol kids, on the other hand, were anything but romantic and quiet—cheering on cowboy heroes like Red Ryder, Roy Rogers, Randolph Scott, and Johnny Mack Brown. During horror movies, they screamed through their popcorn at Boris Karloff, Lon Chaney, and Bela Lugosi, while cringing from monsters that seemed to jump out at the audience from the screen.

Louis Nye managed both the Hoosier and Capitol. Mr. Nye became well known to Capitol kids because of his many promotional gimmicks and showmanship. One of his most memorable promotions was the audience participation stage show, held between features during the Saturday matinee. (Mr. Nye was well aware of the limited attention span exhibited by a theater filled with grammar school urchins.)

Immediately following the end of the movie, while cheers still filled the theater, Louie would walk onstage like a ringmaster. The house lights would come up, and stagehands would push a giant screened drum loaded with ticket stubs near the microphone where Mr. Nye stood. At the far end of the stage, a large painted square easel with a dozen air-filled balloons waited. Each balloon contained a piece of paper identifying a prize. At first sight of the balloon dartboard, the sugar-loaded audience went crazy.

Every kid knew the routine. After thoroughly mixing the tickets with a number of dramatic turns, Mr. Nye, resplendent in his blue suit, white shirt, and trademark bow tie, reached in and pulled a stub. Stepping to the microphone, he dramatically called the number. A number of kids ruined their chances of winning by nervously chewing their ticket stub during the opening adventure feature. The more disciplined kids chewed their fingernails instead, saving their valuable stub for a chance at fame and fortune. The kid with the match would make his or her way down the aisle and climb up to the stage while several hundred peers screamed.

Calming the crowd, Louie would have the lucky youngster give their name. More cheers. Then, like a true master of ceremony, Louie would carefully position the kid on the line that marked the throwing distance from the board. With high melodrama, Louie would hand the contestant three darts. If the kid hit a balloon, he won a prize—usually free passes to the show. Sometimes, there were dishes left over from gravy bowl night that Louie promoted to the winner as "a great gift for Mom." But every kid knew they were there for a chance to win the grand prize.

Hidden in a single balloon was a piece of paper that read: BICYCLE! That was the Holy Grail—the quest that motivated every kid to sit through a Saturday afternoon in a darkened theater. With one well-aimed throw of a dart, some lucky girl or boy could win a brand-new, 26-inch balloon-tire bicycle! With every dart toss, the Capitol rocked. Normally bold rodents on patrol for dropped candy or spilled popcorn took refuge under floor-mounted air vents until the house lights dimmed for the second feature, wary of being stomped by uncontrolled Thom McCann oxfords and Buster Brown shoes. Each time anyone broke a balloon, bedlam broke loose. Louie knew his business. He milked every ounce of suspense out of every throw. Even the kids who missed everything and stuck the dart in the curtain were sent back to their seat amid thunderous applause. Louie made every kid feel like a celebrity. It was simply magnificent!

The stage shows became the magnet that drew us to the Capitol week after week. We each believed our ticket would be drawn next time, so it was back to Nye's fantasyland. Just the sight of those balloons sent us into a frenzy. Like bloated latex fortune cookies, those brightly colored orbs held every kid's dream—a chance to win a new bike!

Although I rarely missed a matinee, my number was never called. My cousin Len Scher, on the other hand, not only had his number called, he won the bicycle! After the show, I walked alongside him on the way home as he carefully guided his new Schwinn down Cleveland Avenue. That was the closest I've ever been to Lady Luck.

As television gained popularity, Saturday matinees faded into history. Today, with videos, multi-channel TV, and countless computer games, throwing darts at balloons to win a bicycle is too quaint and old-fashioned for modern, gadget-oriented, technologically sophisticated youngsters. Maybe it's just as well—times change.

The Capitol Theater is now a hardware store. Thankfully during the conversion, the owners left a portion of the theater's ceiling in its original form. In order to see it, one has to go in the back where they sell pipe. An old chandelier still hangs from the ceiling. One glance and all the memories of Saturday matinees flood the mind: hometown images that became treasures. And though I've never been to Washington, D.C., I've always cherished my frequent visits to the Capitol.

Shoreline Chauffeur

Those of us who lived in the Calumet Region during the '40s, '50s, and '60s were treated to a job-rich industrial smorgasbord that featured steel mills, refineries, small business, factories, shops, and stores. Area communities and neighborhoods were home to thousands of residents who worked, shopped, and went to school. Though many "Regionites" drove cars, a primary mode of transportation was the bus. Whether one needed a ride to the mills, downtown Hammond, Gary, Griffith, or anywhere in between, a Shoreline chauffeur offered convenient, dependable service.

For two bits, blue-collar workers, housewives, students, and patrons of every persuasion rode the familiar yellow and white, diesel-powered municipal limousine. Because our family never owned a car, bus schedules were required reading, with routes and departure times committed to memory. Even though other carriers served Calumet Region residents at the time, by far the most popular and preferred company was the Shoreline—for me, anyway.

Introduced to the bus at an early age, Mom would take us to Chicago's Loop for our annual back-to-school bargain hunt. The bus lumbered along streets with unfamiliar names toward downtown Chicago. Along the way, our chauffeur made numerous stops as wannabe riders waited on corners or by commuter tracks holding transfers, tokens, and coins of the realm.

A favorite boyhood memory involves a bus ride home from Chicago. Following a successful purchasing venture at Goldblatt's, we walked to the bus station to make our connection for the ride home to Whiting. The bus we rode had a single passenger seat up front next to the driver. Still aglow from her shopping wizardry, Mom let me sit aside the driver. Like a co-pilot, I watched the driver shift levers, punch transfers, and make change. Every now and then he'd hit the lever on the fare box. Immediately the small-handled wheel revolved, clicking away and counting the coins that had been deposited through slots in the gable-roofed, steeple-shaped coin meter. To an impressionable 8-year-old, riding up front next to the bus driver was fantastic!

My fondness for the Shoreline grew during the years I worked in the mill. From the summer of 1958 until I left for college six years later, the bus was my transportation to and from work. Even after I purchased an automobile, I would frequently take the bus and forego the hassle of parking in one of the company's lots.

Truly, the Shoreline was a bus for all seasons. During warm weather, windows were lowered, allowing industrial aromas to filter in and out among sweaty riders. Occasionally a renegade wind gust would send diesel fumes upward. When mixed with coke oven dust, refinery vapors, and blast furnace smoke, breathing became a challenge. There were times—when conditions were just right—one could hear mill pigeons cough!

During wintertime, frigid temperatures dictated the closure of windows. Mill workers adapted accordingly. With the bus heater set on open-hearth, riders kept internal thermostats at a comfortable level through frequent nips of libation. Old Granddad and Jim Beam were frequent guest riders on the Shoreline. I don't know about the bus, but the passengers were well-fortified with anti-freeze. Ralph Kramden would've loved driving a Shoreline!

During adverse winter weather, the bus at times was late. In early morning darkness, I stood bareheaded in teeth-chattering, bone-numbing cold, holding an A&P shopping bag with mill clothes and lunch. Mercifully, just before I froze solid, the bus would arrive. As soon as the folding front doors opened, I'd step onto the bus, slip a quarter in the fare box, and search for a vacant seat. On many occasions the bus was crowded and I had to stand. Half awake and shivering, it took considerable effort to maintain one's balance and stability as the bus rumbled along, lurching through Dickey Road's crater-sized potholes on the way to Indiana Harbor. Riding the Shoreline was more than an adventure—it was an expedition!

All in all, I enjoyed those times. Each moment helped shape who I am. Since leaving the mill for the campus and classroom, I don't have occasion to ride a bus. Every now and then however, I climb aboard a scholastic "cheese wagon" when I chaperone a school-sponsored excursion. It's not the same. Still I easily recall the sights, sounds, and fragrance of a mill-bound Shoreline bus crowded with steelworkers. And I think about the kid with the shopping bag who rode the bus and worked in the mill, and the difference it made in his life.

Hometown

I never realized how influential a hometown could be until I went away to college in the fall of 1964. Although Terre Haute and Indiana State University are only 160 miles due south of my home, it was like traveling to another country. During orientation, the 34 residents of Reeve Hall's second floor dorm gathered to get acquainted. I was the only guy from Lake County.

The Resident Assistant asked each one of us to tell a little about ourselves—hometown, high school, college major—stuff like that. From around the room came names I'd never heard of, places like Bedford, Mitchell, Brownstown, Oolitic, Linton. Some towns so small they only had one yellow page in the phonebook. When my turn came, I told them I was from Whiting. "Where's that?" they asked. "It's about 30 miles south of Chicago. Whiting is part of the Calumet Region," I responded.

Immediately, the room went silent. Had I said something offensive? The R.A explained that in parts of Indiana, the Calumet Region had a less-than-favorable reputation. As a 23-year-old freshman, I found their apprehension amusing but unwarranted. To allay any misgivings, I offered to answer questions they might have about the faraway land north of the Kankakee River.

Hesitantly at first, then seemingly all at once, they asked about the Region's lifestyles, environment, and legends. After we got to know one another, I couldn't resist teasing them with stories about living in "Da Region"—and telling a tall tale or two.

I told them about Region wildlife, especially our world-famous six-pound bluebirds. When they challenged the veracity of my story, I casually admitted that Region bluebirds were actually asthmatic pigeons, blue from gasping for air as they flew through clouds of unknown elements from region steel mills and refineries. "That's why we're known throughout Indiana as the Land of Coughing Birds," I explained. After a number of these Region stories, my dormmates accepted the charm of Northwest Indiana with diminished wariness.

Over the course of the year, we traded stories and experiences about hometowns, and I came to understand how important those places are regardless of location, size, or name. More than a collection of buildings, stores, and houses, a hometown helps define who we are. It's our "growing up" place—the place to which we belong. A hometown becomes our primary point of reference, and we eagerly narrate episodes about local characters, places, and events that shaped our life.

How easily memories of bygone days come to mind: my grandparents' house on Oliver Street; Sacred Heart School, where we were taught reading, writing, arithmetic, and discipline—not to mention the fine print in the *Baltimore Catechism*; my boyhood home on Cleveland Avenue; the most important building in town, the Whiting Public Library—Adventureland for the mind; Whiting High School, where classmates and teachers enriched my life beyond words.

I fondly recall the Community Center, the city's "kid place," offering good times courtesy of Andy Yanas and a cast of thousands! That famous landmark and culinary oasis, White Castle, its "Belly-Bombers" and "Slyders" serving as competition for the refineries—a special formula for makin' gas! Businesses like Neal Price's Firestone Store—music, toys, and sports equipment; a kid felt good just going in there. Dave's Drugstore, home of the world's greatest root beer float! Nick's Pool Room, a snooker and pinball emporium for teen guys. Hot Dog Louie's palace of fine dining; Louie's cure-all chili was legendary! Salmon's Barber Shop, Newberry's 5 & 10, and the Victory Restaurant. Standard Diamonds, Little League's field of dreams. The Post Office, ground zero for 46394. Whiting Park, a place for all seasons—skating, swimming, playing, and holding hands without a plan. That's my kind of town!

Even though one moves away to a different city or distant location, there remains a connection, an emotional bond to one's place of origin. And regardless of the number of years or infrequent visits, one fondly recalls their hometown and their youthful, vibrant, exuberant, energetic, and carefree days. Thinking about one's hometown engenders thoughts of effervescent spirit, romantic moonlit walks, and moments to remember. Each recollection is lush with memories of family, classmates, friends, and activities that fill our life's scrapbook, accompanying us like faithful companions all our days.

While others may view your hometown as merely a name or place on a map—ordinary, insignificant—that's okay. What really matters is how you feel about your hometown in your heart and the influence it has had on your life. When asked where you're from, what thoughts make up your response?

To me, Whiting is more than a place to be from; more than a place to return to for a reunion or long overdue visit; more than an attitude, or a perception, or postal address. My hometown is also a journey—a journey of the heart, a journey of the mind, a journey of the spirit. That probably explains why we occasionally look back, scanning the landscape of our life. There seems to be a need to press the pause button, putting the present on hold and giving us time to savor moments past. Somehow, almost instinctively, we know when it's time to savor, and when it is time to continue our life's journey.

By now most of us have been around long enough to understand that the journey should be as enjoyable as the destination; that, as life continues to unfold, we should set aside time to remember private, special moments. By savoring the past, we enrich the present and give purpose to the future. Hopefully, if heaven is kind, our journey will be filled with joyous remembrances of the treasured place called Hometown.

Adolescence to "Adultville"

Sputnik and Me

In everyone's life, there are historic events of such magnitude that they brand the mind. So memorable are these occurrences that one remembers exactly where they were, what they were doing, and who they were with. Regardless of how many years pass, these images are recalled as clearly as a first-run movie. The '40s were a decade of such events: Pearl Harbor, the death of F.D.R., D-Day, V.E. Day, and V.J. Day. My recollections of those times are not quite in focus, as I was too young to experience the full emotional impact of those incidents.

My historical awareness took root during the '50s. The decade began with the Korean War, MacArthur's dismissal, the Korean Armistice, and reached branding iron intensity on October 4, 1957, with a 5-11 alarm called Sputnik—the world's first earth-orbiting satellite. Without firing a single hostile shot, this 183-½ pound, signal-emitting sphere of Russian technology orbited the sky and tore a gaping hole in America's national security blanket. For the first time since World War II, America was thrust in the role of an also-ran. Being #1 in the world was no more. I remember the day Sputnik changed our lives.

We were a month into our senior year at Whiting High School, when the tranquility of our lives and our nation, came to a beeping halt. October 4, 1957, dawned a drizzly, gray Friday. It was the morning's first period class, and I was going about my assigned tasks in the machine shop when our teacher, Mr. George McClure, called the class to his desk. Always pleasant, with a quick smile, his solemn tone matched the dreariness of the day and gave us cause for concern.

"The world will never be the same again," he began. "The Russians have launched a satellite into outer space. It's named Sputnik." Mr. McClure went on to explain what this meant in terms of Russia's military and technical superiority, and how America was shocked by this feat. For the first time in my life, America's self-confidence seemed shattered. I did not fully understand every nuance of Sputnik, but I could tell from Mr. McClure's voice that this was a very serious situation. The unthinkable flashed across my mind: Could Russia overtake the United States? Just the thought caused a knot to form in the pit of my stomach. What a way for our senior year to begin.

By the end of the first full week following Sputnik's launch, we had garnered enough information to initially enter the lexicon of space technology. We learned about elliptical orbits and defined terms like apogee and perigee. We clipped articles and illustrations from the daily newspapers. We read about rockets and boosters and orbital paths. This 23-inch beach ball-sized radio transmitter spawned phrases, jokes, and songs. The entire world was witness to the birth of a new era. For on that first Friday in October 1957, the Space Age was born!

Even though America had been jolted by this technological achievement, it all seemed so far away, disconnected from out immediate concerns here in Whiting, Indiana. That perception, however, changed very quickly.

About two weeks after Sputnik was launched, local newspapers carried details of the satellite's orbit and when it would pass over the Chicago area. The schedule indicated direction, degree from the horizon, and the time of the pass. The senior machine shop students made plans to view Sputnik.

A few days later, on a clear, dark, cool evening in October, several classmates and I met at Whiting Park, walked to the beach, and took up lookout positions, facing east over coal-black Lake Michigan. At the prescribed time, we carefully began scanning the star-filled sky. I sat on the sand to more easily guide my field of vision. A couple of the guys brought binoculars to help in their search. According to newspapers and radio reports, it should be possible to see Sputnik with the naked eye, appearing as a moving star. I decided to test the accuracy of that information.

I leaned back against a small dune and stared skyward. Though I was with favorite classmates, I felt alone. A cool, frisky October wind snuck inside my partially-zipped jacket and made me shiver. The lake, too, protested the capricious breeze and slapped more vigorously at the sandy shore. I continued my satellite search.

Then suddenly, as if dropped into the star field by an unseen hand, I saw it! The small pinpoint of light, more than 140 miles above my eyes, moved silently through the autumn night. Other voices confirmed the sighting. I locked onto this rocket-launched beacon and followed its path across the heavens. My senses were overwhelmed by the vastness of space and seeing the first man-made cosmic vehicle as it traveled beneath the light of ancient stars. Sight came together with sound as I listened to the concert of wind and wave, while friends' voices competed with the whistle of a freight train off in the distance. I used my hand for added balance, and the fragrance of autumn blended with the feel of dry sand as I continued tracking the "traveling companion."

At that moment, I was awed by my insignificance on this planet. How puny and trivial we are; yet, we find solace, comfort, protection, and purpose in all that is seen and unseen.

Today, Sputnik is no more. As a country, we won the race to the moon and have sent machines to explore our solar system and beyond. In time, our national anxiety faded and we regained our self-confidence. Years later, other events would impact my mind and warrant instant recall. Those incidents I would remember in other ways; Sputnik, however, was special. It caused a 16-year-old senior in high school to become a more knowledgeable citizen, a better student, and, helped set him on a journey to understand his place among the stars. Almost five decades later, that journey continues. I still look to the star-filled sky; no longer searching for satellites, but to ponder the majesty, mystery, and wonder displayed before my eyes.

Jalopies and Good Times

I listened as he told his story. The 17-year-old high school junior claimed unfair treatment by local police. With considerable animation, he explained how he was out cruisin' with some friends when he was pulled over by a squad car. "The cop said I was doin' 45 in a 30 zone. The officer never gave me a chance to explain or nothin'. He asked for my license, wrote a ticket, and told me when to be in court. Just 'cause I'm a teenager having some fun with the guys, I get a ticket. I drive a flashy set of wheels, so I'm an easy target. It ain't fair!"

I waited until the level of his indignation returned to normal range before saying anything. But I had waited too long, because he was already talking again. "You ever get stopped by the cops when you were a teenager, Mr. Koch? Were things this unfair when you were a kid?"

Finally, it was my turn. "First of all," I reminded this vociferous adolescent, "life is not fair. In fact, the word 'fair' doesn't even appear in the United States Constitution, so why should it apply to traffic stops? If things were fair, the Chicago Cubs would have won the World Series years ago!" Then I looked the kid right in the eye and said: "Yeah, we got stopped every now and then by the cops, but things were different."

"What do you mean, 'different'?"

"Well, for one, everything wasn't so serious. Sometimes being stopped turned out to be a lot of laughs.

"How so?"

"Because the cars we drove and rode around in were jalopies."

"What's a jalopy?"

"A jalopy was a car with character. And a few flaws. For a hundred bucks or so, a kid could choose any number of vintage street chariots."

"Were they safe?"

"Listen, if it started, and the radio played, we were satisfied. Anything else like windows that rolled up and down, a working heater, functional door latches, and no holes in the floorboards were a bonus."

"How'd they run?"

"Reluctantly. And sometimes the radiator leaked a little, and the engine burned oil."

"What'd you do?"

"We'd fill the radiator with dry oatmeal, and pour a couple of cans of Casite's Motor Honey in the crankcase. After a couple of blocks when the engine heated up, the leak in the radiator would stop and the car smelled like breakfast. The Motor Honey was so thick it clogged the spaces between the worn rings and cylinders. It had a dual benefit: Not only did that petroleum molasses reduce engine clattering, it also lessened oil-based exhaust emissions.

One of the guys bought an old Dodge. It didn't have a door handle on the driver's side, so he wired it closed with a coat hanger and everyone got in on the passenger side. We thought that was *very* European."

"Why'd you get stopped by the cops?"

"We'd ride around singing or acting rowdy, six or seven guys jammed in a little coupe. Sometimes we'd tie a white hankie to the antenna like a flag of surrender. During one Halloween, six of us each bought a gallon of apple cider. We went driving around swigging cider and yelling "Trick or Treat," and were pulled over on Calumet Avenue. The driver, a kid we called Bugsy, was a real character. Genetically, his body contained 200 funny bones.

Anyway, we get pulled over, and the cop comes up to him with his ticket book in his hand like a uniformed carhop. Before the policeman even utters a word, Bugsy says: "Yes, I'll have a cheeseburger, fries, and a large Coke." We're all laughing and giving "atta-boys" to Bugsy.

Bugsy immediately puts on his best poker face and asks: "What's the problem, officer?"

"You're going 50 miles an hour!" the policeman replies.

Bugsy shakes his head in disbelief. "Don't be ridiculous, officer, this car won't run an hour!"

Officer: "OK, wiseguy, follow me to the station!"

Bugsy: "I can't."

Officer: "Why not?"

Bugsy: "Because my mother told me never to go with strangers!"

By now, Bugsy had taxed the lawman's patience.

Officer: "What are you, a comedian?"

Bugsy: "No, sir, I'm Catholic!"

Following his court appearance and a stern lecture by Judge Stodola, Bugsy spent the next four Saturdays in traffic school. The whole episode was broadcast "live" on WJOB ("That's 1230 on your AM dial") from the courtroom. Adding insult to injury, it was re-broadcast later that same afternoon during rush our, so Region motorists could hear the judge's lecture and penance dispensed to wayward drivers.

Reflecting on all this, the 17-year-old said: "So, you guys got along with the cops?"

"Pretty much. Back then, everyone had a more accepting attitude. We were benevolent adversaries. For the most part, we acted silly, not malicious. Occasionally, some do-gooder would have our jalopy followed by a tow truck and ambulance, just waiting for disaster to strike. But it was all in fun. We never had an accident, but we ran out of gas a lot."

"Why, couldn't you afford gas?"

"Basically, that was the problem. Money was tight, and at forty cents a gallon, we'd try and ride around all night on a dollar's worth of Standard Oil's Red Crown. Sometimes, we wound up pushing our 'limousine' to the nearest gas station and pooling finances. If the station was closed, we'd drain the pump hoses. Usually that was enough to get us home.

"That was one of the neat things about being a teenager in the '50s. We didn't worry about driving fancy cars because we were too busy laughing. We didn't care about having a new car; we just wanted wheels. New cars came later. Our biggest concern was having enough money for a few gallons of gas and a large box of oatmeal. The oatmeal came from Mom's pantry. Some of the junkers we bought needed pieces of plywood to cover holes in the floorboards. At times, the brakes didn't brake, and we'd open the doors and drag our feet on the street to slow and stop the car. Like I said, jalopies had character!"

"That was then, Mr. Koch, these are modern times. What should I do?"

"Well," I said, "you can always obey the traffic laws."

Lumber Float

For many of us, growing up in Whiting, Indiana, during the "Fabulous '50s" was the best thing that could have happened to a kid. It was a time filled with sights and sounds, experiences and events that left lasting impressions on young minds. Let me tell you about one of the favorite hangouts—the drugstore.

Aside from providing a sundry of cosmetics, pharmaceuticals, greeting cards, photographic needs, candy, magazines, and the latest comic books, the drugstore featured a soda fountain where the town folk could relax with a cold, carbonated drink and small snack. Situated on corners and other prominent locations along the town's main thoroughfare, these modern-day apothecaries served as a refreshing oasis for the Oil City's citizens.

The drugstore was a store for all seasons and all ages. Throughout the year, shoppers would purchase much-needed merchandise from these contemporary general stores. Wintertime brought half-frozen youngsters in for some warmth and hot chocolate after an afternoon of ice-skating on the park's lagoon. In summer, they came for suntan oils and sundaes.

When Little League season transformed the neighborhood lads into Boys of Summer, one would see hopeful future DiMaggios, Mantles, and Sniders stopping in for a game's supply of their favorite bubble gum on their way to the ballpark at Standard Diamonds. Sporting the name of the team's sponsor on their uniforms, they rivaled the images on the baseball cards that came with the gum.

Following the Friday night football game, as falling leaves ushered in autumn, the city's teenagers would walk the few blocks from the high school field to their favorite drugstore for a post-game nightcap. From gridiron to gridlock, they'd pile in and stake out a favorite spot, or park themselves on a stool in front of the fountain.

Regardless of who was "tending bar," the scenario was always the same. The fountain foreman on duty would start at one end and begin taking orders. Being an experienced professional, this captain of carbonation never wrote anything down. Once committed to memory, the orders were filled with accuracy and precision.

During the time *before* teenagers were viewed as legitimate consumers, and, in an attempt at reducing the teenager's proclivity for mischief, the local drugstores adopted a set of unwritten rules for their adolescent patrons. The kids referred to these fountain rules as the "Teen Demandments." Had they officially been recorded, they would have read thusly:

1. If thou siteth on a stool, thou shalt spend at least a dime.

2. If thou buyest only a nickel Coke, thou shalt stand.

3. If thou chooseth to sit in a booth and partake in time-consuming conversations (regardless of whether thou be the talker or the talkee), each of thee must invest a minimum of thirty cents.

4. Thou shalt not cause the straw's paper cover to become an airborne projectile.

5. Thou shalt refrain from using your straw to blow bubbles in your drink.

6. Thou shalt not suck air through the straw at the bottom of the glass, making slurping noises.

7. Thou shalt not read the magazines or comics, which are for purchase only. This drugstore is NOT the public library!

Even so, in spite of these regulations, the jester would have his day. Fountain orders would be taken amid the normal youthful chaos associated with a "we-shoulda-won-the-game" seminar. Usual requests for cherry Cokes, Green Rivers, Pepsis, and root beer floats were shouted above the din of the teen clamor. Invariably without fail, there was always one kid who didn't have any money. He'd look the soda surgeon right in the eye and order a lumber float.

Anyone who ever toiled behind the syrup rail played straight man to the jester: "What's a lumber float?"

"A lumber float," replied the jester, "is a glass of water with a toothpick!"

Waves of laughter washed across young faces. The now harried fizz-water engineer muttered to himself as to the biological origins of the teenage clown. The momentary distraction enables the nickel-spending standees a chance to "drift" over to the magazine rack and peruse the latest publications. It wasn't long, however, before the sharp eyes of the drugstore owner zeroed in on the comic book-scanning culprits.

"This is not a library. The library is on Oliver Street. Go there if you want to read." (That was one of the neat things about living in Leave-It-To-Beaver,

U.S.A. They not only told you what something wasn't, they told you where that something was located!)

Nowadays, kids go to some look-alike fast food place or any one of a number of franchise restaurants for their post-game gathering. Customers' orders are taken by some uniformed, name-tagged employee with a phony smile, who punches buttons on a computerized menu programmed into a register. Shortly thereafter, the food arrives in disposable containers. No atmosphere, no banter, no ambiance—nothing. Order. Pay. Wait. Pick Up. Next!

Some folks call that progress. Not me. I prefer the old-fashioned way. Give me a drugstore with a real, honest-to-goodness, mix-it-right-in-front-of-you soda fountain, piloted by a seasoned veteran who knows how to flavor phosphates and enjoys repartee with the customers. Give me a marble-topped counter fronted by a row of swivel stools waiting to caress the vertical smile face of thirsty patrons. A place where a kid, short on cash, can saunter in, sit down, look the "barkeep" right in the eye and say: "Gimme a lumber float!"

Cruisin'

During an informal discussion with my twenty-first-century students, I mentioned how, as teenagers, we'd go cruisin'. They were unfamiliar with the term, so I explained. Cruisin' is what you did with a carload of buddies, usually along the main drag of town. You'd "cruise" up and down the street, checking out the chicks, comparing cars, and occasionally "peeling out" from a light in a mock drag race to impress other cruisers. Not brain boggling, I admit, but when you're part of this scene, life doesn't get much sweeter.

Living in the "Region" in the late '50s and early '60s, cruisin' became a major part of the teenage summertime menu. Throughout the area, there were a number of drive-in restaurants and we expanded our cruisin' range to include pit stops at these burger oases. We'd be there long enough to chow down some fries, siphon a Coke, check out the carhops, and look over the roadsters and ragtops. As a bonus, we'd hear the latest gossip about who was doing what with whom—and how often!

On any given evening, the guys would assemble at cruisin' headquarters—Art's Drive In at the intersection of Indianapolis Boulevard and Calumet Avenue, commonly known as Five Points in Whiting. Parked in the back row, a decision would be made as to what chariot to ride in (usually the one with the most gas in the tank) and who would ride shotgun. Vehicles left behind would be locked and watched over by friendly carhops.

There was a pre-determined route and routine featured by cruisers. Depending on where one lived, there were major considerations as to street selection and sequence of drive-in visitations. We lived in the northernmost neighborhoods of the Region, so our travels took us south and east. On a silent internal signal, the cruise crew would pile in the designated street sled and head out. The official cruisin' itinerary was a map to adolescent adventure: From Art's to Son's Drive-In at 169th Street and Calumet Avenue in Hammond; then on to the Drive-O-Matic for a frosty cold A&W root beer. The game was to confuse the carhop until she lost count of how many mugs were to be returned. These heavy glass mugs, which came in a variety of sizes, became prized souvenirs.

As soon as we had "mugged" the carhop, we headed for Kelly's and Serenade, two drive-ins located almost next to each other on the southwest corners of Indianapolis Boulevard at 169th Street in Hammond. Sometimes we'd backtrack a few miles north on the boulevard to The Fat Boy Drive In and wolf down one of their half-ton cheeseburgers. Usually though, we'd park at Kelly's and watch the asphalt Romeos role-play James Dean or Marlon Brando as they sat in their souped-up jalopies and customized cars. With their cars' paint and chrome surfaces Blue Coral-polished to a high luster, these guys were the center of attention, wearing sunglasses long after dark.

After a couple of tunes on WLS, an order of fries, and a round of Coca-Colas, we'd head for the Pow-Wow. The Pow-Wow was a rectangular shaped drive-in placed in the center of a paved lot one block east of Kennedy Avenue on 169th Street. Its glossy white enamel exterior was highlighted by bands of flashing pink neon on the building's perimeter. On the roof's peak, a multicolored neon starburst revolved in the night sky. That drive-in had great tomato burgers; I believe I personally lowered the inventory considerably throughout the summer.

If the evening was still young, we'd cruise to the Patio, or the Frost Top. Both of these drive-ins were in Hessville. The Patio did business at 169th Street and Parrish Avenue; the Frost Top enticed hungry motorists traveling along Kennedy Avenue near 175th Street. On special nights, customized cars would rally at The Blue Top in Highland, just south of Ridge Road on Indianapolis Boulevard, or Sammy's in Gary. Depending upon the amount of funds available, gas in the tank, and local gossip, the cruisin' schedule would be modified to include two additional pit stops.

Regrettably, there's not much cruisin' done today. Most of the drive-ins—movie and restaurants—are history. Instead of carhops, motorists talk to a grid opening in a lighted menu sign, orders repeated back in what sounds like a nasal-damaged underwater gargle. Everything is handed to you through a small opening in the drive-thru window— like passing food to an outcast. No carhops, no souvenirs to collect, little social interaction with anyone. The face in the window has your computerized order bagged and ready to push out to you. Order. Pay. Food. Change. Next! That's the modern way. That's progress. Seems like we're all in such a hurry these days, there's no time to be human. It's all so mechanical.

Too bad the modern generation won't have the opportunity to go cruisin' like we did. There was something very special about going to a favorite drive-in and having a friendly carhop smile while she took your order as you good-naturedly teased one another and enjoyed the repartee. It was quite an era—something very special indeed. So to all the former carhops and cruisers out there: Thanks for the memories!

Cruisers' List of Drive-Ins ('50s and '60s)

Art's Drive-In - Indianapolis Boulevard & Calumet Avenue, Whiting, IN
Hoppe's Drive-In - Indianapolis Boulevard & Atcheson Avenue, Whiting, IN
A&W Drive-In - 3800 Hohman Avenue, Hammond, IN
Son's Drive-In - 6850 Calumet Avenue, Hammond IN
Drive-O-Matic - 7206 Calumet Avenue, Hammond, IN
Fat Boy Drive-In - 168th Street & Indianapolis Boulevard, Hammond, IN
Kelly's Drive-In - 169th Street & Indianapolis Boulevard, Hammond, IN
Serenade Drive-In - 169th Street & Indianapolis Boulevard, Hammond, IN
Pow-Wow Drive-In - 2733 169th Street (169th & Kennedy), Hammond, IN
Patio Drive-In - 3214 169th Street, Hammond, IN
Frost Top Drive-In - 176th Street & Kennedy Avenue, Hammond, IN
Dog & Suds Drive-In - 8100 Kennedy Avenue, Highland, IN
Blue Top Drive-In - 8801 Indianapolis Boulevard, Highland, IN

How many do you remember? What's your fondest drive-in memory?

Senior Prom

As a high school teacher, one of the highlights of the year is prom. As it nears, some of the guys come to school wearing tuxedos. They do that to earn a discount on the tux. Going to the prom these days is expensive. One senior boy told me it would cost him between $500 and $700.

"How come so much?" I asked. "Why is it so costly?"

He proceeded to reel off the expenses: tickets, pictures, limousine, tuxedo, flowers, and spending money. Then he added: "That's without the extras."

"Such as?"

"Such as a pre-prom haircut, tanning sessions, after-prom carriage ride, and a next-day outing at Great America." He paused for a second breath. "A guy's gotta start saving for the prom a year ahead of time."

I was shocked! Five hundred-plus bucks for a high school prom! My mind flipped through years of memory and stopped at Friday, May 9, 1958. Senior Prom. Whiting High School. Madura's Danceland.

I began reviewing the mental inventory of that social high point of adolescence. Hmmmm. Let me think—senior prom. Total cash outlay: a lot less than $500. As I recall, I hadn't planned on going—for two good reasons. First, I was flat broke. In fact, I was more broke than the Ten Commandments. Second, not one girl had answered my want ad for a prom date. Taken together, these reasons made it rather difficult to even *think* about the prom. Things looked bleak, to say the least.

I also had one other problem. I did not know how to dance. That's not really true—I knew one—the famous elevator dance. It was easy; there are no steps to it. You just stand in one spot and hum! Just when it appeared as though I would never promenade, a week before the gala event things changed dramatically!

One of the benefits of attending a small high school is that everyone knows everyone. The enrollment at Whiting High School in 1958 totaled less than 400 students. By the end of senior year, one feels a sense of belonging, of camaraderie, of looking-out-for-one-another. And it was this concern and friendship that made attending the prom possible.

For reasons that still warm the heart, my classmates decided that I *must* go to the prom. Knowing full well my financial limitations, they took it upon themselves to make the necessary arrangements, answering all my arguments.

Several senior girls accomplished what handbills, posters, and newspaper want ads could not—they found me a prom date! Somehow they convinced a young lady in our class to risk her social reputation and allow me to escort her to the senior formal. I argued. They won. Nervously, I asked the young lady. To my utter amazement, she accepted.

The next day, I found an envelope in my school locker; inside were two tickets to the prom. The accompanying card read: "Al, enjoy the prom." It was signed, "Your Classmates." Next item on the agenda—renting a tuxedo. Classmates also took care of the flowers and other ancillary expenses. I didn't know the difference between a corsage and a nosegay, but the girls decided on nosegays. For the guys it was the standard boutonniere.

One of my classmates, Mike Adzima, worked at Topper Formal Wear, and made arrangements for my tux. In less than a day, I had been fitted with a white dinner jacket, black trousers, and blue-plaid bow tie with matching cummerbund. I looked prom-ready. Mike also provided the wheels. Instead of a limousine, our prom chariot was his Dad's '56 Chrysler Windsor. With its gas tank filled with Standard Oil's Gold Crown Premium, it rode like a limo.

The day of the prom was one of those delicious May days, drenched in sunshine and blue sky. Dismissed from school after morning classes, prom couples were given the afternoon to get ready for the evening's festivities. Local hair salons did a bustling business as junior and senior girls were transformed from bobby-soxers into debutantes. Guys spent the afternoon waxing and polishing the family car in preparation for evening's formal affair. Once the cars were ready, it was time for each teenage boy to become Prince Charming: Complementing tuxedos were shined shoes, combed hair, brushed teeth, and a fresh boutonniere.

With some degree of awkwardness, the formally dressed couples climbed into the car and were off. We visited several pre-prom parties where proud parents worked their Bell & Howells and Kodaks overtime. Flash bulbs flashed as regal-looking couples chatted and politely sipped punch while trying to maintain a degree of adolescent sophistication. A dozen snapshots later, we headed off to Madura's Danceland, which had been transformed into a Mardi Gras fantasy.

As soon as we arrived, we could hear the mellow sounds of the Johnny Kay Orchestra. Inside, the dance floor became a showcase for elegant formal gowns and white sport coats. Couples danced, and talked, and shared with one another these magical moments of the high school years.

I actually danced without causing anyone serious injury. This was not easy to do because of all the distractions. Trying to concentrate on your feet while your senses are bombarded by attractive young ladies in strapless gowns, an abundance of cleavage, and provocative perfume requires an iron will. At 17, my willpower had the strength of wet tissue paper! Mesmerized by the music and make-believe fantasy, couples slow-danced and captured moments to remember. All too quickly, minutes became hours and it was time for the prom's finale. Prom couples were called to the dance floor for the Grand March. The orchestra played a final selection and it was time to go.

Following the Grand March, we drove to Chicago's North Side for an after-prom dinner at Honolulu Harry's Club Waikiki. We topped off dinner with a tropical fruit drink served in a hollowed-out pineapple shell. The limit was one per customer, and for good reason—the octane rating of that juice was stratospheric! A floor show featuring grass-skirted dancing girls made every guy there wish they'd brought a lawnmower! After several pictures by the club's camera girl, we headed home.

At 1:30 AM, while Dean Martin, The Platters, and Tony Bennett crooned romantic songs over WIND, we checked out the submarine races on moonlit Lake Michigan from a secluded spot at Bobby Beach. This was our time: Having breakfast before dawn, clutching souvenirs from a nightclub, starry eyes, pink carnations, tired dreamy faces, and soft, quiet kisses at 4:00 AM

The senior prom is a-once-in-a-lifetime experience that fills special pages in life's scrapbook. But as I mentioned earlier, prom can be costly. Some kids cannot afford to go. That's too bad. There ought to be a way for every high school kid to attend the prom who wants to do so; maybe a special fund or some type of sponsorship. Attending the senior prom should not depend on one's financial means. I was very fortunate. For had it not been for my extraordinary classmates, the prom pages in my scrapbook would be empty.

"It's Got a Great Beat and You Can Dance to It!"

American Bandstand made its ABC network debut on August 5, 1957. By the time our senior year began at Whiting High School, less than a month later, we were avid fans. This five-day-a-week sock hop came to us live from Philadelphia in living black-and-white. Hosted by Dick Clark, *American Bandstand* presented the current heartthrobs of the record business, played the hottest hit records, and focused on the world of the teenager.

We immediately made *American Bandstand* part of our lives. Along with listening to the music, we copied fads, adopted fashions, and learned new dances. Kids across America selected their favorite *Bandstand* personality, sending frequent fan letters and gifts. Those of us too shy for such public idolization privately savored the sights and sounds of America's daily dance party. Thousands of teenaged girls swooned over Bob Clayton, and wished they, not Justine Carelli, were his dance partner. Bob and Justine became the show's resident sweethearts. On the other side of the Eat-Your-Heart-Out-Club were the guys who envied Kenny Rossi every time he slow-danced with Arlene Sullivan.

Almost single-handedly, Dick Clark raised the status of teens, and brought respectability to the world of the adolescent. He also established the importance of teenagers as an economic force. Record producers, sponsors, and advertisers flocked to Clark's doorstep, hoping for a chance to promote their company's products on *American Bandstand*.

In the beginning, critics panned the show, warning that rock 'n' roll would corrupt the teenager's mind and lead to social decadence. TV executives snickered when *American Bandstand* was proposed as a network show. They argued that no one would watch a "bunch of kids dancing." The program, they contended, would be a colossal flop. Dick Clark believed otherwise, and within a few weeks, several million teenagers proved him right!

From its initial broadcast through November 17, 1957, *American Bandstand* was 90 minutes of dancing, interviews, chitchat, fan mail, and music from 3:00

to 4:30 PM. So strong were its ratings that ABC inserted newcomer Johnny Carson's *Do You Trust Your Wife?* (later renamed *Who Do You Trust?*) in the middle of Clark's time period from 3:30 to 4:00 PM. *Bandstand* then returned to the air from 4:00 to 5:00 PM.

Seemingly overnight, *American Bandstand* became the teenager's General Store. Dick Clark managed the store, and kept the shelves fully stocked. Throughout the country, a willing, voracious audience of adolescents eagerly devoured the merchandise.

Every afternoon, the sounds of the city echoed with the anthem of *American Bandstand*, Les Elgart's "Bandstand Boogie." This song was the signal for teens of all ages to check in with Dick Clark and check out what was happening with *Bandstand* regulars. Through the power of television, average teenagers from Philadelphia became as recognizable as any public official, and received considerably more mail. More than 30 years later, their names are readily recalled: Pat Molittieri, Frank Giordano, Carole Scaldeferri, Janet Hamill, Little Ro, Joanne Monte Carlo, Rosalie Beltrante (Big Ro), Lou DeSera, Joe Wissert, Barbara Levick, Carmen and Yvette Jimenez, Myrna Horowitz, Ed Kelly, Charlotte Russo, Frank Brancaccio, Dottie Horner, Frank Spagnuola, and, of course, Kenny Rossi, Arlene Sullivan, Bob Clayton, and Justine Carelli.

We watched *American Bandstand* because it made us feel good about ourselves. It also made us feel important in an adult world. There was something special about seeing kids our own age become television celebrities. We secretly wished it could be us. Vicariously through the *Bandstand* regulars, we played out our fantasy scenes: dancing, chatting with recording stars and show business personalities, rating records, receiving fan mail. We pictured ourselves as a "teenscene" trendsetter in fashions, fads, and new dance steps. We knew *exactly* how we'd act in the spotlight of fame.

Contrary to the doom portended by some critics, *American Bandstand* had quite the opposite effect on America's youth. The show that "no one would watch" ended up elevating the self-esteem of countless young people, and promoted positive social values.

In 1957, as a 16-year-old teenager in small-town America, *Bandstand* opened windows to a world I would not otherwise have seen. By consuming my daily serving of American pie, I was presented with new ideas, made aware of current trends, learned how much we had in common with one another regardless of where one lived, and enjoyed more fully the adolescent years. Those were fun, innocent days. Without much sophistication, a substantial amount of naiveté, and the awkwardness normally present during these years, *Bandstand* helped lessen the anxieties of the day, while Dick Clark gave kids a vote of confidence, and assured us that being a teen was a neat age to be.

As usually happens, we grew up, graduated from high school, and went about the task of building our lives. Watching *American Bandstand* became less important. As the years went by, *Bandstand* changed, and so did we. You can't remain a teenager forever. Still, remembering halcyon afternoons, sprawled in front of the TV while listening, watching, and savoring the sights and sounds of *Bandstand*, warms the heart and rekindles reminiscences of yesteryear.

American Bandstand was a vital part of those years, and I wouldn't trade those memories for anything! To Dick Clark and everyone on the show: Thanks—'It's got a great beat and you can dance to it.' I'll give it a 95!

The Last Picture Show

The cutting torches and bulldozers finally brought an end to the "41" Outdoor Theater. After standing vacant and unused for several years, the former drive-in was cleared, graded, and sold. Whatever takes its place will have a tough act to follow. This is truly the end of an era—the last picture show.

The "41" Outdoor Theater, located between Calumet and Sheffield Avenues at 129th Street in Hammond, Indiana, served as the area's entertainment mecca for more than 30 years. Before television became a dominant entertainment force, families would pile into their station wagons and head for the drive-in movie. With the little kids dressed in pajamas, the baby in diapers, and Dad behind the wheel, Mom was free to enjoy a little respite from her domestic duties. Even several trips to the concession stand and restroom failed to dampen (no pun intended) her evening's relaxation. These little treks for bodily comfort and relief always added to the adventure of attending the open-air cinema.

For teenagers, the outdoor theater was the answer to their biological prayers. Almost immediately, the drive-in became known at the passion pit. This wonderfully affordable plot of celluloid real estate became an oasis of romance. Where else, for less than $2.00 a couple, could young lovers find the privacy to practice tactile skills? Every week, wary fathers throughout the Calumet Region toyed with the idea of having their daughters dusted for fingerprints following a date at the drive-in.

There were also several generations of red-blooded American boys who viewed the drive-in as a training ground and test site for a variety of adolescent nonsense. Many of these escapades have become legend over the years. On more than one occasion, we snuck a buddy or two into the drive-in by having them hide in the trunk of the car. This ploy worked well until the time one of the guys stopped off at Hot Dog Louie's for a bowl of that famous chili before going to the movies. Once inside the trunk, the excessive bumpiness of the ride, along with the natural percolation of digesting chili, caused an uncontrollable release of human exhaust that nearly asphyxiated the two freeloaders. Alerted by the frantic pounding inside the trunk, one of the ticket-takers turned us in. Just goes to prove that "You can't fool Mother Nature!"

Regardless of these periodic setbacks, we tested the management's patience many times. Double-dating, we'd pull in and park backwards! This always brought the theater's deputies out in force. Another time, after finding a discarded female mannequin, we sat her up in the backseat wearing only a baseball cap. One of the guys play-acted like Romeo and made "advances" toward her. It didn't take long before several police officers surrounded the car. They nearly passed out laughing when they realized the prank. I can still hear the wolf whistles that followed the beleaguered employee as he carried off our well-endowed, au naturale gypsum princess. For us, it was just another night of cheap thrills!

The first time I went to the "41" I watched Rock Hudson battle it out with James Dean in *Giant*. It rained throughout most of the show, and we had to keep starting the car to make the wipers work. It's important to keep the windshield clear when you're with a carload of buddies, and you want to see the movie. When you're alone with your steady girl, you go to the drive-in and pray for rain.

Like other social relics, the drive-in theater was made obsolete by changing lifestyles and accelerated technology. But in its heyday, it was the best. It's difficult to drive past that property and not think about youthful times, warm summer nights, top-down convertibles, buttered popcorn, and a sporty Oldsmobile Starfire. Jogging the memory brings back images of speakers that didn't always work, voracious mosquitoes that feasted nightly on preoccupied moviegoers, the intermission song ("Let's all go to the lobby"), and the flashlight brigade that patrolled the drive-in in order to discourage any horizontal recreation. Melancholy thoughts and wistful feelings flood the senses as one remembers the silly times, good times, and fun times shared with boyhood friends. For an instant, you flashback to days long past and recall the sweetness of a first date, the scent of perfumed hair, the touch of angora, starry autumn nights, and soft, quiet goodnight kisses at midnight.

Each spring, we used to wait for the "Closed For The Season" sign to be replaced with a full marquee advertising the coming attractions. From then on, evenings would be brightened by the yellow electric arrow flashing toward the drive-in's entrance. That sight alone raised adolescent temperatures several degrees.

Today, there are ultra-modern multiplexes where patrons can watch a film in complete air-conditioned comfort. Somehow, it's not the same. One rarely sees a kid at the concession counter wearing pajamas. Bringing a plaster lady to an indoor multiplex wouldn't have the same effect. And hiding in the trunk won't do you any good at all. Still, there is one carryover from the drive-in. The last time I went to the multiplex, there was some bozo sitting close by who had obviously eaten a very large bowl of chili!

Nick's Snooker and Pinball Emporium

As soon as a guy became a freshman at Whiting High School, he was automatically granted membership at Nick's—the store-sized country club for teen boys. Located a couple of doors east of Sheridan Avenue on the north side of 119th Street, this sanctuary for pubescent males was a place where a kid could unwind and relax after a hard day of adolescence. Except for Nick's wife and daughter, this was strictly a male domain. Decorated in early American dinginess, Nick's didn't offer much in architectural splendor or décor. What it did offer was the comfort and latitude of an adult-free haven where a guy could smoke and cuss and carry-on without being hassled by grownups.

The front windows of this urban clubhouse were landscaped with a number of potted plants. Tenaciously, they survived like a mini forest, nourished by a mist-like, olive oil-based humidity. A few of the more exotic horticultural varieties thrived on the defused sunlight which filtered its way through windows coated with layers of old cooking grease, tars from smoked cigarettes, and a generous deposit of industrial-generated grime. It was rumored that these panes had never known the cleansing caress of Windex. The bare wooden floor was well worn with little attempt made to hide the scuffmarks left by thousands of schoolboy shoes. Daily maintenance with a well-used broom kept the dark, soil-stained floorboard comparatively free of debris.

Upon entering this adolescent snooker and pinball palace, one's sinuses were immediately cleared by breathing suspended leftover airborne droplets ejected into the atmosphere from one of Nick's featured grill entrees. Nick's menu wasn't extensive—burgers, fries, an occasional grilled cheese, and a couple of concoctions listed as "specials."

Because there was but a single porcelain lifesaver in the closet-sized restroom, orders for "specials" were limited to one per day. Using the backroom lavatory left lasting impressions. This was a basic, functional comfort station: a wash basin with no hot water and a cold water tap that dripped incessantly; a well-worn vitreous throne sporting a moisture-stained seat. Attached to the wall was a blotchy mirror devoid of reflective quality. The 6-foot-square room was illuminated by a single bare bulb; its switch had long ago failed so it burned constantly. The most striking accessory in this headquarters for relief was the battered, mildewed, empty dispenser for Doughboy prophylactics. This device gave the place the ambiance of a teenage truck stop.

Snooker was played at a penny a minute, on a first-come, first-play basis. Nick would write your name and the time on a chalkboard. When you finished, you paid—no arguments. In spite of his unsophisticated recordkeeping system, Nick was accurate. Every now and then, Nick would give you a few minutes on the house.

The pinball machines were another story; they *never* gave anyone a break. The appetite of those coin vultures was insatiable. They ate dimes voraciously. Every evening, teenaged pinball wizards would feed coins to these electrified beasts of buzzers, bells, and flashing lights, hoping to win free games. A few achieved victory, fingers weak from frantically working the flipper buttons hours on end. Most, however, quit after their limited finances had been consumed by the Bally and Williams monsters. In final acts of frustration, dominated by vigorous shaking, pounding, and swearing, the beaten players were left staring at the flashing TILT sign.

Entertainment was not limited to pinball and snooker. Nick also provided his young patrons with free TV. Placed strategically in a darkened rear area of his establishment was a deluxe 16-inch black-and-white Motorola and wooden bench seating. As soon as school was out, guys would head for Nick's to sit in shadows illuminated by the television's phosphorescence screen and check out the latest fads, fashions, and music on *American Bandstand*. In between munching snacks and sipping soft drinks, they would joke and kid one another about important teenage topics—girls and associated activities. These daily video visits with Dick Clark's General Store, kept Nick's grill skills well-honed, as orders of burgers disappeared down hungry adolescent gullets.

To a first-time customer, the initial impact on his senses was exhilarating! Immediately, these human sensors were awash in a torrent of stimuli. Eyes were flooded with a rainbow of colors from neon pinball machines, lighted snooker tables, and from the room itself. Sounds from television, energized flippers and bumpers, colliding ivory spheres on green felt-covered slate tables, and lively young voices showered ears with good vibrations. Aromas from cigarettes, grill grease, and every nook and cranny offered a smorgasbord of fragrance. When blended together by the youthful observer, the overall result was intoxicating! This guy-only sanctuary was what being a teenager was all about.

Welcoming each new customer to this pubescent parlor was Nick himself. He'd ask you your name and explain the rules. It didn't take long before you realized that when aggravated, Nick could swear up a storm. Even though his language on occasion was saltier than his burgers, Nick was fair-minded and seemed to genuinely enjoy his youthful clientele.

In retrospect, the times spent in Nick's Snooker and Pinball Emporium were welcomed respites from the sometimes traumatic adolescent years. The hours spent in Nick's played an important role in our socialization, and enhanced our identity and sense of belonging with our peers. But like most things in life, those times passed too quickly. After graduation it was time to move more deliberately into the adult world. One day you realize that your turn at being young is over; that you no longer belong to those times. Still it's nice to look back, to see what you can see; and it warms the heart to touch those things, of what we used to be.

A Store Where the "Price" Was Always Right

It was a store for all seasons. Long before discount stores, mini-malls, name-brand outlets, and giant shopping centers, one place featured the right stuff at the right price. Located in the heart of Whiting's business district, it was one of the townspeople's favorite places to shop. An orange-red neon arrow pointed the way to the entrance, and letters of the same colored neon spelled out the store's namesake: FIRESTONE. And while that brand of tires was certainly sold there, everyone referred to the store by its proprietor's name, Neal Price.

Neal Price's was headquarters for sports equipment, radios, televisions, paints, cameras, small appliances, automotive needs, and phonograph records. If ever a store defined hometown America in the 1950s, it was Neal Price's. Like a living calendar, the store's window displays announced and celebrated holidays and seasons.

In October, Price's windows were aglow with RCA's color telecasts of the World Series. It was standing room only each day after school, as kids of all ages crowded the public sidewalk to view the Fall Classic on the innovative rounded iconoscope of the latest electronic appliance. Like season ticket holders, youngsters and grown-ups alike watched the annual battle between Dressen's Brooklyn Dodgers and Stengel's Bronx Bombers.

During the Christmas season, windows showcased electric trains, dolls, toys, sleds, skates, and gifts for Mom and Dad. Beckoning shoppers and passers-by alike to window shop and be childlike again was a miniature winter landscape, complete with cotton-based snow, ornament-laden Christmas trees, tiny houses illuminated with colored lights, Santa's toy-filled sleigh, and soaring reindeer, as well as a Nativity scene.

When spring arrived, future major leaguers headed to Neal Price's to purchase the essentials for the field of dreams. To Little League ballplayers, the store was their diamond supplier. Sporting needs from A to Z could always be filled at

Price's. Whether the activity involved gridiron, court, lane, field, fairway, or frozen pond, community athletes shopped for their equipment at Neal Price's.

Always on the lookout for products to entice additional business, Neal dazzled customers by presenting them with a snapshot of themselves, developed on the spot with the new Polaroid camera. Regardless of product or season, shoppers could always count on quality, fairness, and courtesy from Neal Price.

A generation of teenagers feasted on rock 'n' roll records served up at Neal's record department. In those days, kids could audition the latest "operas" in listening booths next to the counter. With headliners like Elvis, Jerry Lee Lewis, Ricky Nelson, and the Everly Brothers filling speakers across the land, the audition booths were rarely unoccupied. When kids exceeded the two-person, two-records per booth limit, management personnel would arrive and reduce the occupancy.

Savvy business owners know that it takes more than merchandise to be successful. What made Price's so popular then (and for several decades after, so memorable) were the employees. Along with Neal Price, the store was managed by Jim Grass. Assisting Neal and Jim was Lulu Kammer. Working together, they gave the Firestone Store a vibrant, energetic vigor that made customers feel welcome, appreciated, and valued.

As kids, there were times when we overstepped bounds and taxed tolerance and patience. Somehow, Team Price always managed to treat us with courtesy by understanding our adolescent shortcomings. Over time, we grew to respect and admire them. Occasionally, while shopping for the latest turntable sounds, we sought their advice. Willingly they offered counsel, helping us to more clearly comprehend and cope with teenage concerns. Jim Grass was especially good at relating to young people. He was always a positive influence on adolescent lives. Had he decided to do so, Jim would have made an outstanding teacher.

Neal Price's closed many years ago. But in its heyday, it was the best, the very best. All these years later, it's not possible for me to pass that building without "seeing" the displays, remembering the purchase of my Wilson baseball glove, our family's first television set (a 16-inch black-and-white RCA), the seven-transistor pocket radio I got my dad for Father's Day, and all the 45's and albums that are still part of my record collection. Most of all, I remember Neal, Lulu, and Jim; they helped many of us grow up, and by doing so, enriched our teenaged years. I loved the Firestone Store. Truly, it was a place where the Price was always right!

Goodbye Bobby Beach

When the Hammond Marina opened in 1991, it ushered in a new era. This elegant, 1,113-slip facility transformed an industrialized shoreline into a recreational boating showplace. The $23 million enterprise was an investment in the future, and civic leaders hoped that it would become a financial jewel. But as we celebrated this new beginning with festivities and fireworks, we bid farewell and said goodbye to the hallowed ground that gave rise to the Marina, Bobby Beach.

If one wanted to name a place synonymous with summertime, adolescence, submarine-race watching, beer, and romance, it would be Bobby Beach. Only the drive-in movie witnessed more cupid calisthenics. While lacking movies and a refreshment stand, Bobby Beach had one overriding attraction—free admission! Countless Casanovas guided their Simonized street chariots to the sands of Bobby Beach for biological maneuvers. Before heading home after a date or an evening of cruising, it became the destination of choice. Amorous couples would search out a favorite location to practice and refine tactile communication skills.

Occasionally, a novice would be brought to this lakefront pleasure land under the guise of watching submarine races. Such a ploy required considerable salesmanship by the pilot of the street sled. Wary young ladies had to be convinced that such nautical observations were honorable and proper. A guy would go to great lengths extolling the virtue of these nightly vigils. Some of the more desperate Don Juans evoked reasons of national security, and how it was the obligation of every couple to check the beach and maintain America's freedom, keeping one's homeland secure. Not too many teenaged maidens had the courage to jeopardize the country's safety, so they did their patriotic duty.

For veterans of sand and smooch, it doesn't take much to recall long ago summer nights spent with a special someone at Bobby Beach. This particular parcel of real estate had the most valued quality: location, location, location. How many prom couples savored the golden yellow moonlight as it slow-danced on midnight blue Lake Michigan waves, while listening to romantic teenage love songs on car radios? Late-night disc jockeys dedicated tunes and wished submarine-race watchers moments to remember as they serenaded young lovers until dawn.

How many guys remember clutching a church key, partying with their buddies, slugging down warm beer bought at Chicago's Last Liquor Store? Ingesting six-packs of Schlitz and Primo resulted in noisy, rowdy, boisterous adolescent seminars on the sand at Bobby Beach. Rumor had it that, at one time, the major automobile makers wanted to use Bobby Beach as a site for testing shocks and springs. As soon as the word got out, they had to change their plans: Too many stud muffins volunteered!

Over the years, Bobby Beach became *the* place for makeouts. Even today after so many years, names are recalled and images return. The sights and sounds of youth (a time to enjoy the greenness of life, the exhilarating experiences of adolescence) come to mind and are recalled like good friends, keepsakes and treasures of the heart. Frequently, these memories are awakened by hearing favorite "oldies" on the radio, seeing a well-kept vintage convertible or coupe, or perhaps catching the scent of a long-forgotten perfume. Whatever triggers these remembrances gives cause to dust off priceless souvenirs from younger days and experience their delight once more.

Like the outdoor theater, carhops, soda fountains, and other places of our youth, Bobby Beach is no more. In its place is a state-of-the-art marina. But 30 or 40 years from now, I wonder if anyone will remember the marina with the same degree of affection that some of us hold for Bobby Beach. I know progress is necessary and change is inevitable if a community is to thrive, but I only hope we are smart enough to keep sufficient places where young romantics can watch submarine races, savor golden-yellow moonlight as it slow dances on the lake, and share keepsake moments with each other.

Riverview

Back in the good ol' days of the '50s and early '60s, along with getting a driver's license, buying a car, signing up for the Draft, and paying federal income tax, you knew you were grown up when you took your best girl to Riverview Park on a double date. Riverview Park, a name spoken with reverence, was synonymous with cheap thrills and good times. Long before theme parks like Six Flags, Disneyland, Walt Disney World, and Bungee Jumping Land existed, Riverview Park was the place for thrills.

Every day, Two Ton Baker, the official mouth for the park, filled black-and-white television screens throughout Chicagoland, extolling the fun and excitement of a day at Riverview. Bordered by Western, Belmont, and Clybourn Avenues, Riverview was the place to be for amusement park rides, food, frolic, and fun. An evening at Riverview was like being beamed to another universe. The park itself was raucous, noisy, sideshow gaudy, and unsophisticated. It pulsed and throbbed with adventure, anticipation, and excitement.

Each day, Riverview was witness to false bravado, as adolescent and young adult Tarzans sought to impress nubile urban Janes with devil-may-care ambivalence on carnival rides that tested one's common sense. Squeamish guys wore phony masks of courage as they climbed aboard the Fireball roller coaster. Girls had it made, they were *supposed* to scream and squeal. Virile young studs had to appear as invincible armored knights unaffected by the mile-a-minute ride of the Fireball. After the ride ended, girls casually re-combed their hair, while the guys picked bugs from their teeth. It was grand!

Riverview was budget friendly; seventy cents bought two tickets to the Pair-O-Chutes. Pulled straight to the top of a 200-plus-foot tower, the lucky couple was released to "float" downward under Army surplus parachutes. This ride always tested one's ability to keep partially digested hot dogs whey they belonged. Every now and then, a Pair-O-Chutes patron lost their lunch or their water on the way back to earth. But at thirty-five cents a person, you couldn't beat the thrill.

After extensive sampling of the menu items offered as part of the "Taste of Riverview," one was in awe of amusement park cuisine. Somewhere there is scientific evidence that steel mill soot and assorted particles of industrial waste on hot dogs and cotton candy actually adds to the taste. What's more, it was probably more nutritious than some modern health foods. Without question, the additional sprinkles of iron ore dust that settled on edibles more than met an average daily requirement of that mineral.

The cool thing about being a teenager is that one's system is able to digest every compound known to science, except calf liver. (How else could one explain the ability to voraciously gulp down two dozen White Castle Slyders without becoming incapacitated?) As kids, we forgot about germs. Germs were something your mom worried about, and she obviously had never eaten at an amusement park. It was rumored that the food at Riverview contained the same immunizing enzymes discovered in Hot Dog Louie's chili. There was an urban legend about a kid who ate Riverview hot dogs, Hot Dog Louie chili, and White Castle "Belly-Bombers" just before riding the Whip. He blew up on the second turn!

The ride that did me in was the Wild Mouse. The "victims" rode in cars built for two. The cars were cantilevered, riding on rails like a mini roller coaster but at a much lower speed. What made The Wild Mouse diabolical was the way the cars were built and balanced: seating in front, wheels in back. The cars turned sharp square corners on the elevated track, whipping car and riders around with bone-wrenching force. One had the sensation of overrunning the rails and plunging to earth. At thirty-five cents a ride, the Wild Mouse encouraged patrons to "mouseproof" their digestive tract by guzzling ample quantities of Pepto-Bismol.

As one matures, other interests and activities displace amusement park thrill rides. One day you realize it's not important to violate your bones on the Flying Turns or the Tilt-A-Whirl. The desire to be plastered against the wall of a moving rotor, like some bug about to be squashed, vanishes. About the same time, you lose the thrill of getting soaked on the Chutes, and of rocketing up, down, and around elevated roller coasters. This common sense coming of age usually occurs after adolescence meets up with adult responsibilities.

To be honest, I don't recall when Riverview closed down. One day, long after the fact, I read about it in an old newspaper article. Still, the park served us well in our youth. Every now and then I flip through the cognitive "pictures" in my mind's memory album, seeing once more the Whip, Rollo Plane, Stratostat, Comet, and the Hot Rods that Two Ton Baker drove in his TV commercials.

Wistfully, I think how neat it would be to turn back the clock and cruise through the Tunnel of Love, or enjoy the space ride with that special someone on a warm summer evening. But that's not possible. Today, amusement parks are high-tech, state-of-the-art, and modern, priding themselves on the variety of rides, cleanliness, and safety. Admission prices to these theme parks are higher than Riverview's parachute jump. I wonder what they'd say at Walt Disney World if an old Riverview veteran ordered a hot dog or cotton candy and asked for a sprinkling of that famous Riverview seasoning? Chances are they'd think you're goofy. But when you think about it, being Goofy at Walt Disney World is a pretty good deal!

Cookie and the Crumbs

For me, high school, rock 'n' roll, and *American Bandstand* all arrived at the right time. As full-fledged adolescents, we were ready to embrace TV shows, movies, music, foods, and fads that defined our generation. As kids of the 1950s, we identified heroes, idolized personalities, and imitated celebrities. After seeing *Blackboard Jungle*, teen moviegoers adopted "Rock Around the Clock" as their anthem.

While kids shared a few of their favorite television programs with adults, that wasn't the case with the emergence of rock 'n' roll. This music featured hard-driving repetitive beats, unintelligible rhythmic sounds, and lyrics focused on youthful concerns: cars, school, sock hops, and nonsense. Slow dance records zeroed in on relationships and teen romance. In no uncertain terms, bobbysoxers and greasers staked their claim to rock 'n' roll. The message on the adolescent clubhouse door was clear: NO GROWN-UPS ALLOWED!

As young consumers eagerly shelled out eighty-nine cents for the latest hit records, parents cringed. Rock 'n' roll ushered in a new wave of technology, and even the phonograph changed to entice this newest generation. Shellac-based 78-rpm records were replaced by the new 7-inch 45-rpm vinyl disc. Portable record players with a modern oversized spindle enabled young rock 'n' rollers to listen to their music in the privacy of their room. Many adults complained about the "hoodlum" music being foisted on their children. Some contended the words were dirty, detrimental to the nation's morals, and would create a generation of juvenile delinquents in its wake. Kids didn't sweat the editorials. What teenagers liked about rock 'n' roll was how it conveyed emotions, saying things about subjects that they were unable to express. All of a sudden, timid teenaged boys, without self-conscious embarrassment, confidently sang along or lip-synched words of longing and love.

Almost from the get-go, rock 'n' roll was derided and ridiculed by those who believed the best music came from Broadway and Tin Pan Alley. Rock 'n' roll lyrics certainly lacked precision and polish. The simple melodies, chords, and catchy phrases that flooded AM radio in the '50s weren't encumbered with multi-syllabic words or complex rhymes. Instead, the emphasis was on an infectious repetitive beat and spontaneity.

Another criticism centered on the fact that rock 'n' roll performers were new, inexperienced and unsophisticated, unschooled in musical fundamentals and theory. All too often, the one-hit artist was compared to an experienced, proven performer with an extensive discography and recording success. But such criticism only served to solidify youthful allegiance to rock 'n' roll. The "oldies" didn't realize that freshness and newness is what made rock 'n' roll so attractive. Almost overnight, in schoolyards, street corners, and neighborhoods throughout America, ordinary kids formed groups and garage bands, and began performing the songs of their generation.

Many who aspired to rock 'n' roll stardom road-tested their vocal talents in high school washrooms, taking advantage of the resonant qualities offered by terrazzo and vitreous china. I, too, dreamed of rock 'n' roll fame. Together with three classmates, a vocal quartet was formed. We were certain we would be showcased on *American Bandstand*. We fantasized about our appearance: After dazzling the audience and accepting accolades from Dick Clark, we would casually stroll to the autograph table, sign 8x10 glossy photographs, and make small talk with the *Bandstand* regulars. It didn't take long for us to become legends in our own mind.

The quartet's name was Cookie and The Crumbs. We used every opportunity to harmonize. Some of our best work was done in front of the porcelain lifesavers in the washroom across the hall from the machine shop. Had a record producer happened to stop in, we would've been offered a recording contract on the spot. But that didn't happen. Cookie and The Crumbs never made it to *American Bandstand*. To be honest, we never made it out of the bathroom. All our doo-wop, shoo-be-doo-be-doo, and whapa-nin-nins echoed off vacant stalls in the school's comfort station and faded into silence.

Still, our attempt was not a total loss. A year later, when a name was needed for our team in the school's bowling league, Cookie and The Crumbs made a comeback! Instead of a successful debut on *American Bandstand*, we performed on the lanes of the Whiting Community Center. We led the league for a few weeks like a one-hit-wonder before slipping into oblivion. It doesn't make any difference if it's a street corner, washroom, stage, or bowling alley; when it's over, it's over.

There is a happy ending to all this. In 1966, another group called Cookie and The Crumbs actually made a record on the Vest label entitled "My Dream of You." Hopefully, it doesn't sound like it was recorded in a washroom!

Life Lessons:
Passages

To Be a Turtle

Some kids are born with a silver spoon in their mouth and enter school with a prepaid ticket to Easy Street in their pocket. Others come blessed with extraordinary talent and are immediately pronounced gifted. The vast majority, however, arrive without pretense or fanfare and accepts whatever life offers. By the time I began first grade it was obvious that I was neither wealthy nor gifted. After several months of observations and assessment, my level of ability was determined and noted in my performance record. Before the end of my second year in school, my achievement would be graphically displayed for all to see.

Today educators are very cautious and careful when identifying student deficiencies. An inaccurate assessment or miscalculation can cause serious injury to a child's self-esteem, and may permanently scar the kid's psyche. But in 1947 when I started school, such concerns were not addressed. It wasn't long before a kid was grouped, marked, and labeled.

At the time, parochial school was the sovereign domain of the nuns. These ecclesiastical heaven-helpers administered God-fearing, iron-fisted discipline, expected strict adherence to rules, and demanded rote memorization of subject matter; all hallmarks of their instruction. As students, we were organized, classified, and chastised. And according to Sister, if we lived saintly lives, we could look forward to being canonized.

In second grade, after assessing my reading ability, Sister placed me in the last of three reading groups. Group 1 had the best readers. These were usually girls. Group 2 included most of the boys and a couple of girls who acted like boys. I was in Group 3. As a matter of fact, I believe I was the only kid in Group 3. To chart our reading progress, Sister decorated one of the classroom bulletin boards with colored paper, depicting an outdoor scene. This construction paper tableau portrayed blue skies, puffy white clouds, deciduous trees, a white rail fence, and a lush green meadow. Upon this background were cutouts of different birds, each named for a particular student and placed in the scene according to reading level.

The best readers were Cardinals. Flying high in the sky, they soared to the heavens. Cardinals were all in Group 1. Group 2 had three levels: Bluebirds, Robins, and Sparrows. Bluebirds flew among the clouds, challenging the Cardinals. Robins nested in the treetops, looking enviously at the cloud-hopping Blue-birds. Sparrows sat on the fence, longing to become Robins or Bluebirds, or perhaps even a Cardinal.

Students looked excitedly for their name. I looked, too, but could not find mine, even among the Sparrows. Then, at the bottom of the fence, in the meadow portion of the bulletin board, I saw my name. It was printed on the shell of a lone turtle. I was the poorest reader in class. Now everyone knew how slowly I read: I was a Turtle.

Reading for me was difficult. I stammered and stuttered and struggled, trying to read while Sister stood over my desk with her pointer, tapping the wood each time she heard an error. Tap, tap, tap. I became the Little Drummer Boy. I wanted so much to please her and avoid incurring her wrath but the harder I tried, the worse I read. Seeing me labeled a Turtle made a few kids giggle. Most remained silent, knowing what it symbolized. When reading time came, Sister would heap praise on the Cardinals and Bluebirds. She encouraged the Robins, and pushed the Sparrows to improve, but the Turtle was never asked to read.

After school, Mom listened intently as I related my plight. She sensed my anxiety, and offered consoling words and a reassuring hug. She told me everything would be okay. Mom believed everything happened for a reason, and that it was up to us to find the sunshine. "God sees good in everyone," she concluded. That may be true, I thought, but God's eyesight is so much better than mine! I didn't really want to go back to school, but second-graders rarely drop out, so I had no choice. The Turtle returned.

Despite my best efforts, I continued to struggle. Sister recommended that I repeat second grade if my reading ability didn't improve. That summer, I took remedial reading at the public school. By September, my reading had improved dramatically! My stammering and stuttering stopped. I was not only promoted to third grade, but I began to make the Cardinals nervous.

Years later, while randomly thumbing through a volume of the encyclopedia, I came across the heading for Reptiles and began reading the entry about turtles. Feeling a strange kinship, I continued reading. "Turtles are the slowest moving of all reptiles." Not exactly a morale booster. "Turtles withdraw into their shells when frightened or threatened." This was especially true if the turtle attended parochial school. It was called survival! The article went on, extolling the virtues of the turtle, and I was almost sorry I had invested the time, until I came to the last line: "In order to make progress, the turtle has to stick his neck out."

Wow! There it was—the sunshine Mom had told me about so many years before. A turtle risks his life every time it takes a step. Life is about taking risks.

Without risking, without trying, we have nothing, become nothing, and are nothing! At last, a surge of belated pride finally dispelled the shadows of early failure.

Deep inside, a mind trigger releases long-stored images. For a brief instant, again I see the stammering second-grader, feel the humiliation of being labeled a Turtle, hear Sister's painful words and sense the emptiness of isolation. But just as quickly, these images are replaced with memories of consoling words and reassuring hugs. Throughout life, we are constantly challenged and tested, risking the substance of our character, overcoming adversity to achieve desired goals. And it is comforting to look back at those long-ago beginnings and know Mom was right: It's okay to be a Turtle. It's really okay.

Dog Tags and Tattoos

By the early '50s, America was involved in the Cold War. Now that the Soviets had built their own atomic bomb, the cloud of nuclear war hovered over the entire world. We soon learned the balance of power was precarious.

Not satisfied having developed the atomic bomb, scientists on both sides of the ocean were racing to build the Super. The Super was the name given to the hydrogen bomb. Thousands of times more powerful and destructive, the hydrogen bomb was sought as a deterrent to any misguided adversary. Almost immediately, terms like A-bomb, civil defense, fallout shelter, Geiger counter, radiation, and H-bomb earned permanent inclusion in our everyday vocabulary.

As early as the fifth grade, we were well aware of the destructive nature of the atomic bomb, heard wonderful things about the new nuclear age, and listened to a foreboding, stomach-churning introduction about the power of the H-bomb. Hearing Sister tell us about the horrors of war before recess really took the enjoyment out of one's Twinkies.

Back then, by the time parochial school kids reached fifth grade, they knew the signals. When Sister stood in front of the class to say something, it was *important*! And if she fingered her rosary while she spoke, it meant all eyes up front, accompanied with a seriously pious facial expression. Wisecracks were put on hold, smiles turned off, and breathing reduced to basic survival needs. Even the class prankster, Louie Windledorf, kept still—and he always had at least a half-dozen earthworms wriggling in his corduroys.

Sister was telling us once more about the destructive force of the atomic bomb, rehashing events that lead to the end of World War II. Then without missing a beat, she segued into the terrible holocaust possible with the hydrogen bomb. She concluded her narrative by revealing the purpose of her presentation. First, a school-wide essay contest was to be held. The topic, of course, was the H-bomb. "What would you do to make the world safer? How could we prevent a nuclear war?" Obviously, entries must have a substantial religious flavor. Winners from each grade would be eligible for the diocesan finals. No more than two hundred words. That was no problem as most of us didn't know many more words that that.

"Next," Sister's voice dropped an octave and took on a serious tone, "in the event of a national emergency, everyone should know their blood type in case they need medical attention. Because many don't know, you will have a chance to have your blood type tattooed on your side, free of charge."

I tuned out Sister right then. I knew Mom didn't like tattoos, so national emergency or not, I would have to take my chances. When I tuned Sister back in, she was talking about everyone getting a dog tag similar to the kind used by the military. Sister continued: "It will have your name, address, and a "C" for Catholic. After an atomic attack, identification might be difficult. The dog tag will help identify you." Sister failed to mention that, in the event of an atomic attack, most of us would become a bunch of 10-year-old crispy critters. She went on to say that each dog tag came with a neck chain so we could wear it along with our blessed Scapular. In all honesty, I don't recall if we paid for the tag or if it was free like the tattoo. All I know is that I received mine a week later, stamped stainless steel. Along with our holy pictures and *Baltimore Catechism*, we were prepared in case of an atomic attack.

When the tattoo crew arrived, they went right to work. They set up in the downstairs cafeteria/meeting room. Kids who had signed up were sent downstairs. They formed a single file line, holding their information card. Like a precision drill team, the tattoo crew would check the card, tell the kid where to stand, have him or her expose an area just above the waist, and zap!

Blood-type tattoos while-U-wait! Because I hadn't signed up, I wasn't allowed to go downstairs; this was not a spectator sport. I didn't know if I had made the right decision until I heard the school bully passed out as soon as they placed the tattoo gun against his side. Kids who saw what happened said Bully Bonehead turned green before keeling over. Had Mom allowed me to get tattooed, I would've needed the Last Rites.

Anyway, they chose the finalists for the essay contest and I was the fifth grade winner! I had pulled out all the stops, laying it on thick, employing the intercession of apostles, saints, and a whole host of heavenly helpers. Sister was impressed. Well, almost. After I read my winning entry, Sister took it and tried to read it. She couldn't decipher it. Keep in mind that this was before my know-how-to-type days, and at the time, my left-handed penmanship resembled the scratching of a nervous chicken. When Sister realized she couldn't read my essay, she crumpled it up and threw it in the wastebasket. The second-place winner was a girl whose handwriting was exquisite. Sister sent her entry to the diocesan finals.

All in all, everything worked out fine. Although I perfected the duck-and-cover technique using a newspaper to protect my head as I hid under my desk, we were never attacked, so I didn't miss anything not having the tattoo. To this day, I have my dog tag. It's on display in the recreation room sans chain. And the following year, as a sixth-grader, I learned how to type. Isn't America wonderful?

Summer School

Each year, as students (and teachers) across America eagerly await the end of the school year, anticipating a much-needed vacation, and the newest class of graduates concerns themselves with commencement and diplomas, thousands of other youngsters prepare for summer school.

To some, summer school is an opportunity to pursue the Holy Grail of adolescence: the Driver's License. Others view vacation-time classes as a chance to get ahead, to take advanced coursework, and accelerate their studies. For most of us, however, summer school meant remediation, a time to re-take subjects failed during the regular school year. Having to attend school during summertime is the ultimate challenge of youth. By the time I graduated from high school, I was a seasoned veteran of summer school. Let me tell you about the first time.

I cannot hear the words "summer school" without remembering the summer I spent in the Whiting Primary building with Miss Stewart. Second grade had been traumatic for me. As a fearful, nervous parochial school kid, I stuttered and stammered to the extent that my progress in reading was woeful. Admittedly, I was intimidated by Sister Perpetua. She towered over us like a giant penguin squawking at the slightest evidence of misbehavior. Every outburst sent waves of panic racing down one's spine, leaving the stomach tied in king-sized knots. Adding to my discomfort was a mild case of asthma, an over-enthusiastic bladder, and my left-handedness.

Sister did her best to correct my biological flaws, but met with limited success. As the year progressed, I didn't; I continued to fall behind in both writing and reading. I'm pretty sure that if Special Education had existed back then, I would have been in it. To her credit, the good Sister at Sacred Heart School tried valiantly, but I did not improve. When school ended for the year, Sister recommended I be held back and repeat second grade.

A few days later, my Mom talked with Miss Stewart and explained the difficulties I was having in reading. Mom asked if I could be enrolled in her summer reading class even though I went to a different school. Miss Stewart said yes.

On the first day of summer school, I apprehensively entered the building, climbed the gray-toned terrazzo stairs to the second floor, and timidly walked in

Miss Stewart's classroom. Like Sacred Heart, there were desks to do class work, but Miss Stewart also had a row of small wooden chairs in front, near the chalkboard, arranged in a semi-circle with a larger chair in the middle. Her teacher's desk was placed off to one side.

Evelyn Stewart welcomed us to her class. This summer, there would be 12 small apostles—eight girls and four boys. She talked to us about reading and writing, and what she had planned for us during the summer. We went to work immediately.

It was at the blackboard, while practicing the Palmer Method of handwriting, that Miss Stewart noticed I was left-handed. My circular and oval chalked "slinkies" pitched opposite from my classmates. I waited for an expected scolding but none came. Miss Stewart just smiled and said, "Albert, you're doing fine." I liked Miss Stewart.

When it came time to read, we'd sit on the small oak chairs. Miss Stewart sat in our midst, listening to those selected to read. I dreaded reading aloud. I finally found the courage one day to tell Miss Stewart I wasn't a good reader. She told me not to worry, that we were there to learn. At reading time, I'd sit on the end, hoping she wouldn't notice me and not be called on to read. Miss Stewart outfoxed me. She had *everyone* read. When a student's turn came, the others were asked to follow along silently. As I listened to my classmates read, I realized they had difficulty, too. I watched Miss Stewart help each student. Using a kind, gentle, reassuring tone, she encouraged, guided, and praised each of us.

The first time I read aloud in class, I only stammered twice. When I finished, Miss Stewart did an incredible thing. She patted my shoulder, looked at me and said, "You're going to be an excellent reader." Because of her kindness, my confidence zoomed! As the summer unfolded, my reading skill improved dramatically. Now I couldn't wait to come to Miss Stewart's class. I couldn't wait to be called on. I *wanted* to read!

When summer school ended, I was reluctant to leave Miss Stewart's class. On our last day in class, she gave each of us a bookmark, indicating our performance. Mine had a gold star and the words: "EXCELLENT READER!" After handing out our report cards, she thanked us and wished us well. On the back of my card, Miss Stewart wrote a note to my Mom: "Albert is a fine boy, who will do well in school. I enjoyed having him in class." In September, I returned to Sacred Heart and entered third grade. My stuttering and stammering had stopped during the summer and never returned.

That was more than 55 years ago. I still have that report card, and I've never forgotten Miss Stewart. She was the teacher who helped me improve my reading.

Several years ago, during the renovation of Whiting's schools, I attended a school-sponsored auction, purchasing a familiar-looking small oak chair. Well-worn after many years of use, it serves as a tangible memory of a truly magical summer. Aside from love, I cannot think of a greater gift than teaching someone to read. To all the Miss Stewarts out there: Thanks.

Lent

In parochial school, just before Ash Wednesday, Sister would have us make a list of our favorite treats. Each year we were encouraged to give up something for Lent—our personal statement of penance. For 40 days, we would deny ourselves candy, bubblegum, Saturday matinees at the Capitol Theater, or listening to *The Lone Ranger* radio adventures. These acts of self-denial were designed to help us travel the road to salvation.

Our official rulebook, the *Baltimore Catechism*, spelled it out in no uncertain terms: "No free gate passes to heaven!" In order to make it safely to the Promised Land, one needed Sacrifice, Suffering, Penance, and Prayer. To a playful seventh-grader, one out of four wasn't bad. After all, if a .250 average was good enough to play for the Chicago Cubs, it was more than adequate for the short season of Lent.

These brief forays in abstinence were made in addition to attending daily Mass and the Stations of the Cross on Sunday afternoons. Lent was major league, big-time asceticism. By eighth grade, my list of give-ups was so extensive, it even impressed Sister Superior. And every kid in class wanted Sister Superior on their side, knowing—with one swing—she could knock out the teeth of a charging lion and render it unconscious!

Not only was I willing to forego my addiction to Dots, Jujyfruits, Butterfingers, Johnny Mack Brown, and the Durango Kid—but I also included television! This was my grandiose attempt to be a parochial Lenten legend. Needless to say, I caved in to temptation constantly. Even though proprietors of neighborhood grocery stores draped their candy counters in Lenten purple shrouds, I nevertheless found an ample supply of my sweet-tooth cravings at a pagan-owned establishment just outside of town. Shamelessly, my breath reeked of jellied candies and chocolate-coated peanut butter. The fact that I snuck in the Capitol Theater wearing a disguise shows I had the willpower of a starving shark. And please don't ask me about watching TV.

My entire eighth grade year was a disciplinary disaster. But just as I was about to tumble headlong into the abyss of the terminally incorrigible—a miracle! I was

116

saved, paroled, given clemency! I graduated, and immediately the recurring eight-year nightmare of being chased and attacked by a giant penguin stopped.

When I entered public high school, I found that Lent was no big deal. No one asked you to make a "give-up" list or talked about penance. Lent didn't have the impact of grade school days. What you did was up to you. And for the first two years of high school it wasn't much. Then during my junior year, my Dad asked if I wanted to go with him to 6:30 Mass each morning during Lent. In a spirit of bravado, I said yes.

As a teenager, one of my favorite pastimes was sleeping. Getting ready in time for school was tough enough; waking up before 6:00 AM was brutal. I struggled each morning to keep my commitment. No matter what I tried, my head was always anchored to the pillow and reluctant to break the bond. Groggily, I'd stab at the alarm, paralyzed with sleep. More than once I wished I'd given up Butter-fingers instead. Forty days was a long time. Easter seemed so far away. I tried to speed things up; the second week of Lent I colored eggs.

Somehow, I made it without missing a day. After six weeks of Lent, I mentally reviewed my give-up list and reflected how I did. It was a mixed report card. No, I didn't abstain from White Castle Slyders. No, I wasn't able to do without Ande's Pizza. No, I watched TV. Yes, I'd kept my promise to Dad. For some inexplicable reason, I felt more grown-up, more responsible, and thankful for having shared with him the prayerful tranquility of morning Mass.

Years later, I realized the full impact of that youthful experience. Like the changing colored crystals of a kaleidoscope, fulfilled promises take on diamond-like brilliance. What began as an ordinary Lenten expression of self-discipline evolved into a treasured lifelong lesson that continues to nourish and enrich my life. Lent became a season of opportunity, a chance to strengthen values, a time to perform necessary character maintenance, and reinforces life's purpose. Lent is church medicine for what ails the soul. Penance is the healing which renews us all.

Admittedly, it's been a while since anyone asked about my Lenten give-ups. No one checks up anymore. Still, I'm thankful that once upon a time, a father asked his son a question that made all the difference. And somewhere, far beyond the stars, my father is very pleased.

No Deposit, No Return

Although television had already staked its claim to America's living rooms by the early '50s, the main source of entertainment for youngsters remained the movies.

As parochial grade school scholars, we looked forward to our weekly respite from scholastic regimentation and ecclesiastic discipline within the confines of Whiting's Capitol Theater. At the Saturday matinee, kids from every neighborhood came together and cheered on screen heroes. For an admission price of fourteen cents, patrons were feted to a full afternoon of celluloid adventure: two full-length feature films, the News of The Day, a cartoon, a peril-packed serial, and Coming Attractions. Between features, on-stage dart-throwing contests and other skill-testing events offered lucky contestants free passes and a chance to win the grand prize, a new Schwinn bicycle. To hometown kids, the Capitol Theater was headquarters for good times.

The only problem was figuring how to come up with enough money to partake in this weekend extravaganza. In addition to the ticket price, a kid needed ample funds for a supply of popcorn, Dots, Jujyfruits, Tootsie Rolls, and a couple of Coca-Colas. As a rule of thumb, fifty cents would do nicely, six bits put a kid in candy heaven, and a dollar—actual folding money—made young moviegoers feel like Rockefeller.

Money in our household was scarce, to say the least. As hard as I tried, I never convinced Mom how necessary the Saturday matinee was to my overall well-being. I visualized fourteen cents as spending an afternoon with Johnny Mack Brown and Tarzan; Mom pictured a loaf of Silvercup bread on the dining table. If I wanted to go to the show, I had to find another source of revenue. Borrowing was out of the question. I had to get money the old-fashioned way; I had to work for it.

As soon as the Coming Attractions hit the screen, I knew I had to be part of the action next Saturday afternoon. That meant I had a week to generate the needed cash. Being 11 years old presents limited options. In my family, we didn't get an allowance. In lieu of any weekly stipend, we were fed, clothed, and housed. All things considered, that was a pretty good deal. So movie money had to come from an outside source.

And outside is exactly where it came from. One of the neat things about growing up in those days is that neighborhoods came complete with empty lots and alleys. Because there was no family car, we walked everywhere. To save time, we took shortcuts, always on the lookout for "stuff."

Back then, all soft drink bottles were returnable for deposit; two cents for Nehi, Pepsi, and Coke, and a nickel for quart-sized Canfield's bottles. On Monday, the search began. Like an urban pack rat, I checked trash bins, garbage cans, and vacant lots—particularly along well-worn footpaths. I was determined to see the latest adventure of the Durango Kid.

Finding a bottle here and a bottle there, I'd carefully bring them home, wash them clean, and place them alongside the other glass strays in my cardboard box corral. Once a source was discovered, it was checked several times during the week. Thirsty neighbors meant I'd visit the Capitol. Understanding merchants took my empty pop bottle knowing I hadn't bought soda in their store. One of the most understanding grocers was Pete Condes; after a few trips he'd hand me the coins, wink, and say, "Enjoy the show."

This may sound odd, but I learned valuable lessons while scrounging for deposit bottles. Store owners and grocers became respected friends. I learned self-reliance, perseverance, and positive thinking. Hunting for discarded pop bottles helped me appreciate the value of money, the necessity of determination, and appreciation for hard work. Sometimes vacant lots and neighborhood alleys teach lessons as valuable as those taught in classroom.

I doubt if any kid today prowls about looking for take-back bottles. Most are "No Deposit, No Return" disposable plastic. Aluminum cans offer some reward, but it takes lots of cans for a movie ticket these days. Most kids have other financial sources without patrolling alleys for stuff.

Personally, I loved those times. They've become part of my life's scrapbook. It would be worth a king's ransom to live those days again, but it's not possible. Like bottles today, there's "No return."

Turning Points

Turning point. This phrase is used to emphasize a place, decision, action, or event that causes a marked change in circumstances or one that influences the overall outcome of things. Turning points are retrospective in nature. Rarely does one realize their importance at the time they occur or immediately visualize their full impact on a given situation. Only after careful review of the occurrence or contemplative soul-searching does one identify specific happenings as turning points.

Sports broadcasters identify turning points during their post-game analysis. Critical errors, crucial base hits, a game-saving catch, clutch free throws, managerial decisions, and coaching judgments determine whether a team wins or loses; whether individuals celebrate victory or sustain the sting of defeat. Turning points are unpredictable. One never knows when they will present themselves, or to what degree they will influence a particular outcome. At the time they occur, many turning points are disguised as ordinary everyday commonplace bits of life. Sometimes they arrive with an element of surprise. More often though, turning points just show up and demand immediate attention. It is the individual's responsibility to be prepared, ready to act upon such opportunities with appropriate effort, intelligence, and precision.

Many times, turning points in life are unexpected, traumatic, perhaps even brutal. Such devastating events call upon one's deepest reserve of faith, perseverance, commitment, and dedication. In their wake, these unpleasant turning points leave painful memories that gnaw the spirit and bring turmoil to one's mind. But in their aftermath, such moments add strength to one's character.

At other times, turning points drop in like welcome guests, filling one with happy thoughts at each remembered moment. When looking back on these times, one is able to review the circumstance with fondness. From time to time, all of us experience such turning points. When you find a few quiet moments, reflect on those events that changed your direction along life's road, and consider how they have influenced and impacted your life. To get things rolling, permit me to tell you about a few of my own turning points. By the way, if I don't keep things in chronological order, it's because I was born at a very early age and sometimes I get mixed up.

Several turning points involve teachers, educators who, throughout my formative years, imparted confidence, encouraged excellence, served as mentors, and instilled a love of learning. These outstanding individuals willingly gave their best so that I might learn, grow, and live. Along with these teachers were classmates who gave support, encouragement, and friendship. One particular class at Whiting High School, the Class of 1958, captured respected values and long-lasting friendships that continue to sustain and nourish classmates almost 50 years after graduation.

Among the critical markers that changed my life's course was not being accepted into military service, after trying to enlist in the United States Army for conscription in the Vietnam War. That rejection provided an opportunity to enter college and pursue a degree in education. How different my life would have been, save for an acute case of common hay fever. Because of heaven's intervention, I fought ignorance on a tranquil campus while others bled and died on Asian battlefields.

The most important turning point in my life was meeting the lady who became my wife and has shared my life for more than 40 years. Rarely has any man been more fortunate or favored. We met as teenagers when she was a high school senior. She came into my life and gave it purpose and direction. She has enriched my life beyond all expectation. Together—and that's the key word—we've shared life's experiences for more than four decades: Parenting our children, building positive family values, caring for elderly parents, supporting each other in times of crisis and sorrow, and enjoying the frequent rainbows that brighten our marriage. Initially ours was a chance meeting, unplanned and unexpected. Luckily, we took time to get to know one another.

Turning points have made their presence known throughout my lifetime. An illness that nearly took a child from us was conquered so that the child healed to continue his life's song. Devastating maladies and terminal diseases took beloved parents, despite medicine's best efforts. As a family, we did all we could; we gave our energy, time, and, most of all, love. But there are inevitable turning points we cannot influence. In the final analysis, this is the essence—the meaning of family.

Several years ago, a near-fatal automobile accident presented another turning point. The lives of our entire family were jeopardized by an inattentive motorist who smashed into our car as we traveled to a birthday celebration dinner. Though there were some very serious injuries, all survived and healed. I took the hint and mellowed out. The accident encouraged retrospective considerations. I reaffirmed the importance and treasure of loved ones, family, and friends. I hope the next turning point of this magnitude is delivered a little more gently.

For those turning points hidden in the future, we can only try to be prepared to meet whatever challenges or demands they present. Hopefully, when the books are audited, the record will show that we gave a good account of ourselves and chose the proper course. Turning points are the personal landmarks along the road of life. May we all be granted a most enjoyable and fruitful journey.

The Wall

From the day it opened to the public in November 1982, the Vietnam Veterans Memorial in Washington, D.C., has profoundly affected all who've stood before it. Referred to as "The Wall," 58,132 names are chronologically engraved, in the order of their deaths, on two walls. Each wall is 246.75 feet long, joined together at an angle of 125 degrees. Beginning at ground level, the walls rise to the height of 10.1 feet at the vertex. Each wall is comprised of 70 panels of black granite, polished to form a mirror-like surface that reflects sky, ground, and all who come to pay their respect.

Architect Maya Ying Lin designed the Wall while she was a student at Yale University. Her intent was for the memorial to be honest about the reality of war and be for those people who gave their lives. She wanted something that visitors could relate to as on a journey or passage, leading each individual to their threshold of remembrance. She believed the memorial should not be embellished. The names would become the memorial. After more than 10 years, the public has made the Wall the most visited site in the nation's Capitol.

For thousands of Americans not able to visit Washington, D.C., a one-half scale replica of the Vietnam Veterans Memorial was built so others could still experience the positive benefits that contact with the Memorial evokes. The "Moving Wall" stands 6 feet high and is 250 feet long. It lists all 58,132 names. Several years ago, the Memorial made its initial visit to Northwest Indiana as part of the rededication of Wicker Memorial Park in Highland, Indiana.

And so, on a Saturday morning in early October, I stood facing the wall as a unit of military personnel presented the colors and sounded taps. I had come to find the name of a friend, to see his place on the wall. Entering the information tent, I gave the name to a young lady who looked it up in the Memorial's directory. On a small slip of white paper she wrote the name and location. While I was inside the tent, it began to rain. "Do you know how to find the name?" she asked. I nodded yes.

Outside, a number of visitors stood with umbrellas. Some veterans wore old jungle fatigues; others wore street clothes, using hats to ward off the rain. I walked bareheaded through the downpour along the west wall of the memorial to panel 16W. I counted down to line 42. At first I didn't see the name. I rescanned the panel. There, leading line 42 was the name I came to find: Lawrence Michael Dart.

I met Larry in June 1966 at Inland Steel. As college students, we were part of the summer workforce assigned to plant labor crews. Larry was from Iowa and had come to the mill to help defray the cost of his senior year. Throughout the summer, we traded stories about campus life as we shoveled and raked and swept our way toward September. What I enjoyed most about Larry was his die-hard allegiance to the Chicago Cubs. Each day we'd take turns naming former Cubs players. He had a quick mind and an insatiable sense of humor. He was able to take an idea and improvise a scene that had everyone laughing. *Saturday Night Live* could've used Larry Dart. He was an intelligent, decent 21 year-old college kid looking forward to completing his studies and graduation. When the summer employment stint ended, we went our separate ways.

Several years later, I met one of the guys from our summer labor crew. We talked about those days and traded stories about the guys we'd worked with. When I mentioned I'd lost track of Larry, my coworker told me how Larry had been drafted after graduation and was later killed in Vietnam.

So here I was, reading his name on the Wall, remembering his mischievous smile and laughter during brief golden moments of a summer long past. Automatically, I began reading other names. Name after name, panel after panel—in the pouring rain—thinking about all those lives lost; all those hopes and dreams, promises unfulfilled, families torn apart, life songs left unsung. Touching the wall, feeling the cool stone washed by the morning autumn rain as if each name was being cleansed by the tears of grieving loved ones.

I walk slowly along the length of the west wall. There is a feeling of poignancy, a connection with the past, a spirit that fills one with heartfelt emotion. Among the crowd of visitors I am alone with my thoughts.

Almost reverently, I walk across the rain-soaked ground as I take my leave. I pass others on their way to the wall and I'm glad for the rain, as droplets and tears blend together. I hope one day we all come to understand Vietnam and the price exacted by this conflict. By doing so, we'll not only pay tribute to our fallen heroes but also honor the generation of veterans who survived the war and carry both physical and emotional scars. The Wall is indeed a journey and a passage. It is also a chance to heal our hearts and remember extraordinary courage, friendship, and youth. Lawrence Michael Dart—rest well, my friend.

Lenten Gift

At first glance, when one considers the somber tone of the Lenten season, with its focus on fasting, sacrifice, and prayer, the concept of receiving gifts seems out of place. Throughout these 40 days, emphasis is placed on renewal of one's commitment to heaven's purpose. For many, Lent is the "give-up" season, God's diet plan. Like an ecclesiastical version of New Year's resolutions, many of the faithful decide to forego favorite foods, refreshments, and earthly indulgences. Others make a pledge to attend Lenten services, or volunteer to help friends and parishioners in need of assistance.

Beginning Ash Wednesday and for the following six weeks, Catholics especially are reminded of their origin and destination, encouraged to inventory their relationship with God, and challenged to improve the quality of their life's journey. Lent affords the opportunity to exercise the spirit, strengthen the Faith, and spiritually re-tune one's thoughts, words, and deeds. Lent is divine aerobics for the soul.

In my home, one learned about Lent early. Although Lent was not formally addressed in Father McGuire's *The New Baltimore Catechism, No. 1, Revised Edition*, it didn't matter. Mom and Dad taught us about Lent, chapter and verse. By word and example, we learned Lent was a no-nonsense affair, a test of self-discipline and commitment. The season of penitence meant additional trips to church and meatless meals.

Back then, Fridays were *fast* days—no meat. During Lent, Wednesdays were also *fast* days, increasing purchases of halibut at the local A&P. Mom was expert at preparing Lenten meals. Vegetables, rice, noodles, tuna, salmon, and a variety of soups all made frequent visits to our dinner table. For six weeks, King Oscar and his brisling sardines were celebrities. (To this day, a favorite culinary delight is sardines and Swiss cheese on saltine crackers. Sometimes doing penance isn't so bad.) But not everyone was happy. Until Lent ended, Charlie the Tuna was one of America's Most Wanted. Always looking over his fin, Charlie became the "Chicken of the Sea."

Daily Mass, Friday novenas, Saturday evening Holy Hour, and Sunday afternoon Stations of the Cross were an integral part of Lent. Mom decided we should be in attendance for all. Her decision was non-negotiable—we went. As a young-ster, the thought of curtailing listening to favorite radio programs was Lenten sac-rifice above and beyond the call of salvation. A few years later, when the resident eighth-grader tried to give up watching TV, it proved impossible. Instead, Twinkies, candy, and gum were substituted in place of shutting off our newly acquired picture-radio.

As a grade school acolyte, Lent provided additional opportunity to directly participate in church services. Mornings when I served Mass for Father Daniels, Dad and I walked together. Sometimes on the way home, we'd stop at a small neighborhood grocery and buy a couple of glazed donuts for breakfast. "What about Lent?" I'd ask. "Doc," my father answered, "I don't think a couple of donuts will hurt." Pop was right; they were delicious!

Through adolescence into adulthood, Lent has continued to provide its annual spiritual checkup. Each year, beginning Ash Wednesday and culminating Easter Sunday, we're allotted 40 days to review, reflect, renew, and refresh our humanity. After all these years, I still draw upon lessons taught so long ago. Admittedly, my "give up" list isn't very extensive. Previously favored food and drink turned unfriendly some time ago, and were quietly dropped from the menu. In appreciation for those lessons, at morning Mass I prayerfully remember loved ones who have passed on. By doing so, I continue to use the gifts presented during my formative years.

Like I said, at first glance, receiving Lenten gifts seems out of place. Looking closer, however, one sees treasures waiting to be presented. With all its somber tones and foreboding events, Lent generously offers the faithful gifts that enrich the spirit, nourish the heart, and nurture the soul.

Benchmarks

As far back as I can remember, Mom always used the Great Depression as her benchmark for adversity. Surviving those bleak economic times left an indelible mark on her character. All other experiences were measured against that standard of hardship, as she often said, "I made it through the Depression, and I can make it through this." ("This" was whatever the current difficulty happened to be at the time.)

She believed that survival in spite of formidable challenges strengthened one's character and gave one toughness and determination to call upon in troubled times. As usual, Mom was right. Over the years, I watched her deal with difficult situations that should have overwhelmed her, only to witness her steadfast Faith and tenacity until she overcame the problem and accomplished her goal. The word "quit" was not in her vocabulary.

Understandably, growing up in a family where lessons were seasoned with stories about the Great Depression had lasting impact. By adolescence, we knew the value of a strong work ethic, commitment to task, standards of excellence, and supplication. Making excuses became an endangered activity. We learned how to organize assigned duties and manage time. We were taught to accept responsibility and strive for improvement, whatever the job. Vicariously, the Great Depression became our benchmark, too.

As life unfolds, we often have to face uncomfortable situations. In many ways, character is measured by how we conduct ourselves in trying times. True, I didn't have to endure depravation, but I have dealt with some unpleasantness. Still, I believe I'm way ahead of the game. Without question, there are more pluses than minuses. This positive philosophy is due in part to another of Mom's favorite sayings: "Things can always be worse!" She felt it didn't pay to dwell on one's troubles. Doing so hindered progress, wasted time, and gave doldrums the advantage.

I've often wondered how Mom managed as well as she did, especially in her later years. Living alone after Dad died, she cared for herself and maintained a neat-as-a-pin home. On occasion, when I'm battling a nasty cold, someone is nearby to bring medicine or prepare a cup of hot tea; Mom did all those things for herself. She was reluctant to bother anyone unnecessarily. Her resolve was incredible; her spirit indomitable.

I mention this because since she's been gone, I've come to appreciate her qualities even more. Born shortly after the turn of the twentieth century, her values reflected the strength and character of earlier generations. Today we're spoiled with conveniences brought about by technology. Fulfillment of our needs and comfort is readily available through countless appliances, gadgets, gizmos, and doodads. What would happen, if all of a sudden, we had to do without and had to rely on self-perseverance to see us through adversity? What consoling benchmark values would we call upon for sustenance? Would we have sufficient Faith and strength of character to face difficult challenges?

Periodically, we are confronted with serious illness, trauma, and the death of loved ones. And every so often, Nature delivers spirit-crushing devastation. When these events occur, some people are able to sustain the particular tragedy and go on with their lives. Others are emotionally and spiritually broken. But some have within their heart a reservoir of Faith so strong and deep they overcome their sorrow, and give courage and comfort to others. Benchmarks.

Throughout life each of us is tested in many ways—at times, well beyond our understanding. Somewhere, we're being evaluated on how we deal with these reality checks. Hopefully, when the final score is totaled, we'll receive a passing grade. Every now and then, when things get difficult, I think about Mom and how she lived her life. Automatically, I silently ask: "How am I doin' Mom?" I take comfort in that question, knowing that she has become my benchmark.

The Question

I hadn't planned this. My intention was to complete some errands and take the most direct route home. But traffic and trains tested my tolerance, and made other roads more attractive. As I stopped at the intersection for the stop sign, I realized where I was, and on the spur of the moment, decided to make a short visit.

Parking on the gravel shoulder alongside the fence, I walk the short distance to the gate opening. By now, I'm familiar with the pathway that leads to the final resting place of my parents. It is late afternoon on a cold, slate-gray day in November. The wind churns up the remnants of autumn. Crispy brown oak leaves randomly sail in the air like small rudderless boats. Most of the flowers have long since given up their blossoms, as winter makes its bid for the landscape.

I continue my walk through the neatly arranged rows of headstones. Each name on these granite directories reflects a family's final tribute to their loved one. In muted shades of gray and rose and black, these stone tablets give silent answer to the haunting question: "Will it really matter that I was?"

The chrysanthemums planted in front of my parents' grave during an earlier visit in late summer are burnished from near-winter weather. The remaining flowers seem to huddle together in defense of the snow and cold that is sure to come. I approach the now-familiar gravestone with the family name and read once again the inscribed words:

FATHER—ALBERT A. 1903–1965
MOTHER—ANNE M. 1908–1990

Recalling the day of my mother's passing, an unspoken thought makes its presence known: Twenty-five years after my dad died, they are together again.

Down on one knee, I brush away leaves from the stone's base. Thoughtfully, I trace over the carved letters with my fingers, feeling their shape and texture. The stone is cold and lifeless. Suddenly I am startled by movement close by. A ground squirrel's refuge has been disturbed and he rustles through dormant plants and dried leaves searching for another. Even among the lifeless there is life.

Silently, I read once more the brief words cut into the coarse-grained quartz. Images and scenes flash strobe-like through my mind. Snatches and glimpses and snippets of living focus and fade like fragile snowflakes. I try to hold on to these thoughts, but they dissolve and vanish in the briefest of moments. Alone in the waning daylight, I speak words they cannot hear and offer prayers I know they do not need. These two faithful servants now reside with angels. Retracing my path to the gate, I know I will not return until springtime. For now, there is no more to do. Although the day is dry, my face is wet; there are some things you cannot hide, even from yourself.

When I was an altar boy and served funerals at Sacred Heart Church, I thought graveyards were for the deceased. I was wrong. I know now they are for the living. For when we visit the final resting place of our loved ones, it gives us pause to confront ourselves by asking the haunting question: "Will it *really* matter that I was?"

Hand-Me-Downs

Just like clockwork, before the start of a new school year, annual back-to-school ads flood TV, fill newspapers, and spill out of radio speakers everywhere. Manufacturers and retailers put on the "hard sell" in hopes of enticing consumers with school-age children to buy the latest fashions. These attention-getting ads stress the importance of having new clothes so kids will feel good about themselves and look forward to going to school. Some eager-to-please parents overheat their budget so their child can make a fashion statement. I guess that's okay if one can afford to do so, but I can't help remembering how it was when I was in school.

Instead of designer, name-brand clothes, the majority of my scholastic wardrobe was hand-me-downs. As the third son in succession in my family, I knew a year or so ahead what I would be wearing to school. As long as my brothers continued to grow, I was guaranteed a fresh supply of duds. Mom was an expert at altering and mending. She wasn't into new; money was scarce. When it came to clothes, her motto was: "Neat and clean!" I admit there were times when all the buttons weren't alike, and once in a while the thread color didn't quite match, but we always went to school neat and clean.

Hand-me-downs became part of our family's value system. We were a domestic version of Lend-Lease. Shirts with frayed cuffs were touched up on Mom's trusty Singer or converted to short-sleeve. Torn-out buttonholes were repaired and made good as new. Corduroy pants with playground-scarred knees were patched and mended to withstand a school year's quota of recess. Jackets, sweaters, hats, and mittens were recycled through Mom's hand-me-down factory.

I suppose some kids might not like hand-me-downs. Wearing used threads might lower their self-esteem, make them feel inferior, and not as good as the other kids. It might even make some people think one is poor. I didn't mind at all. To me, hand-me-downs were a tangible symbol of family love. Each brother-tested, refurbished article reflected shared kindness. I was glad to have something "new," and I always wore these donations with pride.

To this day, I can picture my mother carefully mending a torn sleeve on a shirt that would soon have a new owner. I can still hear the mechanical melody of her foot-powered treadle sewing machine as she carefully guided a newly-set trouser cuff around the threaded needle. Remembering the loving, caring hands that sewed and mended the clothes that kept me comfortable and warm has become part of my hand-me-down treasure. You don't get those feelings with new, store-bought clothes.

Today, a number of name-brand manufacturers produce high-priced ragged, ripped, faded, and torn garments, selling a contemporary pop culture version of the "mock-poverty" look. Kids can now come to school flaunting skewed afflu-ence and self-esteem by bragging about the cost of their contrived indigent fash-ions.

As might be expected, hand-me-downs became our family's trademark. In addition to clothing, Mom and Dad handed down their values and principles. They treated our skinned knees and mended our feelings when things didn't go as planned. By their example, hard work, and allegiance to God's will, they handed down to their children the essence and purpose of life. Unselfishly, they provided us with the chance to do better. Somehow they learned the secret and understood the wonder and magic of hand-me-downs, sharing it with their chil-dren. It was one of their most important gifts.

Today, you don't hear much about hand-me-down clothing; everyone wants new. With modern lifestyles, schedules, and activities, there isn't time to sew on a needed button, mend a torn sleeve, or hug the hurt from a child; we're all too busy. Nationwide, the traditional two-parent family is in diminished supply these days. According to current studies, many have been replaced with single-parent households, unmarried couples, latchkey kids, and in some instances, nothing at all. Sadly, society has too many unwanted children.

Some may think that hand-me-downs are an indication of tough times. I think it's just the opposite. Hand-me-downs are evidence of the best of times—the very, very best.

Respect

Not too many years ago, respect meant to feel or show esteem. Sometimes it conveyed heartfelt consideration. When one exhibited respect, a particular deference, courtesy, admiration, and honor was evident. For a long time, respect for someone or oneself was highly sought after and prized. In May 1967, a song entitled "Respect" became a number one hit across America.

Those of us who grew up in the dark ages (before living rooms were illuminated by television screens) understood at an early age what respect was all about. Respectful behavior was what we were taught to exhibit in the presence of adults, in our community, and especially at school. To disrespect one's elders was to disrespect and diminish oneself.

Those vitally important lessons began at home long before we started school. From little on, we were assigned things to do, helping out around the house. These household chores served as a foundation upon which one's character was built. As we grew older, we were given added responsibilities and duties. Little by little, these family-centered tasks engendered feelings of belonging, elevated self-worth, and provided a bounty of personal satisfaction. These daily responsibilities made one acutely aware of the importance of cooperation within a family. The most important lesson we learned, however, was that respect was not given—it was *earned*. I mention this because of the way some view respect today.

Turn on TV and one will hear athletes chide opponents about not giving them respect. It sounds so ridiculous listening to overpaid players posture about respect. If they want respect so bad, let them earn it. During any newscast, some act of violence will be reported. When the culprits are taken into custody, often the crime committed has to do with someone's skewed concept of respect. Gang-bangers blast away because rivals didn't respect their turf or their colors. Hot tempered motorists attack one another because of a "disrespectful" lane change or some imagined affront. Schoolkids fight because someone "dissed" them; a classmate made fun of what they were wearing or what they said, laughed at them, or mocked some personal characteristic.

Too many misguided people demand respect. They perceive respect as if it's fast food: They want respect and they want it now! Unfortunately, they haven't learned a fundamental lesson. Today, a disturbing number of individuals believe respect can be acquired by brute force or threat of violence. It cannot. Respect has to be earned. It has to be cultivated and nurtured through positive, constructive actions. Respect, like love, has to be genuine—without pretense. Respect has to be earned over a long period of time through acts of kindness, generosity, understanding, tolerance, patience, decency, unselfishness, and compassion.

True respect is not achieved easily. It exacts a high price. It requires a lifelong commitment to high ideals, constancy of faith, and allegiance to cherished human values.

I'm not sure how kids learn respect these days. It's obvious, though, that there's room for improvement. Many demand respect but don't have a clue how to earn it. It's too bad we can't turn the clock back and teach these youngsters some old-fashioned lessons about family-shared chores. It wouldn't be a cure-all, but a youngster who has scrubbed floors, helped with the family laundry, washed dishes, and kept the yard clean will become a responsible kid who will earn respect one day.

Sadly, today too many young people put a price on everything but value nothing. The demand respect, but don't respect themselves. Somewhere along the way, these youngsters were not taught how valuable they are, how important they are, how much of a difference they could make. Maybe one day we'll realize that television, movies, video games, and computers cannot raise kids. Maybe one day the family will be whole again. Maybe one day we'll learn how important respect is—to ourselves and to one another.

Family

Mom's Cure-All for School Absenteeism

Absenteeism is a chronic problem in many schools. Copious hours and money are spent each year trying to curb and find a solution to this problem. All kinds of strategies have been tried: after-school detentions, in-school suspensions, Saturday breakfast clubs, parental involvement committees, grade-point penalties, fines, verbal and written reprimands, incentive plans, awards, and recognition programs for perfect attendance. All have been partially successful for a limited amount of time. None, however, resolved the problem with any finality. Perhaps it is time to bring back Mom's Cure-All for School Absenteeism. A brief historical review of Mom's philosophy concerning school attendance will help clarify what follows.

I know I'm old-fashioned; I can't help it. I was born prior to World War II, before television, computers, and Dr. Spock. When I was a kid, school attendance was NOT negotiable. You went every day there was school and arrived on time, prepared! You did your schoolwork, behaved, came home, and did your homework. Case closed. Whether I particularly liked this routine was immaterial. My task was to go to school and learn. Sometimes learning is not fun, but like awful-tasting medicine, it's good for you, so you take it.

Rarely did anyone in our house miss school. In order to stay home from school, you either had to be sick enough to receive the Sacrament of Extreme Unction or you had died. On those rare occasions when you qualified for absence with an approved disease (Mom kept the list), you spent the whole day wearing pajamas in bed. Maybe she would let you listen to the radio—maybe. To earn radio privileges, your body temperature had to be over 102°F.

My brothers and sister learned early that any keep-you-home-from-school illness having to do with the digestive tract qualified for an enema—commonly referred to as "The Treatment." Mom would scan your features, feel your forehead, and make her medical assessment. Once the verdict was in, you knew something else was going in, too! Mom would fill the enema bottle with a cleansing solution handed down for generations from Czechoslovakian cattle farmers. (Years later, I discovered that these same ingredients were used to clean tar from whitewall tires.) With the enema bottle hanging upside down like an IV, Mom proceeded to hose out the afflicted exhaust system. This was immediately followed by a lengthy porcelain novena from the recipient. From then on you NEVER were too sick to go to school. Once you'd experienced the scourge of the homemade Liquid-Plumr, no germ on earth could make you sick enough to stay home.

But like I said, I'm old-fashioned. As a living fossil, I'm supposed to adjust to the current generation. Still, after almost four decades in the classroom, I find it difficult on occasion to do so. What perplexes me are modern-day parents who seem so eager to call their children off from school. On any given school day, the attendance office sounds like a telemarketing boiler room as call after call comes in. Excuses, excuses, excuses.

The other side of the absenteeism coin is truancy. Kids cut school at the drop of a hat. Anything, these days, seems better than going to school. Joy-riding with friends, spending the day at downtown museums, walking the malls, playing arcade games, or sneaking back home after everyone goes to work fills the truant's agenda.

I am convinced that schools would save big bucks by making a small adjustment in the way they attack AWOL students. Instead of utilizing secretaries and deans to chase down these adolescent MIAs, schools should install several enema stations manned by no-nonsense nurses. Every time a kid is truant, plays hooky, or fakes an illness, he or she becomes the recipient of this therapeutic procedure. Think about it. For the first time in academic history, the schools would be the *hoser* instead of the *hosee*!

In no time at all, epidemic absenteeism would end and schools could put this problem behind them (no pun intended). True, this might be a sore spot for some (oops), but eliminating truancies (ouch) would be well worth the discomfort. If nothing else, schools would get to the bottom of this problem (forgive me) once and for all. And kids, when asked how they feel, would answer: "Exhausted!" And that's not "punny!"

A Dog Named Sam

Stories abound with exploits of famous dogs. Books, movies, radio programs, and television shows have related the adventures of such canines as Rin Tin Tin; Roy Roger's dog, Bullet; Sergeant Preston's Yukon King; and of course, Lassie. These brilliant four-legged fur bags always came through, saved the day, and caught the bad guys, all for a little affection from their master and a generous, deliciously nutritious helping of ground horse.

People love their pets, especially dogs. Every year, Americans spend billions on doggy needs—from teething toys to tombstones. Anyone who has ever owned a dog knows how quickly it becomes part of the family. Regardless of breed or size, the pooch is pampered, petted, protected, and praised. Owners are quick to extol the merits and virtues of their cur in a never-ending stream of: "My dog this," and "My dog that." It's human nature to boast about things one's proud of; the truth is all dogs need a good press agent. They require someone, usually their master, to get the word out to the world about their wonderful, striking, amazing, well-trained, intelligent qualities. That's why I'm writing this, to tell you about a dog named Sam.

Sam came into our family as the result of a religious experience. Well, sort of. On the way home from a Friday evening novena, Mom found this pint-sized, bedraggled, flea-infested puppy whimpering alongside the curb. Its black coat was matted and dirty. Obviously abandoned, one look in its sad brown eyes and Mom was hooked.

After a generous amount of warm milk, Mom took the mutt downstairs to the basement. Immediately the laundry area became puppy-cleaning headquarters since Mom had this rule: Live in her house clean or else! While she prepared the puppy's bathwater, I was recruited for duty and sent to Richards' Pharmacy for germicidal soap. The platoon of fleas that had taken up residence with the orphaned canine street urchin was about to meet its demise. After several baths, sudsy scrubbing, and soapy shampoos, the street pup passed Mom's exacting inspection.

I don't recall how we decided to name our dog Sam, but we did. All this occurred when I was in seventh grade. Sam would be part of our family for the next 12 years. All in all, Sammy lived a pretty good life. Interspersed between his normal diet of "horse a la horse," Sam feasted on leftovers from the dinner table. Occasionally Sam helped himself, like one Thanksgiving when he got into the turkey remnants from the family meal; he picked the bones of that old bird clean. Though he was severely verbally scolded, it took three days for the smile to leave his face.

Sometimes Sammy ate things he wasn't supposed to or ate things that weren't even food, like Crayolas! Whatever the attraction, Sam chewed up a veritable waxed rainbow. He gnawed through cornflower blue, mulberry, peach, and his personal favorite, carnation pink. Paper and all went down Sam's gullet. He had the most colorful droppings in the neighborhood—talk about marking one's territory!

Sam also loved pizza. Actually, he was addicted to it. Countless times I tried to sneak in a pizza after working late in the steel mill. No such luck. Though Sam was sound asleep in the basement, his nose would signal an oregano alert. Like a thief in the night, he would quickly appear, drooling.

Sam was a majestic-looking beast. He was a mongrel with class. He had the stature of fine pedigree, though his ancestry was a Heinz-like blend. Nevertheless, Sammy carried his 25-plus pounds with dignity and grace. His silky black coat with white forefront gave him an elegant, endearing look. Sam knew who his master was. Unlike the children in the family, Sam *always* came when Mom called. He grew into a faithful companion, and was trustworthy and obedient—most of the time.

As with humans, age took its toll on Sam, particularly his teeth. At age 11, his teeth deteriorated and had to be removed. Sam took it all in stride. He learned a whole new diet, but kept his protective nature and guarded our home from strangers. His once-ferocious bark was replaced with "Wuffle-wuffle-wuffle." One time he went after a delivery man, clamping his toothless gums around the man's ankle. Sam tried to be vicious, but after several minutes he hadn't even worked up a red spot. The delivery man asked to come back again.

As I said, Sam was with us for a dozen years. He was an orphaned throwaway that captured the hearts of our family. There wasn't anything fancy about Sam. You'll never see his story in a movie or watch his exploits on TV, but like most pets, he stars where it matters most: in the hearts and minds of those who shared his life. Some pet owners, after their pet has passed on, remember them through pictures or old collars. While I don't have those things, I did keep a box of Crayolas!

Mom's Garden

It must be spring! Seed catalogs are arriving in the mail and garden center ads are filling newspapers, encouraging folks to plant, cultivate, and garden. I know they don't mean me. If the food supply depended upon my agricultural abilities, the country would be on the verge of starvation; I have trouble growing hair, let along edible crops. But in every family there is usually someone who is gifted with a green thumb. In our family, it was Mom. During World War II, her victory garden was a profusion of vegetables. Whatever seed was sown thrived. I'm convinced that pictures of Mom's garden devastated the Nazis, demoralized the Japanese, and helped shorten the war.

Regardless of where we lived, Mom always found room to plant a few horti-cultural goodies. Before too long, bountiful plantings filled the chosen space. After Dad died, Mom bought a small house with a fair sized backyard. That yard became prime real estate for her garden as she staked out an area for her home-grown produce. She grew parsley for her soup and cucumbers and tomatoes for salads.

Mom adhered to a single gardening principle: "If God wants it to grow, it'll grow." That was the reason her garden acquired two permanent residents: a blue spruce evergreen and an apple tree. The evergreen began as a wild, wind-blown sprig that took root in the middle of the front lawn. The apple tree arrived after Mom had made applesauce and buried leftover remnants in the garden. Instead of decomposing into organic nutrients, one apple seed decided this was home and within a few years, had grown into a tree. Mom dug up the wayward spruce sprig and transplanted it to a corner of the garden. It, too, flourished.

As the years moved on, Mom recruited me to help cultivate the garden. Immediately I became a regular viewer of garden shows on public television; I wanted to be ready. I envied the professionals. They had the latest gardening tools, scientific methods, and up-to-date technical know-how. Mom's garden, in contrast, was a scaled-down Spartan version of the made-for-TV agronomy.

When spring signaled the earth with its warmth, we'd prepare the soil and dis-cuss the year's plantings. Our inventory of farm tools included a pitchfork, two old tablespoons, and our bare hands. One year, we grew potatoes—by accident.

The garden became the landing site for peelings and scraps from whatever fruits and vegetables Mom used. Organically, this was good fertilizer. A few potato scraps took the hint from the apple tree and grew into plants, which bore potatoes. Mom called these her "surprise spuds"!

Each year, we anticipated spring. After the cold, dreary, shut-in days of winter, we looked forward to a change in routine. Setting the garden was tangible evidence that a new season was at hand, a renewal for all living things. We knew, too, that sunshine and outdoor activities would become part of our daily tasks. Working in the yard and tending the garden always invigorated the spirit with replenished energy and purpose.

One memorable spring, the apple tree blossomed, and a robin made her nest in the boughs of the blue spruce. By now, both trees dominated the garden and planted vegetables had to plead for their share of sunshine. Mom was in the garden on her knees, preparing to plant cucumbers. Using her trusty tablespoon, she scooped out the soil. I was in charge of dropping in the seeds. The tomato plants were already in place. Here the roles were reversed: Mom directed, I planted. Later that summer, there would be a variety of homegrown tomatoes. Onion sets were in, too. For a novelty, I planted one eggplant alongside the tomatoes, remembering Mom's adage, "If God wants it to grow, it'll grow."

The bright spring sunlight created a cascade of garden shadows as it filtered its way through the branches, dodging the leaves and blossoms of the apple tree. Mom continued preparing the soil for the tiny vegetable seeds, enjoying the shower of warm sunshine. Without looking up, she said, "OK, you can put in a few seeds." Instead of cucumber seeds, I grabbed a branch of the apple tree directly above her and shook it, causing a downpour of apple blossom pedals. Like flower snowflakes, they settled in her hair and landed all around. A few fell in the holes with the cucumber seeds. Momentarily startled, Mom looked up, smiling and holding her tablespoon shovel, and asked, "Do you think they'll grow?" My response was quick: "Like you've always said Mom, if God wants them to grow, they'll grow."

It turned out to be the best garden of all. The cucumbers were terrific. The tomatoes were delicious. The onions and parsley had just the right flavor. Even the eggplant was choice. Later that spring, Ms. Robin added three more voices to the songbird chorus, and in the fall, the apples ripened just in time to be baked in pies.

Once again, spring beckons the spirit to the garden, offering the bounty and abundance of life to those who faithfully tend the soil. For some, springtime is very special. Speaking without words, this season showers the heart with apple blossoms, remembering treasured moments in Mom's garden.

The Carbonated House

As an avid do-it-yourselfer, I pride myself in the knowledge that I can handle most any task. Not only can I read a rule and measure, but also regularly assembled the kids' Christmas toys without resorting to drugs or booze. It was with considerable confidence, therefore, that I approached the remodeling of our house. So when it came to building a recreation room in the basement, I decided to install an old-fashioned soda fountain rather than the conventional wet bar.

Locating a vintage soda fountain in a defunct drugstore wasn't too difficult, nor was the transportation of the unit to my garage. In a few weeks, after considerable cleaning and refitting, I was ready to install the unit in the basement. With a Herculean effort and substantial block and tackle, I pushed, slid, and coaxed it into position. After carefully connecting the drain and water lines, I was ready to attach the carbonator, the neat little machine that makes the fizz water. (Carbonated or sparkling water is made by atomizing water in measured quantities with carbon dioxide gas that's no less than 90 pounds of pressure per square inch.)

Since I didn't have a factory-built carbonator, I decided to build one out of sundry spare parts. (I am a machinist by trade, and machinists believe they can build *anything*. This is not true, but we believe it anyway.) Ignorance prevented me from knowing that I needed a check valve on the cold water supply; the check valve prevents gas from flowing backwards out of the carbonator and keeps a constant water pressure of 90 pounds in the carbonator tank. But like I said, I didn't know that. Consequently, I filled the homemade carbonator tank with water and energized it with 90 pounds of CO_2. After a few minutes, when I judged the water to be carbonated enough, I turned off the carbon dioxide tank. It was at that moment that things got tacky and I lost control of almost everything.

Without the check valve to restrain the gas, the 90 pounds of pressurized carbonated water back-flowed and rushed furiously out of the tank into the main water supply. Fed by the abnormal pressure (and my technical ignorance), the entire water supply of the house was now carbonated!

Meanwhile, as all of this was taking place in the basement, my wife, oblivious to my labors, was upstairs ensconced on the almond-colored vitreous throne in the family comfort station. At the exact instant when the water supply was reach-

144

ing its full potential of carbonation, and with pressure building from the 90-pound injection of CO_2, my lovely, docile, unsuspecting wife flushed the toilet.

Rarely has anyone witnessed such an explosion and eruption! Mount St. Helens was minor league compared to this! To tell you the truth, I didn't know my wife could scream that loud. The poor lady thought the toilet had blown up under her. By the time I got upstairs, she had both arms tightly wrapped around the toilet as if it were a porcelain life preserver, and she was babbling to the Alka-Seltzer-like water in the bowl as if fervently praying a novena.

It took several minutes to calm her down and explain what had happened. When she regained her composure, I reassured her, "No, it wasn't an earthquake, just a small technical oversight." I comforted her by saying that, to the best of my knowledge, no one had ever died from an exploding toilet. And yes, she could release her grip on the toilet; carbonators do not give off aftershocks. She icily spoke words to me that I hadn't heard since my days in the steel mill, and in no uncertain terms conveyed to me what she thought about the "best of my knowledge."

What more is there to say? Most of the swelling on my head was gone in a couple of days; she was kind enough not to leave any scars. That weekend I went and bought a factory-made carbonator. Still after all these years, she's more than a little sensitive about what happened, especially when I refer to this gaseous domestic explosion as my most "sparkling" achievement!

Shoes for Mom

Sometimes when you give of your time and offer to help someone, you wind up receiving most of the benefit. Often these tokens of goodwill seem ordinary or insignificant, yet in their aftermath one is left with a precious, priceless gift. I've come to call such experiences "Heart Moments." Let me share one with you.

Having a day off of work, I promised Mom I'd take her shopping for a new pair of shoes. Now I am not a shopper; I rarely shop for anything. And I know next to nothing about shopping for women's shoes. Nevertheless, at 9:30 AM, Mom and I climbed into the cab of my pickup, fastened our seatbelts, and headed for a mini-mall on Chicago's east side.

Mom was in her 80s, a tad over 5 feet tall, and tipped the scale at around 102 pounds. She spent the majority of her years acquiring and refining survival skills. Her resourcefulness enabled her to survive The Great Depression, marriage, four children, a series of demanding jobs, and the renovation of three houses, while shopping at every type of imaginable store. In short, Mom's a seasoned pro. When it comes to shopping, she's Hall of Fame material and I'm strictly minor league. Oh, I can handle hardware stores and lumber yards, and I've even managed to transact a degree of retail grocery business under close family supervision if the list isn't too long (although I still can't deal with coupons). But when it comes to regular "stuff-type" shopping, forget it!

The shoe store targeted for our merchandising madness opened at 10 AM sharp, and we arrived a few minutes later. The lone saleslady was busy preparing the store for the day's business, and because we were the only customers, left us to fend for ourselves. This particular palace of soles was set up for self-service. Each aisle had rows of shoes arranged according to size and gender: Men's, Women's, and Children's. We wandered down a couple of aisles until we located the women's section.

"What size, Mom?" I asked. She's always impressed when I ask the correct technical shopping questions.

"Six and a half," she replied.

I scanned the vertical rows of shoes, found the general area, and guided Mom to the battle zone. Mom claimed her eyesight wasn't what it used to be, but this lady knew—*sensed*—quality when it came to spending. If you were lucky enough to see her put hard cash on the table to buy something, you could bet the farm that she had analyzed, scrutinized, and economized the item.

I helped her select a series of shoe styles to try on. (This store had one of those little shoe-benches for you to sit down and try on shoes while attempting to keep from falling off the pint-sized seat.) Actually, Mom selected the shoes; I simply retrieved them from the higher shelves as they were beyond her reach.

Each pair was followed by her assessment: "Too narrow," "Wrong color," "Too 'cheesy,'" "Wrong heel," "Wrong style." Shoe after shoe fell to the wayside, discarded for poor workmanship, price, or personal preference. With several dozen pairs of ladies' shoes on display, I had the feeling that I was going to handle all of them. The game was on: Select. Inspect. Try on. Discard. Next!

As we continued our shoe search, I noticed several boxes of shoes marked with the letters "TAPS." Not attaching any special significance to these tagged shoes, I entered them into Mom's inspection and try-on derby. Bingo! (Forgive the use of this quasi-religious term; sometimes I just forget myself.) To my surprise and delight, she found a pair of the tagged shoes to her liking. These particular shoes were sturdy, stylish, comfortable, and, best of all, the price was right.

While Mom put on her old shoes, I took the chosen pair to the checkout counter. The saleslady looked at the tagged shoes, glanced toward my Mom, and smiled. "These are tap dancing shoes," she said, "are you sure she wants these?"

"They'll be just fine," I replied with a wink. "Mom starts her dancing lessons tomorrow."

Riding home, Mom asked, "What did you and that saleslady find so funny?"

"She was somewhat amazed that you bought a pair of tap shoes."

"I bought what?"

"The shoes you bought are for tap dancing. You're supposed to take them to a shoemaker and have the metal taps put on. Which shoemaker usually works on your tap shoes?"

I watched as the realization washed over her. She looked at me, tried to say something, and then started to laugh—we both started laughing. Bone-shaking, eye-watering, sidesplitting laughter filled the truck cab and spilled out onto the street. Laughing like ticklish hyenas as comical images and amusing scenes flooded the senses. I could just picture my sweet mom in her favorite housedress, clicking up her geriatric heels on the old *Morris B. Sachs Amateur Hour*, tap dancing to an accordion rendition of "Tea for Two," while the host, Bob Murphy, says to the viewing audience, "To vote for 'Tap Dancing Annie,' please call…"

It took the better part of four miles for us to regain our composure. We were still suffering aftershocks of laughter when I pulled up in front of her house.

Every so often we experience special, spontaneous episodes of life that nourish and enrich the spirit. Without any conscious intent or forethought, we memorize these moments and savor them again and again. And so it was with Mom's tap shoes. Thanks for the memories, Mom.

A Watch, a Window, and Wonder
Beyond the Stars

A short time after my father passed away in 1965, Mom gave me my grandfather's pocket watch, which my dad had kept since his father's death in 1924. The gold Hamilton watch was presented to my grandfather upon his retirement from Whiting's Standard Oil Refinery. A reception held at the family's home on Oliver Street was attended by coworkers and close friends, and a group photograph was taken outside on the front lawn to mark the occasion. In the picture, Granddad proudly displays his new timepiece, surrounded by family and well-wishers. Captured forever on the photographic plate are images of his dignity and courage—a strong work ethic personified.

Everyone wants to be noticed once in a while, and remembered after we're gone. Today we have video recorders and digital cameras to save and preserve important occasions and memorable moments. But during my grandfather's lifetime, optical instruments were limited, producing grainy black-and-white photographs that filled family albums and scrapbooks. To enhance this sparse historic record, keepsakes were passed along to family members as tangible reminders of a loved one's life song.

I never knew my grandfather. Peter Koch had been deceased 17 years when I was born. But while I never heard Granddad's voice or saw him when he was alive, I have his gold watch as a memento of his life. Engraved on the back are these words:

Pete Koch
From P.S. Employees
1924

Pete was a plant supervisor who treated everyone with respect. Years after he passed away, former coworkers would reminisce, expressing kind words to his son and grandson whenever they'd meet uptown. Shortly after his retirement, Granddad succumbed to a fatal illness. Aside from a few faded pictures, his watch has become his legacy. It symbolizes honor, integrity, and moral character, reflecting his decency, commitment, and values. Now displayed in a glass case, the watch hasn't worked in years, its hand stopped at 17 minutes past one o'clock. Even so, after 80-plus years, the watch still gives the correct time twice each day. Keepsakes and photos bridge generations, sustain familial connections, and serve as reminder of times past.

Long before Mom gave me my grandfather's watch, I was aware of his name and place within the community; since first grade at Sacred Heart School, I knew. Every morning at Mass before school, I would look at the stained glass window by the confessional on the east side of church and read the words: "In Memory of Peter N. Koch." (My grandfather's middle name was Nicholas.) The family purchased that window as a memorial to his life.

In hometown churches throughout America, one sees a directory of parishioners whose dedication, commitment, and generosity helped build their church. Through stained glass images of saints, families provided lasting tribute to loved ones. Granddad's window depicts St. Peter holding the golden keys to heaven's gate. In grammar school, when it was time to receive the Sacrament of Confirmation, I chose the name of Peter.

A major benefit of living in one's hometown is a sense of connection with generations past, belonging to the present, and planning for a hopeful future. Much of what we enjoy today—much of what we treasure—is due to the efforts of those who came before us. These early citizens, our relatives and friends, exhibited a fierce determination to make a positive constructive difference. They worked long and hard to provide for their family, especially their children. By the fruits of their labor, their children and their children's children would be afforded additional opportunities, enabling future generations to more fully enjoy the liberties and freedoms pledged by the United States.

Many great-grandparents and grandparents came to this country from foreign lands. These immigrants sacrificed and struggled unselfishly, working tirelessly toward fulfilling America's promise. These individuals helped form the character of this country—morally, socially, and spiritually.

Growing up, most of us have been told stories about the people, places, and events that are part of one's family history. Even without having been there, we can sense what it was like and what it took to survive and succeed in earlier times. As we grow older, recollection of those stories—like old photographs—lose sharpness and slowly fade. Even so, through stained glass and an old pocket watch, I can see and touch part of my grandfather's life.

Whatever stories of his life are left untold, whatever songs left unsung will have to wait for now. Perhaps one day these too will be known; for now, a watch and a window are enough. As I said, I never knew my grandfather, and that is part of the wonder beyond the stars.

Laundry Room Learning Center

Learning centers are part of every school today. Special areas are set aside in libraries or classrooms where students can pursue tasks to develop thinking-and-doing skills. School districts spend substantial sums of money to purchase age-appropriate materials so students can take advantage of this modern educational innovation.

When I was in school, we didn't have learning centers. Our thinking-and-doing lessons were taught at home by our parents. (For those ultramodern human units not familiar with such terms, "home" was the place where the family lived; and "parents" were the married couple of opposite gender who accepted responsibility for preparing their children to live positive, constructive lives.)

In our house, the learning center was headquartered in the basement by the washing machine and laundry tubs. The entire basement, however, became a "field laboratory" to practice tasks learned and refine skills taught. Perhaps it seems odd to locate such an important educational oasis in the basement, but it was the best environment in which to learn. Let me tell you why.

Traditionally, Monday was wash day. Tuesday was ironing day. Wednesday through Saturday were do-whatever-has-to-be-done days. Sunday, of course, was a day of rest. In ancient times (before Permanent Press and automatic washers and dryers), laundry required a full onsite commitment. Clothes were washed in a conventional wringer-type washer. They were rinsed, wrung, and hung to dry, held by clothespins on wash lines strung throughout the basement.

From little on, everyone in our family did chores. By the time I was in eighth grade, I was a full-fledged laundry helper. Because both Mom and Dad worked during the day, laundry was a Monday evening affair. Whenever I was scheduled for learning center duties, they would begin as soon as the supper dishes had been tended to and the kitchen put in order.

Load after load was placed in the sudsy Maytag. Laundry tubs were filled for rinsing or for soaking tough stains in chlorine bleach. While clothes washed, clotheslines were wiped clean with a damp cloth. Low-hanging steam pipes from the furnace were also wiped to keep any dirt from settling on the freshly laundered clothes while they dried. Old newspapers lined the bottom of the wicker laundry basket. Countless editions of the *Chicago Daily News*, *Chicago Herald-American*, and *Lake County Times* readily accepted the batches of wringer-damp clothes. American Family Flakes, Fels-Naptha soap, Linco bleach, Climalene detergent, and liberal amounts of elbow grease were stock items in the laundry learning center. These were the washday weapons of choice against ring-around-the-collar, gamy sweat socks, and whatever dirt had soiled the family apparel.

Amid the rhythmic sounds of agitating water, the steady hum of the machine's electric motor, and the driving gears of the wringer, the home-based learning center came alive. As we did the laundry, Mom and I talked. With wash-and-rinse cycles as background, we'd exchange ideas about living and life. While hanging the clean-scented laundry with wooden clothespins, Mom would relate stories about family and friends, occasionally interrupting her narrative to correct my technique and improve my clothespin skills. When the week's wash was done, the final task was wiping the basement floor with Climalene, lest any dust take up residence on the wet hanging clothes. Shortly before midnight, the basement learning center would be still.

Listening to Mom's experiences and hearing family stories provided me with a treasury of riches. At home we learned appropriate social, moral, academic, and religious values. By word and deed, our parents taught us proper behavior and showed us positive, constructive ways to conduct our lives. We learned, too, that there wasn't anything magic about having a well-kept home or finding clean clothes in a dresser. Such things were the result of hard work, taking pride in one-self, having a positive attitude, and pursuing a desire to make things better. That may sound like pretty heady stuff—most ideals do; but these ideals, these values, are some of the benefits gained from the Laundry Room Learning Center.

In a way, I feel sorry for today's youngsters. For with all the gadgets, technology, and materials available in their high-tech media centers, I doubt they'll ever come close to the level of understanding acquired by those of us who were fortunate to be taught in a laundry room learning center.

Now, laundry is done anytime, almost automatically—just a few minutes to set the dials and push the buttons. The old-fashioned wringer washer is now a museum piece. And I can't recall the last time I heard of a kid hanging clothes, let alone wiping the basement floor. But perhaps the saddest part of this whole scene is what's happened to the concept of family since I was a boy. These days, not many kids get the chance to hear their parents' stories. I was very lucky; the images and sounds and fragrances of those days are mine to keep always.

So impressionable were those times that today my keyboard and Maytag share space in the laundry room. After the dials and buttons have been set and pushed,

I sit at the keyboard and finger dance with letters. With motors and pumps and water all in motion, it brings back bittersweet memories. What I wouldn't give for the chance to return to my boyhood learning center and listen once more to my favorite teacher.

November's Song: A Remembrance

My dad was born on November 13, 1903. That seems so long ago, but memories freeze time and aging is put on hold, releasing time from its dominion. Everybody knows that unless one becomes famous, achieves national prominence, or gets a place on the holiday calendar, most of us will live out our lives in a mostly uneventful fashion. The remembrance of our lifetime will be left to family and friends on an occasional, informal basis. As important as some of us think we are, deep down we know that after we're gone, they'll never shut down the post office, close banks, curtail business, or give us even the tiniest snippet of recognition on the evening news.

But memory is a treasured human characteristic, and as we grow older, we tend to firm up our grasp on remembered experiences and give added distinction to loved one and friends who have passed on. This is about treasured experiences—and it's about remembrance.

My father died in 1965. At the time, I was 24, newly married, and just starting my sophomore year in college. Immediately upon hearing the terrible news of his fatal heart attack, I left for home. I'll never forget that rainy September night as I drove northward; thoughts and feelings flooded my mind.

Automatically, I inventoried moments shared with my father. I replayed our last meeting: Dad helping me pack the car prior to my leaving for campus. I recalled our last conversation: He told me to be careful and drive safely. I reminded him to take it easy and that I'd see him on the weekend. I pulled images from memory and flipped through remembered times: playing catch in front of the house, trying to capture his elusive knuckleball; his willingness to loan scarce pocket money when I experienced frequent adolescent cash-flow problems; bowling privileges at the Community Center; cheering my questionable talents as a Little Leaguer; arguing the merits of Cubs vs. Sox (Pop loved the Chicago White Sox); the countless times when, as a boy, I'd meet him on 119th Street as he walked home from Standard Oil and we'd share the journey together.

Through rain and rheumy eyes, I traveled homeward. Each mile of roadway brought additional memories. All those ordinary, take-it-for-granted episodes of living took on special importance as the finality of the situation took hold.

As a grade school choirboy on Christmas Eve, Dad walked with us to midnight Mass. I recalled the time when I was about 10 years old when he defended me from an older boy who tried to bully me around. Bits and pieces of a lifetime flashed by; how he held my hand as a child, and his tolerance when I tested his patience as a teenager. I recalled him borrowing my convertible, top down, and losing his favorite cap to the jet stream that flowed over the car. I called to memory the image of him at our wedding a few months prior to his heart attack: full of life, vibrant, joking. I recalled, too, Mom telling me of his tears when I left for the Army. And I saw his joy a few days later, when Uncle Sam returned his youngest son to civilian life. Suddenly, no more moments; his life's song silenced.

I reached further back in time, searching childhood files, and a long forgotten scene played out in my mind. In our family, everyone did chores. As a young kitchen helper, I was given the daily task of peeling potatoes for supper. It didn't take long, however, for the novelty of the job to wear thin and become "unapeeling." Every now and then, Pop would have to pry me away from a favorite radio program and remind me: "Peel the spuds, Doc." Reluctantly, I'd get the potatoes from the basement storage box and start peeling. I know this may sound odd, but peeling the supper spuds helped me appreciate our family. To this day, I enjoy peeling the supper spuds.

Our four children never knew my father. They would have enjoyed their grandpa and would have shared many happy moments together. He was a good and decent man with a gentle manner and kind heart. The kids would've loved him. I know I did.

In the years since he's been gone, I like to believe he'd be proud of his family: sons, daughter, their spouses, and, of course, his grandchildren. There isn't a day that I don't think about my late parents or remember them in prayer. Each November when Dad's birthday comes around, I reflect on his life and think about all he gave us. Mom's special time comes in April.

To all whose parents are still with them, I trust you treasure their presence, appreciate their efforts, and savor the resonance of their life's song. To those whose parents have passed on, I hope you remember them with kindness, setting aside any grievances or ill feeling, aware that, like us, they came flawed with human frailties but now add flame to heaven's stars.

At first glance, November is not the most glamorous time of the year. Its early darkness, leafless trees, and frequent biting cold aren't attributes that uplift spirits. Even so, November is a time of remembrance, a time to celebrate the life songs of those fortunate to mark their birthday in the autumn of the year.

Mom's Aerobic and Exercise Program

At my annual checkup, Dr. Feelgood recommended an increase in exercise to help thwart my expanding midriff. Stated in layman's terms, if my input is greater than my output, then my upkeep will be my downfall. For one who recently nudged closer to LXV, I believed my current grunt-and-groan activities were more than adequate in my personal battle of the bulge. However, when Doc Charge Card scanned my anatomy, he concluded a reduction of frontal tundra is warranted.

I freely admit being a snack food addict. I've proven countless times that eating just one potato chip is impossible without having someone staple my lips together. And over the years, I've assassinated dozens of Twinkies, Ho Hos and some of Dunkin's finest Donuts. One of my fantasies as a kid was running off with Sara Lee to live happily ever after in Blueberry Muffin Land.

In my much younger days, I would load up on pizza, hot dogs, "Belly-Bombers," chili, cheeseburgers, french fries, and wash it all down with a healthy quantity of liquid refreshment. My steel mill lunch bag bulged with five sandwiches, supplemented by several cups of coffee and a quart-sized thermos of cold milk. I metabolized food at the speed of chomp. Digestion became my favorite hobby. I scoffed at those who warned me of putting on extra pounds.

No matter how much I shoveled in, I knew a fat attack was not in my future, for I was a full-time member of Mom's Aerobic and Exercise Program (MAEP). In this exercise program, fat was not allowed! Perhaps now, however, after viewing the scale's statistics from my latest weigh-in, it's time to sign up once more for MAEP.

The premise of Mom's conditioning program was simple: Work repels fat. The harder one works, the trimmer one stays. Like a personal trainer possessed to fitness, Mom shouted out motivational slogans: "Keep your bones in motion!" "Work those muscles!" "It's better to wear out than rust out!" "Search for dirt!" Her training facility was home. Her exercise program—housework.

Mom subscribed to housework as a vehicle for fitness. Each task was designed for both fine and gross motor development, muscle kinetics, and to raise one's level of domestic skills. Each time we cleaned windows, washed walls, scrubbed linoleum, waxed floors, vacuumed rugs, dusted furniture, scoured kettles, dried dishes, hung laundry, shoveled coal, sanitized the bathroom, mowed the lawn, pulled weeds, swept sidewalks, raked leaves, removed snow, ironed clothes, and in general, policed the area, we tuned and toned our body.

Mom's exercise program didn't require fashionable, color-coordinated, specially designed clothing. Nor did we need exotic training aids or body-building devices. MAEP clients wore mended hand-me-downs, nicknamed "housework tuxedos." Group photos looked like Fruit-of-the-Loom discards. Training equipment consisted of abundant supplies of soaps, cleansers, scrub rags, dust cloths, buckets, and brushes. Participants were expected to supply copious amount of elbow grease and energy. Sweat was encouraged.

Before too long, patrons of Mom's Aerobic and Exercise Program exhibited noticeable results. They increased their level of physical stamina, acquired and refined essential domestic skills, elevated feelings of self-worth, developed a strong work ethic, took pride in their accomplishments, and projected an overall positive attitude. Granted, Mom had a captive workforce, but such shortcomings were more than offset by bowls of homemade soup, served to her cadets at the end of the workday.

Today, there are dozens of videos promoting physical fitness. Movie stars, models, athletes, celebrities, and TV personalities pitch their particular type of exercise program. Set to everything from Bach to the Beach Boys, people of all ages, from every walk of life—sporting body shapes and sizes ranging from beauty to beast—dance, sing, and follow along in hope of maintaining svelte profiles or regaining control over bovine bodies. Some boost their image by purchasing the latest workout fashions from head to shoe. Admittedly, some look terrific. Others pursuing personal fitness goals pay good money to sweat in modern workout centers. Committed to tone up, they climb, pull, tug, lift, row, press, and strain against brightly polished chrome-plated equipment as they wage their personal war against sag and bag. Numerous mirrors provide the cellulite assassins a constant visual assessment as to their progress. Still others exhibit their fitness quest more openly, using public parks and streets. Their personal dedication to good health is inspiring.

Unfortunately, there are too many whose primary exercise is the five-mile sit. Perhaps some of these couch potatoes should consider adopting Mom's Aerobic and Exercise Program. Although Mom's program is not glamorous or as technologically up-to-date as modern fitness parlors or exercise videos, engaging in the program's activities will achieve healthy levels of fitness. Every participant receives the bonus of a clean house and a neatly trimmed property. If there are young children in the family, involve and encourage them to partake in this program of domestic exercise. By sharing, teaching, and working together, a family enhances values and strengthens love. Try getting *that* from a video.

Attic Treasure

One of my favorite boyhood heroes was Red Ryder. Billed as "America's Famous Fighting Cowboy," his adventures filled radio speakers, comic books, and Saturday matinees at the Capitol Theater. Living with his aunt, the Duchess, and teamed with his sidekick Buckskin and Indian ward, Little Beaver, Red Ryder fought the good fight. He turned bad guys every which way but loose. Astride his horse, Thunder, with red hair and red shirt flashing across the screen, we cheered every time Ryder saved the day. By movie's end, the Capitol Theater echoed with Little Beaver's refrain, "You betchum, Red Ryder!"

When periodic financial shortfalls prevented me from watching my hero on the silver screen, I followed Red Ryder's adventures in comic books. For a dime, kids could purchase the latest escapades of Superman, Green Arrow, Batman and Robin, Captain Marvel, and favorite western heroes. Because Mom wasn't a fan of comic books, I had to use my grade school buddies' personal libraries.

In spite of Mom's warnings that comic books would corrupt the mind and render me incorrigible, I devoured issue after issue. Throwing caution to the wind, I read every word—including advertisements. One such ad caught my attention: an offer for an official Red Ryder Daisy BB gun. This lever-action air rifle was a replica of the carbine Red Ryder used in his movies. It had an authentic-looking blue-black metal barrel and a simulated walnut-grain hollowed-out plastic stock to hold 1000 BBs. Two strands of genuine rawhide were knotted to the metal ring above the trigger mechanism so young Red Riders could hook their carbine over saddle horns or Schwinn handlebars. A deluxe model came with a compass mounted in the rifle's stock, along with a supply of bull's-eye targets. From the moment I laid eyes on it, I wanted that BB gun.

I pictured myself drilling BBs in the target's center. Cleverly using my leg as leverage, I'd deftly cock the rifle, and with one slick-smooth motion, bring the carbine to eye level, sight the target, squeeze the trigger, and simultaneously hear and watch the BB find its mark. So much for fantasy; there were two major problems. One, I didn't have the $8.95 for the rifle; two Mom *hated* guns.

To solve the money problem, I began scouring neighborhood alleys for discarded deposit bottles. This technique had earlier worked when I was in desperate need of an Ovaltine waxed seal, so it was back to the alleys. In those days, 12-ounce pop bottles were worth two cents; large Canfield's bottles, a nickel. All summer I trekked alleys, and by early September, I had enough for the BB gun.

The second obstacle, Mom's dislike for firearms, would be dealt with later. First things first—it was time to go carbine shopping. I bought my treasure in Whiting at the Western Tire & Auto Store next to Standard Drugstore, across the street from the State Bank of Whiting. Although I couldn't afford Daisy's deluxe model, I did have enough money left over to buy a dozen cellophane packets of BBs. Bull's-eye targets weren't included with my air rifle but I figured I'd find suitable substitutes.

As soon as the coast was clear, I smuggled the air rifle inside the house and hid it in my bedroom closet. But in spite of my precautions, Mom found the gun. Try as I did to convince her that the BB gun would only be used for target, Mom was not sold. When I asked for one good reason why I couldn't keep my Red Ryder carbine, she replied, "Because you'll shoot your eye out!"

End of discussion.

Shortly thereafter, the BB gun vanished. I knew better than ask where it went. Mom worried about me losing an eye, but I valued my life! Case closed. Every now and then, however, I'd think about my BB gun and wonder where it was. Several months later, I finally got up enough nerve to ask Mom about the rifle. She told me she had hidden it inside the house. One day, she promised, she'd tell me where, but for now that information was classified.

Somewhere along the trail of life, Red Ryder lost his importance, and so did the BB gun. High school, steel mill, college, and married life took priority, leaving boyhood fantasies far behind. A couple of years after Dad died, Mom sold our house. With her kids now married and on their own, she no longer needed such a big place. One day, long after she had moved and settled into her smaller home, I asked about the infamous BB gun. She told me she hid the gun out of fear that I would hurt someone or myself.

"Where did you hide it?" I asked. "I looked everywhere in that house."

"What I did," Mom replied, "was take up a couple of attic floorboards and bury the gun under the rock wool insulation, so you couldn't possibly find it. Then I re-nailed the boards and forgot about it."

Then she told me exactly where she had hidden the gun. For all I know, it's still there. Today that BB gun would be worth a handsome amount, considering it was brand-new when Mom hid it in 1954. I don't know if the present homeowners ever found Red Ryder snoozing among the insulation—it's been more than 50 years! I wouldn't mind getting it back after all these years as a souvenir of youthful days. Who knows, one day someone may discover an unexpected attic treasure. If that happens, I hope for old time's sake they say, "You betchum, Red Ryder!" I also hope they're careful not to shoot their eye out.

The Best Birthday Ever!

When you're a little kid, birthdays are a big deal. It's the one day each year when your family treats you like a celebrity. Relatives you rarely see fawn over you and carry on like you're the greatest. While you're not enthralled with having to kiss your old-maid aunts, you do it to show appreciation for the birthday gifts they've brought you. Of course, they always want to see the toy they bought you the year before; how do you tell these wonderfully generous ladies that the wind-up farm tractor they bought at an after-Christmas sale fell apart? Mom usually came to the rescue and distracted them by offering something to eat. Once food was mentioned, farm tractors were quickly forgotten.

Kids learn early that hugging and smooching relatives is all part of the birthday game. Even so, when you are 10 years old and your birthday is in January, you hope for cold and pray for snowy weather severe enough to keep rouge-cheeked aunts at home; they can send the presents via UPS!

The highlight of any birthday party is everyone singing "Happy Birthday" to you while seated at the table directly in front of Mom's homemade cake, decorated with special frosting and burning candles. As soon as everyone finishes singing, you're supposed to make a wish and blow out the candles. It's a good thing birthday wishes aren't always granted. When I was 10, I wished for a horse like the Lone Ranger's!

As soon as childhood is over, birthdays take on a different look. Toys are replaced by clothes. Later, clothes are replaced by cold cash (still my favorite). Regardless of the gift, each birthday I would receive a card signed by Mom and Dad. I can't explain why, but I've saved almost all of them. Mom would always write the date on the card and add a little note for best wishes and blessings. Packed inside a box stored in the attic is my treasury of birthday greetings: Every once in a while, I open my personal archives and re-read Mom's and Dad's words. If you've ever read old cards and letters from loved ones, you know what feelings are engendered; enough said.

Too quickly, another birthday approaches; time to add one more ring around the tree. Though I've accumulated more than a six-decade supply of birthdays, only a few carry a lasting impression. That's the way life is—we remember moments rather than days.

On my 11th birthday, I had a mini party. To mark the occasion, I received a small-sized pool table. My cousin and a few grade school classmates shared cake and ice cream. As a special treat, Mom prepared a batch of her homemade potato chips. Long before I heard a now-famous slogan, when it came to Mom's chips, "I couldn't stop eating 'em!" In addition to the pool table, Mom and Dad gave me a small penlight. In 1952, having your own flashlight was pretty impressive.

All in all, it was quite a birthday. We had an impromptu 8-ball tournament and feasted on the world's greatest potato chips, cake, and ice cream. Because it was a school night, the party ended before 7 o'clock. After a stab at some homework, I fell asleep listening to *Suspense* on our Zenith console.

Over the years, I've celebrated birthdays in a variety of ways: Setting pins at the Whiting Community Center as a teenager, enjoying an after-work banquet of White Castle Slyders; working as a machinist; cleaning steel mill sewers; taking final exams in college; teaching school; and just hanging around the house, doing whatever.

Now, when I mark my day of genesis, I take everything in stride and play the day by ear, informally. My preferred uniform of the day is sweatshirt, blue jeans, and sneakers. I try to spend the day as quietly and low-key as possible; a party animal I'm not. But that doesn't prevent me from remembering birthdays past and recalling loved ones who shared those moments with me.

It's been awhile since I faced a candle-laden cake as well-wishers sang "Happy Birthday" to me, and that's okay. At this point, I wouldn't want to jeopardize the safety of partygoers or set off smoke alarms. Receiving warm wishes from friends and love from family members more than compensates for a flaming cake; no birthday could be richer. At some point during "my day," I'll inventory personal memories and offer prayerful thanks. Then I'll carefully return these treasures of the heart to their keeping place until next year. But before the day ends, I'll make a special private wish (no, it's not for a horse). And finally, like I've done each year, I'll savor the day just passed and deem the current birthday the best ever.

Orphan Annie Goes Home

She was orphaned before she was 5 years old. The mysterious circumstances surrounding her mother's death and the disappearance of her father would never be fully investigated or resolved. The year was 1913, and throughout southern Indiana coal towns, concern was for living, not dying.

Anne and her two younger sisters were taken by a state agency and placed separately in foster homes. The youngest child, at 8 months of age, would die from scalding milk mistakenly fed to her by an inexperienced attendant. Anne's remaining sister was adopted by an uncle who then left the United States to return to his native Europe, living out their lives on a farm in Czechoslovakia. Anne was in her 50s when she finally located her sister. While her sister's letters were heavily censored by that country's communist government, they corresponded faithfully until her sister's death a decade and a half later.

Anne was taken north to the Calumet area by a family looking for better paying employment. She would eventually live in Whiting with seven different families, spending her childhood and adolescent years as a kept orphan. Anne was never adopted.

Because she never had a family to call her own, Anne often experienced feelings of loneliness. At age 6, she earned her keep by babysitting the younger children in the family that had taken her in. Moving from family to family made lasting impressions on her. Throughout her life, she would share stories about how she was taught to live, work, and pray. Anne told of happy, loving days and of people who befriended her with kindness. She also told tearful stories of hard times—working long hours, of not having enough to eat, and suffering ills that robbed her of stamina and strength. These "when I was a little girl" stories reflected a poignant desire to be part of a family; to be cherished and loved.

Surprisingly, despite her fragmented childhood, Anne grew up with strong feelings of self-worth and self-esteem. In contrast to the adversity she faced, Anne maintained an incredibly strong faith in God. Religion became the bedrock upon which she built her life. Following her eighth grade year, Anne wished to enter the convent of the Sisters of Providence but poor health prevented her acceptance.

Because of economic hardship and pressing financial need, Anne left school at the end of her sophomore year at Whiting High School. She found secretarial work in Chicago and studied business at the Barret Institute at night. Such a demanding schedule required a commute between Whiting and Chicago comprised of train, bus, and streetcar. Fourteen-hour days were the norm as she worked, studied, and survived. In spire of fragile health (devastating seizures, a heart attack at age 20, and an ulcerated stomach), Anne's fierce determination, coupled with her unshakable Faith, sustained and strengthened her resolve.

The country, too, had fallen on hard times. Jobs became scarce as the Great Depression tightened its grip on the nation. Fortunately, Anne found work at the Majestic Radio Company in Chicago, and struggled to live on a few dollars per week. The year was 1929, and her life took a major turn. Even with commitments that left little time for socializing, Anne met a young man from Whiting, Albert Koch. Their mutual affection blossomed, and after a four-year courtship, they were married in September 1933.

Never in good health since birth and nagged by chronic maladies, Anne was advised by doctors to forego any thought of having children; childbirth would place her life in jeopardy. When her husband passed away in September 1965, they had been married 32 years and had four children. Thankfully, for my two older brothers, younger sister, and me, Mom put her trust in God. She was a charter member of heaven's HMO.

Growing up in our family meant everyone did their share. The gospel according to Mom was straightforward: No free lunch! By her example, we acquired a strong work ethic. Anne had a master plan, rules to guide and help us live Christian lives. Mom *never* sent us to church when we were little; she took us! Anne taught her children how to work and how to pray. We knelt in front of so many candles we were flame-toasted by first grade.

Using religion as a nucleus, Anne taught her children respect, decency, and kindness. She instilled self-discipline, honor, and a sense of fair play. She prepared her offspring to be self-reliant and independent. Every lesson was presented as a gift. Mom encouraged us to risk, to use our imagination and skill in a positive constructive manner. She tempered every lesson with goodness and compassion. She cultivated in her children an attitude to help others willingly. And though she could be firm and demanding—make no mistake about it, Anne was a tough taskmaster—her actions were always clothed in maternal understanding. Anne was one orphan who always helped others before thinking of herself.

As happens with most families, kids grow up and move away to build their own lives. Sometimes a son or daughter stays close to home to lend a hand. I was able to do just that. It was love returned.

During the years since my father died, I helped Mom do the necessary maintenance and chores around her home. As the years moved on, I made a habit of checking on her at least twice a day. Sometimes by telephone but usually by stopping in to see her: an early morning visit after Mass before going to work and at suppertime, when we would visit and talk about the day's events. Mom was an avid radio listener. It kept her informed and exercised her mind. Over a bowl of her homemade soup, we'd discuss the current state of affairs. Those conversations have become treasures of the heart.

As seasons changed and darkness came early, Mom would leave a small light on so I could more easily find my way. When leaving, I never said goodbye. Mom didn't care for the word; it sounded too final. So instead I'd say, "See ya." "See ya" has a gentleness all its own. Mom liked "See ya."

On August 9, 1990, Anne suffered a massive stroke. She peacefully passed away the following day. She was 82. Everyone who knew her teased about how hard she worked. Mom always liked to keep busy doing something; she didn't believe in wasting time. Her house was always neat and clean, her housekeeping skills legendary. I mention this just in case some heavenly employee is listening, and they meet up with Mom. She'll be easy to identify. Just look for the lovely little lady with silky, snow-white hair. She'll be the only angel holding a dust cloth.

She's earned her peace and is an orphan no more. Mom and I enjoyed each other's company and I know one day we'll talk again. Until then, I'm sure she'll keep a light on for me. Rest well, Mom. See ya.

Working:
Pay for Play

Fun in the Factory

Long before there were theme parks like Disneyland and Six Flags, America's working adult males found an outlet for their foolishness in factories across the land. In large industrial complexes, petroleum refineries, manufacturing plants, and workplaces of every description, employees (mostly male) used these surroundings to stage pranks on unsuspecting candidates. Such shenanigans were the sustenance of sanity. This goofiness became the blue-collar glue that held the American workforce together and provided the stuff of which legends are made.

Every day, every night, every shift—throughout steel mills, assembly plants, oil companies, businesses, and corporations—allegedly adult men would frequently allow the mischievous little boy lurking in their psyche to come out for recess and play. Acts of juvenile silliness and dangerously stupid, creative stunts would fill volumes in the library of horseplay.

Many times, this proclivity for mischief was a way to release tension or to "get even" with a coworker or supervisor for some imagined wrongdoing. Sometimes it was to ease the boredom of sameness. And once in a while, it just felt good to be silly. Working in a place filled with exotic equipment and machinery, it doesn't take long before an employee saddles up and goes horsin' around. And no amusement park, circus, or carnival ever offered better entertainment or escapism than the industrial playgrounds of Northwest Indiana's steel mills.

The type and degree of occupational nonsense depended on the shift schedule. Dayshift was reserved for docile acts of inane misbehavior like the leaky coffee cup trick, greasy handle caper, hidden lunch bag, or misaimed coolant hose (squirting an unsuspecting machine operator right between the eyes). The reason for such a low-key approach to mayhem was that many of the guys working dayshifts were busy making bonus, trying to impress management in hope of being considered for foreman (or fill-in flunky, when a foreman was off). Other workers called these guys "animals." They took everything seriously. They were the "lifers," guys who used metal lunch pails. Everyone else was a "short-timer" or "brown-bagger."

Prime-time horseplay took place from 4:00 PM to midnight. By five o'clock, the gung-ho bosses had gone home, so the laid-back nightshift took command of the Good Ship Mischief. Unless there was a "Triple-X" rush job (a job that needed to be completed yesterday!) or an emergency breakdown, things went along an unhurried pace.

Working midnights, commonly referred to as the graveyard shift, meant eight hours of whatever. Employees were not allowed to sleep, but like many other things they were not allowed to do, they slept anyway. One thing they did shy away from, however, was work.

Machinists are very precise individuals. Because of this trait, every stunt or practical joke is given careful analysis, a degree of sophistication, and an element of cleverness. The intended victim is thoroughly assessed. This follows the machinist's axiom: "Plan your work and work your plan." Take the Dog Food Caper, for example. This practical joke involved convincing a coworker to eat dog food for lunch. It certainly livened up the dayshift.

Like modern soap operas, some pranks took an entire week to play out. Monday was "Victim Setup Day." Tuesday was "Reinforcement Day." Wednesday was "Victim Participation Day." Thursday was "Victim Solo Day." Friday was "Maybe-We'll-Tell-Him-and-Maybe-Not Day."

Lunchtime was fun time. During the allotted 30 minutes, guys would eat, sleep, talk, relax, or any combination thereof. Usually, the same guys would share a lunch place—a table, a machine, or any convenient bench. This particular scene was staged in a small maintenance area of the shop. The cast included Bill and John, two journeymen; Paul and Al, two apprentice kids; and, the foil of the prank, a fitting floor helper we called Starch. On one nondescript Monday, the five of them sat down to lunch. The game was on.

The two veteran machinists put the caper in motion. As everyone unwrapped their sandwiches and began eating, Starch noticed that Bill was opening a can of dog food. What the unsuspecting Starch didn't know was that earlier, Bill had removed the label from his can of corned beef hash and replaced it with a label from a can of dog food.

Bill casually offered some to John: "Have some dog food, John."

"Thanks, Bill, don't mind if I do," John replied, scooping a large spoonful onto a paper plate. "What kind is this today?"

"Strongheart. The ol' lady found it on sale, so she bought six cans."

Starch was in shock. "What the hell are you eatin', Bill?"

"What's it look like, Starch. Can't you read a label?"

Bill offered some to the co-conspirator apprentices. "No, thanks," they replied. "We're on a diet."

"Ah, you kids don't know what's good for you," Bill chided, "this is terrific stuff."

Tuesday was a replay of Monday, except the two apprentices now accepted Bill's offer and put a healthy glob on their cold cut sandwiches. "Delicious!" "Yum-yum!" they chorused, bad acting and all.

Starch just sat there and watched the apprentices devour the dog food-labeled hash. You could hear his mind shifting gears, trying to figure it all out. On Wednesday, Starch's curiosity got the best of him; he asked Bill for a small taste. "That's all you're getting, Starch. You didn't want any the other day."

Starch nibbled at his sample and found that he like the taste of it. John closed out any doubt Starch might've had in his head by saying, "It's a heck of lot cheaper than buying corned beef hash, and it's got all them vitamins."

The guys couldn't wait until lunchtime Thursday. Sure enough, Starch had his can opener working around the rim of his container of Strongheart. "You guys want some?" Starch offered.

"Not today, thanks," Bill replied, "the wife made chicken salad."

"Any of you guys want any? There's plenty here. Don't be bashful." Starch continued to offer. Everyone declined. "Okay, more for me," Starch boasted.

The guys watched as he literally wolfed (no pun intended) down the entire contents of the can. He topped off his meaty little feast with some potato chips and a large Coke. "I had my wife buy 12 cans. Saved almost two bucks over the price of the hash," Starch said. He was beaming.

By Friday at noon, everybody in the shop was making barking sounds at Starch. He took them as a compliment to his insightful frugality. By two o'clock, he'd heard every dog joke known to man. Then, in a moment of weakness, one of the guys spilled the beans and told Starch he'd been had. The prank took on added life when several other guys made up phony illnesses and diseases one gets from eating dog food.

Starch went home an hour early, sick as a dog—complaining of a growling stomach. For a while the guys in the shop called him "Strongheart Starch," and teased him about trees and fire hydrants. The two engineers of the prank were quite satisfied with themselves. By the look in their eyes you could almost guess what they were thinking: "What'll we do for an encore?"

Rust-Free Pigeons

Years ago, to help defray college expenses, I worked as a laborer in the steel mill. It was back-bending, sweat-dripping, dirt-shoveling, broom-sweeping, window-washing, sewer-cleaning, paint-covering, office-mopping work; and I loved every minute of it. Although I was 24 years old when I was hired as summer help, I was no stranger to the mills. After graduating from high school, I had been a full-time employee for six years, working as a machinist apprentice, then journeyman. When the opportunity to pursue a college degree presented itself, I put away my calipers and coffee cup and headed for the university campus. Now, as a college student, I had returned to the "scene of the crime," taking up shovel and broom.

I enjoyed being a laborer. Free from the tension of class work (and precision machining), I found piloting a rubbish-hunting wheelbarrow relaxing. Every day was a new adventure. One day might find me shoveling slag from a rolling mill, while on another I would be cleaning office walls, moving furniture, or washing a foreman's car. For the most part, laborers worked straight days, and being assigned outdoor work on a summer's day was close to hog heaven.

The boss in charge of the labor gang was a good man named Leo Noel. He had a good sense of humor and treated men in his crew with dignity and respect. As soon as he found out that I had previous mill experience, he teamed me up with another college kid, Jerry, who was about 20 years old. He dubbed us "Batman and Robin" because of the television show that was popular at the time. Jerry and I hit it off immediately. He was a student at Purdue University and I was at Indiana State. We were to be "partners in grime" for the summer. It was soon obvious to our foreman that his "Dynamic Duo" required minimal supervision once assigned a job, performing the given task with little or no additional assistance.

Leo liked that. To reward our efforts, we were given the more responsible jobs. Granted, one didn't have to be a rocket scientist to be a laborer, but it did require some degree of self-reliance and cognition. The problem with Jerry and I was that, at times, our creativity and proclivity for nonsense distracted us from the task at hand. A case in point involved painting the company's cyclone fence.

174

On a clear, hot summer day, Batman and Robin were assigned to paint the chain-link fence that marked the outskirts of the mill's property. It was an 8-foot high fence topped with barbed wire that ran several hundred yards. Sent to work in this "no-man's land," we were told to paint as much of the fence as possible until quitting time. Jerry and I grabbed our lunches and placed 20 gallons of aluminum paint and the necessary supplies in the truck. We hopped on, taking a seat on the tailgate. The truck driver would drop us at the worksite, and return to pick us up at 2:30 PM. As we started to pull away from the supply shanty, our foreman gave the Dynamic Duo his instructions: "Do a good job and don't bring back any paint. When it's time to quit, toss everything but the roller handles in the dumpster—got it?"

"Yessir, Boss. No problem!" Jerry and I chorused. "No return on the paint. Gotcha!"

Jerry and I attacked the job enthusiastically. The plan was to get as much done before the heat of the day reached its peak. The 5-gallon paint buckets were opened, stirred, and readied for the rollers. We had taken a couple of 6-inch brushes, but neither of us intended to paint that precisely.

We painted like men possessed, each of us moving faster than a one-legged man in a cow-kicking contest, paint-saturated rollers covering the wire fabric of the fence. We broke for lunch and then launched our afternoon paint-and-roller assault. At times, we were putting more paint on ourselves then the fence, but this was not the Sistine Chapel. Time and again the familiar steel mill adage played in my head: "Get the job done, don't be so fussy. We're not building watches!"

By 1:30, the monotony of the job and the heat was getting to us. Looking over the landscape, we both noticed them at the same time. Dead pigeons. Dozens of dead pigeons. We formed several hypotheses for their demise. Had the birds been victimized by the high voltage wires overhead? Had they been asphyxiated by coke oven gasses? Were they poisoned? We even suggested a suicide pact as causation but dismissed that as unlikely, given the pigeon's limited vocabulary.

We stood there mulling over these deep philosophical questions when we simultaneously came up with the same idea: Let's paint the birds! We each picked up a deceased pigeon and dipped it in the silver paint, totally submerging it. Holding them by their feet, they looked impressive. "What now?" Jerry asked.

"Let's mount 'em."

"Where?"

"On top of the fence posts. There's enough scrap wire around here. Let see how one looks."

I wire-tied the first bird. Dripping aluminum paint in the bright summer sunshine gave it the appearance of a majestic silver gargoyle. Geez, it looked impressive!

Immediately we set up a mini-production line; Jerry dipped and I wired. In no time at all, we had a length of fence festooned with fantastic-looking aluminized pigeons, dazzling the eye with their rust-free brilliance!

Unannounced, Leo showed up to check our progress. At first he didn't notice. He looked at the freshly painted fence and nodded his approval. Then he looked up, did a slow-motion double-take, stared, and said: "What the @#$%&* are those?" (I've edited his actual words to prevent lawsuits.)

"Those are a newly discovered avian species—rust-free pigeons! Just a small touch of architectural splendor, boss. Pretty classy, huh?"

Remember what I said about our boss' sense of humor? Not true.

"You two 'professors' have about three minutes to get those damn chickens off the company's fence or you'll be cleaning toilets until September!"

Just goes to prove that great artwork is not always appreciated.

There isn't a whole lot more to tell. We took down the soggy steel-mill eagles and tossed them in the dumpster. As the boss got into his car, he was mumbling something about bat-brained intelligence and robin-sized mentality. Driving away, we heard him shouting: "THEY PAINTED DEAD PIGEONS! THEY PAINTED DEAD PIGEONS!"

Plan B: Get a Job

In the summer of '65, I was in desperate need of a job. Newly married and a 24-year-old college sophomore without employment, it was essential that I find work. It was more than essential—it was a matter of survival! The plan for the next three years was for my wife to keep her secretarial job and live in our rented garage flat in Hammond while I went to school in Terre Haute. I would come home on weekends and supplement our income by working in the steel mill on Saturdays and Sundays as a laborer. The major problem back then was earning enough money for the upcoming year of school.

I had started college a year earlier, after working in the steel mill for six years. Beginning an apprenticeship immediately following high school graduation, I earned my machinist journeyman's card four years later. But the ensuing two years brought a gnawing restlessness to pursue other interests, so I entered college to become a teacher. With an avalanche of assistance from friends and family, encouragement and support from my bride, and heaven's kindness, I managed to successfully complete my first year of college. To continue, however, I needed a summer job.

Through various contacts, I had heard that the G.A.T.X. plant on Euclid Avenue in East Chicago had an opening for a machinist. (General American Transportation Corporation manufactured railroad cars.) But I had also heard they weren't planning to fill the position until September. I couldn't wait until September; I needed a job *now*! Already near the end of June, there wasn't time for, nor could I take a chance on, Plan A, the conventional process of applying for a job. The fact that I had never set foot anywhere near G.A.T.X. left me undaunted. I decided it was time for Plan B.

Plan B involved creating a mental hologram in the minds of unsuspecting participants. The objective was to use ordinary, familiar, well-accepted patterns of behavior and carefully chosen verbal and facial signals to convince the other players to correct a series of contrived imaginary errors and oversights, allowing me to achieve my goal—summer employment. A brief review of Plan B:

> GOAL: To procure a machinist job for the summer.
> TARGET: The machine shop at G.A.T.X.
> OBJECTIVE: Convince G.A.T.X. personnel that I was already hired!

On Monday, June 28, 1965, at 6:30 AM, I put Plan B into action. I had completed my research and had rehearsed the cognitive gymnastics I selected for the success of the mission. In short, I had planned my work; now I was going to work my plan! The personnel office opened at 7:00 AM sharp, and I intended to be their first customer of the day.

Dressed in my work uniform, complete with pocket protector, safety glasses, and steel-toed shoes and holding a chest filled with machinist tools, Thermos, and brown bag lunch, I *looked* ready for work. I had my wife drive me to the plant gate. I told her to park a half-block down the street and wait 15 minutes. If I didn't come out of the personnel office in that time, she was to leave.

Entering the plant's main gate, I lugged my toolbox, lunch, and Thermos to the personnel office and went inside. When the lone office employee opened the window for business, there I stood like a model posing for the OshKosh B'Gosh Industrial Calendar.

"What are you doing here?" he asked, startled.

"I'm supposed to start work today," I answered confidently.

"What department?" The personnel man looked bewildered.

"Machine Shop," I answered, clunking my toolbox on the floor. I could almost hear his mind gears shifting, trying to get a handle on the scene being played before him. He looked at me closely, his eyes scanning my carefully contrived ready-for-work costume. Then he spoke: "Who told you to come to work?"

Now it was time to feed him the psychological triggers necessary for the desired responses. In layman's terms, I had baited the hook. Now I had to set it and reel him in.

"The gentleman I talked to back in April when I filled out the application. I was home from college on spring break. I explained to him that I would be able to start work on June 28th. After he processed my application and everything, he told me to report here on the 28th. And here I am."

"What was the name of the man you talked to?" The personnel guy was really puzzled.

"I don't know. Things were pretty busy when I was here, and I just don't recall." I gave him my best furrowed-brow look. The man in the window asked for my name, and began looking through a stack of processed applications. "I can't find it," he said, now more puzzled than ever.

"What do I do now?" I asked, with a look of deep concern and anxiety as I continued to feed him the appropriate body language signals. He searched further. No application. I segued to my frantic, nervous, fidgety Don Knotts impression, as I conveyed an image of grave apprehensiveness about the situation.

The personnel guy was soaking it up like a thirsty sponge. Finally he spoke: "Listen, I just got back from vacation, and things are little screwed up, but we'll get them straightened out. I guarantee it!" His face glowed with a "don't-worry-everything-will-be-all-right" smile. "Would you mind filling out a *duplicate* application?" he asked. "It'll save time looking for the other one."

"I'll do whatever I have to do," I replied.

"They've obviously lost your file so you'll have to get a duplicate health exam from the clinic too. OK?"

"Yes, sir." My performance was Academy Award-worthy!

After filling out the application stamped "DUPLICATE," he sent me to the clinic. There was one problem; I didn't know where the clinic was! There I stood, in the middle of rush-hour traffic on Euclid Avenue, trying to locate the company clinic. Casually I approached the uniformed guard directing traffic in front of the plant and inquired, "Where's the clinic?"

Without missing a beat, he answered: "The red building across the street. Second floor."

In less than a minute, I was handing the only nurse on duty the stamped medical form.

"What'd they do, lose another one?" She queried, shaking her head.

"Guess so," I replied, "I'm supposed to have this one filled out."

"Well, you're all set for work I see. This won't take long." She hurriedly filled in the blanks, initialed the form, apologized for the mix-up, and sent me back to personnel.

"Get your tools, lunch, and c'mon. I'll take you to the machine shop and get you on the payroll."

"Sounds good," I said.

There's not much more to tell. After grumbling to the personnel clerk about not knowing they hired anyone, the machine shop foreman put me to work. I worked the remainder of the summer and earned enough to pay my school expenses.

Looking back all these years later, it's hard to believe I pulled it off. Thankfully, this was pre-computer age. Logically, though, it was the most sensible thing to do. I had everything to gain and nothing to lose. Had the personnel guy called my bluff and told me no, what would I have lost? Instead, I wound up with a good-paying summer job. Since then, I always keep a Plan B handy—just in case.

Blue-Collar Genius

There was a time when I equated creativity and genius with individuals who had attained lofty educational heights. And to some extent, this association holds true. But I'm convinced that the vast majority of clever, creative thinkers are found in the blue-collar workforce.

I worked in the steel mills for almost 10 years. The first six—right out of high school—I was a 17-year-old machinist apprentice, then a journeyman in the main machine of Inland Steel's Plant 1. For the remainder of those years, I was employed part-time on weekends and during college vacations at Inland, Youngstown, and G.A.T.X. Although I've since earned several university degrees, I rank my "steel mill education" near the top. That may sound strange, but there are good reasons why.

Not only did I learn a trade, I also acquired the greatest social education available and developed friendships with some of the most interesting and talented characters this side of anywhere. As I mentioned, the majority of my industrial experience was at Inland Steel, and it didn't take long for me to realize that I was working among the gifted all-stars of blue-collar workers. I suppose one could argue the merits of other trades and professions, and in some instances make some rather convincing arguments. But overall, in my humble opinion, the top of the tradesman's ladder is *owned* by machinists. This is one trade that requires constant manipulative and cognitive precision, day-in and day-out. Working in tolerances other workers have difficulty spelling, the machinist exhibits these highly technical skills with laser-like accuracy. It also helps if you're a little wacky! Ah, but I get ahead of myself.

For those of you who don't know, a machinist is a highly trained skilled craftsman who removes the right amount of material, from the right place, at the right time. Becoming a machinist requires a four-year apprenticeship that includes 8000 hours of on-the-job supervised training on a variety of machine tools and related mechanical assemblies, plus four years of apprentice school that includes 432 hours of related classroom study. If a candidate survives this regiment, he'll work another 4000 hours before he reaches journeyman status.

181

There is one more criterion necessary to become a machinist. The technical term is *stress reduction activity*; in layman's language: horseplay. Such activity was condemned by management but regularly practiced by employees. Included in this broad category of micrometer monkeyshines is any nonsense perpetrated in an effort to maintain one's sanity. It covers both small pranks (the leaky coffee cup and greasy machine handles) and medium-size stunts (pigeon hunting and rat fishing). Grandiose capers included joyriding around the plant in a "borrowed" truck and playing chimes on 20-foot billets with 8-pound sledgehammers.

A few extra-curricular feats became legend, like the clandestine adjustment of work schedules and creating industrial-size polka dots! There were over 300 employees in the machine shop during the '50s and '60s, each with his own unique sense of style. They were talented and dedicated machinists, helpers, and support trades who kept their mind on their work, while their heart was often on the playground. These terrific employees made Plant 1 Mechanical the best department at Inland Steel. These hardworking, creative professional craftsmen took pride in their work and pleasure in their nonsense. They fully understood the need for humor and the healthy, therapeutic effect of laughter. It was a delight to work and share those years with such distinguished, brilliant, imaginative minds; the camaraderie was incredible. In the words of Charles Dickens, "It was the best of times."

The Fourth Wise Man

For many years, Inland Steel decorated their Indiana Harbor property for Christmas. Utilizing the lawn adjacent to their main office in front of the West Annex, the company set up an elaborate display of colored lights and wintry scenes. The centerpiece of the exhibit was a life-size Nativity.

From early December through the first weeks of January, thousands visited the Watling Street display. The increased traffic required extra duty by plant protection personnel to maintain safety. Though the majority of visitors simply drove by, hundreds parked in company lots and surrounding streets and walked the remaining distance. Countless snapshots were taken as parents posed their children for Kodak moments and scrapbook memories. Families approached the realistic-looking manger as close as the protective railings allowed, hoisting their children shoulder-high for a better view. The cold winter evenings were filled with happy voices and radiant smiles, with Christmas music adding richness to an already impressive scene.

In 1966, as a college student, I had worked the previous summer as laborer at Inland. Since I had maintained my part-time employment status, I could work in the mill on weekends and during school vacations. Home for Christmas vacation, I had returned to work.

The week prior to Christmas was spent doing conventional laborer tasks—shoveling, raking, mopping, and sweeping. I had become quite skilled at navigating a fully loaded wheelbarrow, steering deftly around a variety of obstacles along Bar Mill Avenue. And when assigned janitorial duties, locker rooms and latrines sparkled, the result of my manipulative prowess with bowl cleansers and disinfectants.

Before they posted the following week's schedule, my foreman asked if I was interested in working the 3:00-11:00 PM shift during the week between Christmas and New Year's. Since Christmas and New Year's both fell on a Sunday that year, and laborers only worked Monday to Friday, regardless of when I worked I would be off for the holidays. Normally, I would have declined because of my aversion to shift work, but because I was thankful to make the extra money, I agreed. After all, Inland was generous to keep me on part time, so if I could help out during the holidays it was okay with me.

"Whad'ya want me to do?" I asked.

"You're gonna be the fourth Wise Man."

"The fourth what?"

"Wise Man, as in Manger. Come with me. I'll show you."

The foreman and I drove out through the front gate, past the guards, and across the tracks, parking behind the West Annex. From there we walked into the Employment Office. I followed him down a hallway to a combination office/meeting room. There was a desk, telephone, and several tables with chairs. Through partially drawn blinds on the window, I could see the Christmas display.

My task as the fourth Wise Man was to sit inside the darkened office and watch the Christmas display. If anyone went beyond the railings or acted as if they were going to vandalize the Nativity figures or decorations, I was to call Plant Protection. Though the office would be dark, a radio was available for listening. I was not to call attention to myself in any way; I was the unseen observer.

The Monday after Christmas, I reported to the guard in the clock house. He ushered me into the employment office. By 3:00 PM, I was on station, reading a magazine, and occasionally glancing at the display. Until the offices closed at 5:00 PM, there wouldn't be much to do. Visitors didn't start to show up until 6:00 PM. My foreman offered me the day's paper when he made his rounds shortly before 4:00 PM. For the sake of the Nativity scene, it was probably a good thing to be inside; as the fourth Wise Man, I had no gift and was wearing street clothes.

For five days, I sat in the darkened office and watched. Nothing improper happened. What I saw were hundreds of people who came to view a replica of the First Christmas. Amid colored lights, a snowy landscape, wintry winds, and Christmas music, the faces of children, moms, dads, grandparents, and friends glowed with appreciation as they viewed the figures in and around the manger. It was like having a week of Christmas Eves. A few children, encouraged by their parents, left small gifts by the railings for the Christ child. Some prayed, and a few added their voices or lip-synced to the songs of the season, but most just smiled and enjoyed the sights.

Working as a laborer in a steel mill does not usually evoke blissful images. Every now and then, however, a special benison descends upon those who labor, bringing an extraordinary gift of the spirit. Such a gift was bestowed that Christmas. Hardly anyone was aware that a "Fourth Wise Man" was present. During that final week of 1966, I was privileged to witness a living Christmas that would have pleased Hallmark, one that joyfully overflowed with excited children, proud parents, and cheerful visitors. Sometimes, being a laborer is the best job of all.

"He That Hath a Trade"

"He that hath a trade hath an estate." The first time I read those words from Ben Franklin, I was a 17-year-old machinist apprentice. At the time, I didn't fully realize the impact of the quote's meaning, but after earning my journeyman's card, the full enrichment of his words became evident.

Besides being highly skilled, technical individuals, machinists are very creative. Unfortunately, not many people understand what a machinist does. It's not the most glamorous way to make a living; so far, no television sitcom has featured a machinist in a starring role. But several years ago, to help promote the "lighter side" of machine trades, I wrote several poems. Perhaps these will suffice until machinists are recognized for their talents by the entertainment industry. Who knows, one day there might be rock groups named Mike & The Micrometers, Carl & The Calipers, or Feeds & Speeds! How about a TV sitcom, *Murray the Machinist*? Well, you get the idea.

The Machinist

Back when I was 17, on work I had to speculate,
And soon enough, before I knew, from high school did I graduate.

To actually work was quite a shock, for talent I had none.
In school, in lieu of studying, I was mostly fool and fun.

But one bright summer morning, with bath and clean, brushed teeth,
I gathered up my courage, and then I hit the streets.

On doors I knocked, and questions asked, employment was my plea.
Though my feet were hot, and my throat so dry, no one would hire me.

And then, my oldest brother, with wisdom that was keenest,
Said, "Listen, kid, take my advice, and go be a machinist."

A great idea! I think I will; I'll see the program through.
But wait a minute, "Brother, what does a machinist do?"

He handed me a real thick book to read and contemplate,
When I closed the cover, I knew it was already too late.

Oh, it's easy work for some, that's true, but for sure you won't get lazy;
If everything goes according to plan, in four years you'll be crazy.

For milling is thrilling, and slottin' is rottin', and grinding I'm told is okay.
Just keep makin' those pretty blue chips until they take you away.

Well I took the tests, flunked two out of three, and those were only medical.
Evidently I was a physical wreck, 'cause the doctor went hysterical!

The written exams were even worse, but I gave it a valiant try.
When they were over, I knew I did poorly, for I saw the examiner cry.

But in spite of my faults, and all things considered, overall I did just grand.
For they ushered me into the machine shop, and my apprenticeship began.

Before the trade, I seldom drank, a draft I would not draw.
But now at home, the tub I fill, and jump in there with a straw.

My great machinist mind is trained to work all day and slave.
At home, the booze now fills the tub, for that is how I bathe!

You have to be bananas and have that far-off look;
And every night recite the pledge inside the Machinist's handbook.

My eyes aren't always crossed like this, sometimes I see great.
It only happens now and then, when I'm scheduled twelve to eight.

I'm wide awake, I try to fake, while I work and run and race;
I got too close to my coolant pump, and squirted myself in the face.

I read somewhere in one of my books, as I walked out to the gate;
That "He that hath a trade," you see, also "hath an estate."

Those words of wisdom from Benjamin Franklin most assuredly are right;
Even so, I wondered though, why Ben flew all those kites!

"I love the trade," "I love the trade," I recite ten times each day;
And so I end this homily, for there's nothing more to say.

The Great Icebox Giveaway Caper

Sometimes it doesn't pay to be clever, especially when you're trying to unload old refrigerators. Confused? Well, let me "unconfuse" you. (And believe me, this is true. I couldn't make this stuff up if I tried.)

Several summers ago, a friend and I agreed to help an elderly couple with some much-needed home maintenance. For the better part of June and July, we scraped and painted windows, sashes, and trim. We repaired rotted wooden steps and cleaned the house inside and outside. As schoolteachers on summer vacation, we enjoyed working outdoors and it was a welcome respite from the classroom. Everything was going smoothly until it came time to clean the basement.

The homeowners had moved into their house in early 1949. Because there was no attic, the basement became the catchall for everything not being used on the floor above. As best as we could determine, the basement hadn't been cleaned since the Korean Armistice. The owners of this subterranean smorgasbord were veteran newlyweds of considerable financial means. Because of their affluence, little attention was given to domestic labor. Hired help took care of housecleaning, laundry, shopping, and other household chores. Somehow, the basement became a restricted area and was off-limits to the maid, so we were recruited to purge all unwanted trash. In short, everything had to go.

After considerable effort, we entered the basement through an outside door that had been painted shut shortly after the Democrats took control of the White House in 1960. We stumbled around piles of debris before reaching up and finding a pull chain, throwing a little light on the task at hand. Instantly, the incandescent illumination brought an answer to an olfactory question.

Permeating this domestic catacomb was an odor akin to terminally ill sweat socks. A quick glance located the source—dozens of old shoes forming a fermenting leather mountain in one corner of the basement. Removing the shoes at 10 pairs per gasp, it took almost 40 minutes to reduce Dr. Scholl's Summit to ground level. Trash bag after trash bag was filled and toted to the alley. Three decades of accumulated "we'd-better-not-throw-this-out-because-we-might-need-this" were taken to the trash pickup area behind the house. Finally, only three vintage refrigerators remained. This is where my cleverness backfired.

After a brief discussion with my coworker, we decided to donate the refrigerators. I called a used appliance dealer, who inquired: "Do they work? Are they running now? We only take appliances if they are in operating condition." Listening to this conversation on another extension, my coworker shook his head no. Paying no heed to his head-shaking signal, I answered, "Yes!" without hesitation. A truck would be coming in a few hours, so we had to figure out how to convince the scavenger that the three deceased iceboxes were in working order. Not to worry; I had a plan.

First, we thoroughly cleaned the refrigerators, inside and out. Next, we filled all the available ice cube trays and placed them in the freezer upstairs. When the ice cubes were ready, I planned to put two trays in each icebox. When the guys from Ace Appliance came, I would "inspect" the iceboxes one last time. Imagine my surprise upon discovering that ice cubes had been left in the freezer compartment. The men would see the ice cubes and assume the refrigerator had been in service. It was an ingenious ploy, reeking of cleverness. I believed my ice cube scam was foolproof.

Everything went according to plan with the first two appliances. Place and fasten dolly. Check. Remove ice cubes. Load. Two refrigerators were on the truck, happily awaiting a new home. The third icebox was a battle-scarred veteran retired from service the year the Edsel made its debut. Nevertheless, it was clean and "salted" with ice cubes. As the men prepared to hoist it onto the dolly, I went into my third, "Let-me-check-to-make-sure-I-didn't-leave-anything-in-here" routine. I opened the small freezer compartment and, sure enough, some rascal had left a couple of trays of cubes.

"Wait a sec," I said. "I better get these outta here. You don't want these meltin' in the truck." It was a stellar performance. My co-conspirator was cringing in the background. He obviously detected a degree of skepticism from the appliance guys. It was then that the heavy-set truck driver, his curiosity piqued, looked me in the eye and asked: "Are you sure this refrigerator works? It looks pretty old and beat-up!"

Like a moth to a flame, I stayed the course: "Working? Heck, yeah. You saw all those ice cubes. What makes you think it's not working?"

Slowly, the truck driver slowly raised his massive hand, holding the refrigerator's electric cord. His fingers gripped the cable as he flopped it back and forth like a squirming ebony snake. "Working, huh?" he challenged me, eyes dancing, sensing his advantage over a helpless prey. "Kinda tough to do with the cord like this—THERE'S NO PLUG ON THE END!" He paused for a long moment, savoring his victory. "Gotcha!"

Like I said, there are times when it doesn't pay to be clever. Lucky for me, the guys from Ace Appliance had a sense of humor. In spite of my nonsense, they took the refrigerators. I never saw them again but I bet they're still telling coworkers about "The Great Icebox Giveaway Caper"!

Industrial-Size Polka Dots

There was a time when I thought life was relatively normal, and believed that people in positions of authority were more or less intelligent. Working in the steel mill changed all that. It didn't take long to realize that occasionally management went wacko, tilting common sense. It's like being on a planet knocked off its axis and out of orbit. Ample evidence indicates there is an unseen force that takes up temporary residence in the mind of some supervisors, giving them false data that their ideas are sound. They start out okay but wind up like an industrialized version of Dr. Seuss. Eventually when things return to normal what remains are legends that beg to be told to future generations. A case in point: industrial-size polka dots.

The year is 1962. America is vibrant, full of promise. The space race is on, technology reigns supreme, steel mills and automotive plants are going full bore, J.F.K. is in the White House, and "The Stripper" by David Rose is the number one song in America.

Like many legendary events, the polka dot caper began innocently enough; a simple gesture to brighten the otherwise drab work environment of a steel mill machine shop. As its name implies, a machine shop is not noted for glamour. Filled with lathes, boring bars, post mills, planers, shapers, slotters, drill presses, and grinders, the predominant color is gray. In addition to the monochromatic machines, the surrounding work area, with the exception of safety lanes painted traffic-zone yellow and several safety signs, is rather cheerless. After years of accumulated soot, oil, grease, solvent, coolant, cigarette smoke, coffee stains, and spit, the machine shop offered the ultimate challenge to worker morale.

And so it was until one day, in an effort to lessen the visual boredom, the assistant supervisor decided to spruce up the shop by painting the machinery vivid, eye-catching colors. The resident genius of team management thought this would make employees feel better about being at work and make them happier. Actually, the place did need some sprucing up and there *was* a shortage of employee smiles.

Unfortunately, this machine-tool Michelangelo never realized that, along with Scroogish bonus rates, he *was* the problem. This particular supervisor viewed machine shop employees as serfs and lorded over them with arrogant disdain. Had Mr. Wonderful transferred, retired, or died, morale would have shot up higher than a Mercury space capsule. But that didn't happen; instead, he contacted painters.

For his machine tool rainbow he selected orange, white, brown, blue, and pink. Now some of these machines were quite large and covered substantial floor space. And one would think that the new color scheme would be sampled on a small machine first, to see how it looked. Not so with our leader.

Full of confidence, he plunged in whole hog and had the biggest machines painted first. One by one, the shop took on hues never before seen. Complementing the soot and assorted compounds were colorful islands of gloss enamel. The mechanical landscape was awash with a kaleidoscope of iridescence. Awestruck shop employees reported cases of heavy breathing, tingling bodies, and quickened heart rates. Journeymen machinists teased one another and made jokes about their newly decorated machine tool. Watching skilled craftsmen perform precision machining on gaily-colored machine tools was truly a Kodak moment. Employees from neighboring departments toured the shop, eager to see how precious everything looked.

Apprentices got caught up in the newness of the freshly redecorated machines. Conversations went like this: "Well, Larry, are you working on the pink bar or the orange lathe?" Larry would respond: "Neither one, you silly goose. I'm runnin' the chocolate brown mill."

After a few days, one of the guys decided to improve upon the new paint job. Things were a little slow that particular midnight shift when a machinist, fumbling with an empty coffee cup, realized that the bottom of the cup, if carefully cut out, created a neat circle about 2 inches in diameter. He then retrieved a spray can of blue layout dye from his toolbox. (This dye was used to spray a work piece so desired machining operations could more easily be identified.)

Carefully, he took his coffee cup, now resembling a mini megaphone, and placed the small end against the recently painted orange lathe, spraying the surface using the cup as a template. When he withdrew the cup—Eureka, a blue dot! His eyes lit up like a pinball machine. He continued until the lathe was covered with blue dots. He stood back to admire his handiwork. Excited, he called his coworkers to show them his artistry. Waves of laughter echoed through the machine shop in the wee hours of the morning. "Wait'll what's-his-name sees this in the morning," one of the guys said through his laughter.

When the assistant super arrived at work and saw his lovely orange lathe covered with blue polka dots, he was livid. Like a drill sergeant, he threatened reprimand, days off, even dismissal. But he never found out who the polka-dot phantom was. And by the time the polka dots were painted over, everyone in the mill had seen, heard, or cracked jokes about them.

One of the guys said the polka-dotted orange lathe looked like the animal in the kids' book, *Put Me in the Zoo*. That did it. When the assistant superintendent heard *that*, he ordered all machines repainted gray. The machine shop rainbow was over. But by then, it was too late; a legend had been born. And not long after, the assistant super took a leave of absence. Word was he kept seeing spots in front of his eyes!

Apprentice School vs. The Convertible

When I graduated from high school, the furthest thing from my mind was more school. As one who had not experienced scholastic prominence, my immediate objective was to avoid class work and find a job. Many high school grads in the late '50s found work at Standard Oil's Whiting refinery; others applied at nearby steel mills.

Early on, I opted for the mill. Though several family members had long-worked for Standard Oil, I decided to pursue a machinist apprenticeship. Like my oldest brother, I enjoyed working with metal and machine tools. The difference was that he was gifted and talented, while my entry-level skills were marginal at best.

Gainful employment was Plan A. If by some quirk of fate I was unable to find a job by summer's end, Plan B was to join the Army. In spite of impassioned pleas at a number of employment offices, no one hired me. By the second week of August, I began rehearsing how to salute. Just when I convinced myself that khaki was my color, I received the miracle phone call.

Disregarding academic shortcomings and subpar test scores, I was accepted in the machinist apprenticeship program. As soon as September arrived, it was back to school. Beginning the first Monday after Labor Day, and every Monday during the regular school year, we went to night classes at East Chicago Roosevelt High School.

Apprentice school was like high school with ashtrays. From 5:00 to 9:00 PM, apprentices from several companies, representing a variety of trades, pursued studies from math to metallurgy. For the next four years, wannabe tradesmen struggled with physics, economics, industrial safety, shop theory, and blueprint reading. Attendance was mandatory, and an unexcused absence was grounds for dismissal. Management was serious as a heart attack about attendance; they had no sense of humor for apprentices who cut school. I experienced their wrath first-hand following an episode of adolescent irresponsibility.

A few weeks before the start of my junior year, I bought an Oldsmobile convertible. Ebony with a white top, fully equipped, and powered by a four-barreled aircraft engine, the Rocket 98 dripped elegance. Those were the days before gas economy became a concern. Fully loaded, that street sled got around seven car lengths per gallon. I didn't care; it was a flashy set of wheels.

One Monday night in late September, the temptation was too great. Several of the guys wanted to go cruisin' with the top down. Instead of going to school, I played hooky. When I arrived at work on Tuesday morning, I was ordered to report to the assistant general foreman. The moment I entered his office, I could tell he was not a happy camper. Well under 6 feet tall, his fierce demeanor made him seem taller. Obviously, he'd received the school attendance report from the night before.

He let loose a barrage of industrial strength vocabulary that made me edge toward the exit. He was purple with rage. "You stupid this!" "You dumb that!" "Cut school? I'm gonna cut you—right out of the program!" The cigar clenched between his teeth softened by saliva began to droop. Hot ash landed on his shirt causing another verbal eruption. Finally, he sucked air and asked, "What have you got to say for yourself?" His words shot through the air like hot pokers. I was petrified. In near shock, I decided to tell the truth. Clearly, this was not the time for one of my clever excuses. This was "Lord have mercy" time, and I seized the chance for salvation.

I told the boss about my new car, and how I gave in to the temptation of truancy. I explained what I did, where I went, and pleaded for another chance. When I finished, beads of perspiration were fighting for position on my forehead. When I looked at my boss, he was smiling.

"New car, huh? Reminds me of the time when I was about your age. I hot-wired the old man's new Buick and went joyriding. He waited for me in the dark as I was sneaking in the house. He gave me a tongue-lashing I've never forgotten. I didn't think he'd ever trust me, or let me drive again. But he gave me another chance when I promised I wouldn't do it again."

I stood there, aware that I was witnessing a miracle.

"Look, kid," he began, "I know what being young is all about. It's been awhile since I pulled a dumb stunt like you did last night. My dad gave me another chance. He was strict, but fair. I'm gonna give you another chance if you give me your word that this never happens again."

I gave him my word and we shook hands. "Get to work, kid. You need money to pay for that fancy car." I went on to complete my apprenticeship and receive my journeyman's card. Sometimes important lessons are learned by *not* going to school.

Pin Boy

In order to earn spending money while in high school, many Whiting teenagers had part-time jobs. During the days before automation took over—and aside from the usual job fare of stock boy, window washer, movie theater usher, and gas pump jockey—the most lucrative position available to teen boys in the 1950s was pinsetter.

For those too young to remember, pin boys were employed to set pins at bowling alleys. At the time, there were three local bowling establishments: Gyure's, Parkview, and the Whiting Community Center. A complete game of bowling is called a line. For every game a pin boy set, he was paid ten cents, hence the phrase, "A dime a line." On a regular league bowling night, a pin boy could earn $6 by working a double-double: setting two alleys for two matches. Usually though, a pin boy would set a double-single: two alleys, one match. A match consisted of two five-man teams. Each team member bowled three lines—a total of 30 games. An efficient pinsetter would set a match in about two hours. He could also add to his earning by setting pins on weekends for those patrons who enjoyed the relaxation of open bowling.

Setting pins required agility, good hand-eye coordination, physical stamina, alertness, and sharp concentration. It was also a great way to keep in shape—sort of a workingman's aerobics! In the course of setting a complete match, a pin boy would bend over about 5450 times! For each frame bowled, the pinsetter would jump into the pit, return the man's 16-pound bowling ball (a lady's bowling ball weighed a little less), pick up the knocked-down pins, and place them properly in the rack according to the pins left standing.

Each bowling pin weighed three and a half pounds. In setting a single game, a pin boy would lift about 600 pounds of bowling balls and pins. Multiply that amount 30 times, and during one match, a pinsetter handled over 18,000 pounds! The loaded rack would then be lowered, resetting the pins for the next bowler.

Monday through Friday were league bowling nights. Each night was different. Each night was an adventure. Once a pin boy became a regular, he was assigned the same pair of alleys. My bowling home was alleys three and four. Starting at

6:15 PM, the local lane warriors would begin their individual and collective assault on their high game, high series, and match contests. The team names read like a directory of the town's commerce: banks, clothing stores, taverns, jewelers, factories, refineries, funeral homes, dry cleaners, and drugstores. It seemed as though every merchant in the community sponsored a bowling team at one time or another. On league nights, the names of these businesses were proudly displayed above the assigned alleys.

The atmosphere of the Community Center's bowling alley, my place of employment, was intoxicating! Mixed in with the cigarette and cigar smoke were the aromas of assorted talcum powders, alley oil, and bowling equipment and accessories. Topping off this olfactory smorgasbord was the perfume exuded from the various petroleum products used to lubricate bowling alley machinery. To an impressionable 16-year-old pin boy, the scope of this arena was exhilarating!

Wearing their team's logo on colorful monogrammed shirts, adult bowlers of all shapes and sizes showcased their kegler skills. How well they bowled on a particular night determined to a large extent their selection of vocabulary. Understandably, the more "salty" vocal servings added to the overall flavor of conversation.

The bowling alley was smoky and noisy. It throbbed with the sound of rolling bowling balls and echoed with the crescendo of crashing pins. Stationed at the end of the nearly 63-foot runway of lacquered maple and pine, directly behind the triangle of waiting 10-pins was the ever-vigilant pin boy, poised to collect rolled ball and fallen pin. From the outset, pin boys learned that wood hurts, especially when propelled by the collision of a 16-pound sphere thrown at the speed of light!

In addition to nightly aerobics and monetary earnings, setting pins afforded young employees an opportunity to observe and partake in one of America's finest social classrooms. Amid the clamor and organized chaos, the pinsetter worked, sweated, and learned. He watched intently as white-collar and blue-collar workers competed in friendly rivalries, challenging each other with both bowling skills and boasting.

A seasoned pinsetter could identify bowlers by their unique style and body language. There was the arm swinger, the croucher, the backside-shifter, the foot-stomper, the arm-pumper, the hand-clapper, and the genuflector. Each mannerism identified a particular bowler. When coupled with team colors and accompanying vociferations, these combinations of sight and sound presented an unforgettable demonstration of human gyrotechnics. One team's members became so well identified with their gyrations and sounds that the pinsetters nick-named them "Four Grunts and a Groan!"

What made them do it? Why would otherwise normal teenage boys want to set pins? What was the attraction of the pits? Surely there was less strenuous and less hazardous work for them to pursue within the community. So why did they risked getting bumped and bruised, and possibly knocked out cold for ten cents a line? After a year or two in the pits, a pinsetter's fingers were curved, disfigured, and often pinched, as ball and pins took their toll.

A primary reason was money. At that time, being a pinsetter was the highest paying job available to teenage boys. Fringe benefits included the opportunity to develop responsibility and a solid work ethic. It also provided an adolescent male his first tentative steps toward independence. Money earned from their labor paid for high school class rings, senior proms, clothes, and, if you were truly fortunate, gasoline for the family limousine.

Without question, setting pins helped build character. One of the "perks" of the job was for each pin boy to write something profound on the ceiling or wall that surrounded the pits. Each guy autographed, wrote, cartooned, or in some way left his mark. I wrote my name, too. It's been a lifetime since I set pins, but after all these years I can honestly say I loved that job. "Rack 'em!"

Part-Time Labor Pains

As a college student, summer employment was always an adventure. After a year of coursework, lectures, exams, and classroom routine, working in the mill was a welcomed respite. Although some collegians found work in offices and labs, I always signed on as a laborer. I did so because of the variety of tasks assigned to the division of yellow hardhats, but also because one spent the better portion of the workday outdoors. I've never cared much for inside work during nice summer weather; it feels like confinement. So when they asked for laborers, I eagerly volunteered.

Summer work in the steel mill was a great way to stay in shape. It also taught participants how to skillfully use a variety of less-than-precision tools. In no time at all, I became well acquainted with brooms, shovels, buckets, rakes, jackhammers, wheelbarrows, hip boots, sledgehammers, picks, and number two sand scoops (heavy, humongous shovels). During the week, I worked as a laborer at Inland Steel Company; on weekends, I worked part time at Youngstown Sheet and Tube Company. Working seven days a week was brutal, but I needed money to pay college expenses and help my wife maintain our household budget.

As "weekend warriors," we inherited a foreman who did not particularly care for college kids. This particular supervisor had a belittling sense of humor that he used to emphasize his authority over us. The labor foreman always referred to shovels as "idiot sticks." He couldn't wait to say: "Hey, college boy, grab the idiot stick and fill up that hole." Then he'd wait until someone would ask why it was called an idiot stick. "Because," the foreman answered, "it's named after the college boys who use it!" This was followed by exaggerated phony laughter. I didn't want to burst his bubble but he was no Henny Youngman.

In spite of the snide verbal remarks, I liked the labor gang. After working just one shift, even a slow learner knew why they called it manual labor. But sweat aside, the $2.20 per hour wage more than compensated for management's jokes. And come August, I'd have the last laugh, returning to school.

As with most occupations, there are levels of expertise and being a laborer is no exception. We soon realized there were good labor jobs and bad labor jobs. (Bad, however, is not the descriptive word we used at the time.) Arriving at the labor shanty one morning, we noticed a sign scrawled on one of the walls: "Thinking can be dangerous. Just do what you're told!" It was written in several languages.

In spite of the handwriting on the wall, we didn't always heed that advice. One Sunday, my labor partner (and co-collegian) was told to clean the garbage and refuse from the railcar loading dock. Standing on the dock above the tracks, we could see dozens of frisky rats frolicking boldly among the vegetation and trash. "How do you want us to clean that up?" I asked. The boss watched the rats running around, smiled, and said, "You guys go to college, think of something! I'll be back before 10:00 to see how you're doin'."

Alone with our shovels, rakes, and rats, we were left to solve a problem, to "think of something." Not thrilled with the prospect of raking among rodents, we decided the rats had to go. After tying our pants cuffs securely closed with twine, we ventured down to the tracks and surveyed the landscape. Our plan was to smoke the rats out with a small fire; with the rats gone, we could then rake up the refuse and police the area.

To encourage the fire, we saturated the vegetation with solvent found in a barrel by the dock, sort of like putting lighter fluid on briquettes for a barbecue. One match was all it took. The "small" fire quickly turned into a very large one.

Just after company firefighters had extinguished the flames, our foreman arrived, smoldering! Looking upon the scorched earth, burnt rubbish, and sautéed rodents, you could tell he was less than pleased. He got right in our faces and boomed, "I asked you two to clean up the dock, not burn down the plant! Come with me!" We jumped in the back of the pickup and he drove off like a man possessed. We thought we were getting fired. Our foreman had other plans. He dropped us in front an acre-sized parking lot.

The blazing August sun had already baked the asphalt to a griddle-hot temperature. This parking lot was to be our penance. Even though we'd done exactly what the foreman had told us to do, he was livid. Pulling two large outdoor brooms from the truck, he said, "There's one for each of you geniuses. Sweep this lot @#$&*% clean. If I find one stone or piece of glass when I come back at 2:30, I'll fire both of you!" He fired up the truck, spun gravel with the rear tires, and drove off.

Not too far from us was a safety shanty where rock salt, sand, fire hoses, and stuff like that was stored. We walked over and put our lunches inside, safe from the broiling sun. My coworker, Joe, surveyed the lot and said, "There's got to be an easier way. Sweepin' this by hand in this heat will kill us. What'd he get so mad about? It wasn't that big of a fire."

Hearing the word fire, the answers to our situation immediately came to me: Fire hoses. Water. The lone hydrant was less than 20 feet from the shanty and there was more than enough fire hose stored in the shanty. We found the hydrant wrench and began hauling lengths of hose to the parking lot. With hoses connected and attached to the hydrant, we turned on the water. We were soaking wet by the time we figured out how to control the nozzle!

We were done by 1:30. In the time it took to disconnect, roll up, and store the hose, the lot was bone dry. It not only looked clean, it smelled clean. Even our saturated work clothes had dried. When our foreman drove up, we were sitting down with our backs and brooms resting against the wall of the shanty. Before our boss could say a word, I said, "This is the hardest job we've ever had. No one should have to work like that when it's this hot." He smiled. "Well, college boys, I hope you've learned a lesson."

He left us sitting in the sun while he inspected the lot. He returned beaming. "Outstanding! Looks like it was scrubbed!" Then he paused and sort of apologized: "Look, fellas, I wanted to teach you two a lesson after what you pulled back there on the dock. So I gave you a real hose job. I hope there are no hard feelings."

"None at all," we replied. "And you're right about one thing, boss."

"What's that?"

"It was definitely a hose job!"

February Flashback

I'm on my way home, heading north on Cline Avenue. It's several minutes past 4:00 PM as I ride along the elevated concrete ribbon. Snow-filled clouds have called a meeting to decide when to deliver their latest batch of "freezing skid stuff," forcing the late afternoon sun to curtail its allotment of daylight. A cold north wind challenges antifreeze-filled radiators while forcing car heaters to work overtime. It's February, and though the sun sets a little later each day, winter hangs on stubbornly, daring spring to dislodge it.

In the distance is Inland Steel's main office building. As I drive along, steel hauling trucks and other industrial vehicles freely exceed the posted speed limit, regarding 55 mph as a suggestion rather than mandate. In the interest of maintaining the flow of traffic, I simultaneously increase engine rpm and decrease mpg. It's either speed up or risk being tattooed by a tailgating truck's tires.

Like quickly flashing slides, scenes rush by. In tenths of seconds, visions fill my mind's eye, triggering memories of times past. From my mobile vantage point, familiar landmarks come into view: Plant 1, Bar Mill Avenue, Plant 3, Dickey Road, Canal Bridge. Unseen but visualized by lightning-fast thoughts are places that complement and complete this setting: Watling Street, the entrance to Plant 1 Gate, the corner employment office, gravel parking lots, Knight's Bar, Red's General Store, the adjacent coffee shop, railroad tracks, Shoreline buses, the clock house, pedestrian overpass, canteen, and main machine shop.

It's difficult to believe that more than 40 years have passed since I left the mill. Forty years? It seems like 40 minutes. After more than four decades, images of those days are still vivid and alive with fond remembrance. My truck's radio tuned to an oldies station, I hear the voices and melodies of yesteryear. "Theme From 'A Summer Place'" fills my mobile time capsule as I continue homeward, remembering days gone by.

By February 1960, I followed a regular routine when working days: Up by 5:45 AM, a quick breakfast, and then a short walk to the corner bus stop to await the bus to work. Having bought a car the previous summer, I would occasionally forego the luxury of the Shoreline limousine for the comfort of my Oldsmobile

Rocket 88 four-door sedan. Although the car was already six years old, it ran and rode like a Rolls-Royce—well, sort of.

For convenience, I parked in Plant 3's lot and walked across the tracks and fields to Plant 1 where I worked. One particular Friday, it snowed heavily. By 4:00 PM, the thick wet flakes covered everything with an accumulation in excess of 6 inches. The mill looked regal, wearing its winter ermine. In the parking lot, I cleared the windshield, fired up the four-barreled Rocket and headed for home. Traffic on northbound Dickey Road was subdued as motorists cautiously made their way across the canal bridge toward Youngstown. Once past the Mill Gate Inn, traffic increased as additional steelworkers headed homeward.

With the defroster gaining on the snow-fogged windshield while the wipers vigorously slapped away unwanted flakes, the big Olds made its way steadily through the accumulation, following the winding roadway that circled Standard Oil's refinery. WIND-AM was playing "Teen Angel," Mark Dinning's tragic tale of what happened when a girl tried to retrieve her boyfriend's class ring from a car stalled on a railroad track. Needless to say, it was a big hit for both Mark and the girl.

Turning on Front Street, the deep snow challenges the traction of the "Big O." For just a brief moment, I entertain the thought of driving through Whiting Park. Covered in fresh snowfall, the landscape looks like a Currier & Ives print. Instead, I choose 119th Street, a more direct route, I'm eager to get home.

Downtown Whiting resembles a little Alpine village. Storefront signs and display windows illuminate the late afternoon. Their multicolored neon and incandescent lights refract prism-like off falling frozen crystals of ice, enhancing the aesthetics of the winter scene. A final turn by White Castle on Cleveland Avenue, a half-block more, and home.

Once inside, the labors of the day are set aside. As quickly as possible, I'm comfortably sprawled on the rug in front of the TV, watching Ken Rossi and Arlene Sullivan slow-dance on *American Bandstand* to Dion and The Belmonts' "Where or When." It felt good to stretch out and relax after a day in the mill. Dick Clark chatted with a few visitors before introducing the next record. The dance floor was then filled with kids rockin' to Jimmy Jones' "Handy Man." Not surprisingly, I dozed off. When I came to, Dick Clark had been replaced by the evening news.

There was something deliciously ordinary about those times. Like pages in a scrapbook, the more than 2400 days I spent as a steelworker are captured forever in images, sounds, and feelings. Not many days pass without thinking about the people, places, and events that gave substance to youthful years, enriching moments and leaving behind the resonance of life. Like "golden oldies" on the radio, those memories make it yesterday once more.

Exiting Cline onto Calumet Avenue, I head for home. The snow clouds have made their decision and adjourned the meeting; it's already snowing heavily. Instead of going home, I think I'll drive over to Whiting Park and watch the landscape fill with snow.

Parenting

Kids, Crayolas, and Lunch Bags

I believe the early years of school, from kindergarten through sixth grade, are the most important in a child's life. Those years serve as the foundation upon which all other formal education is built. By the end of sixth grade, kids either love or despise going to school. In this relatively short period of time, a child experiences success, failure, approval, disapproval, triumph, and defeat. How their performance in school is affected by such moments is due largely to how they feel about themselves. And the responsibility for building a student's positive mindset falls to their parents. There are many ways to parent a child, but the most effective methods focus on the child's needs first; the child gets top priority.

When the time came for our children to begin school, my wife and I decided to make those days special. Along with an abundance of encouragement, support, and loving hugs, we made a conscious effort to enrich and enhance each day. Working together, we cultivated and instilled in our children positive attitudes about learning, teaching them that the process of education should be both rewarding and enjoyable.

Everyone loves success. It's one feeling we never get tired of. We knew, too, that success builds self-confidence and elevates self-esteem. We focused our efforts and guided our children to achieving these goals. Acutely aware that much of the socialization process, along with the emergence of one's personality, is accelerated and shaped during childhood school days, we seized every opportunity to nourish this potential.

Each day, when the kids came home with their papers and drawings, we listened as they explained purple trees, orange ducks, and a special turtle with wheels ("It helps him go faster!"). We praised their accomplishments, took a genuine interest in their work, and covered the refrigerator door with Crayola art. We rewarded, advised, helped, and encouraged. We read to them and they read to us; then we talked about the stories. There was a family rule: The only days we didn't read were the days we didn't eat!

We taught our children that it's okay to make mistakes. In spite of their best efforts, they may still fail, but that's part of learning, growing, and living.

As each of our four children started school, we did our best to ensure that they got off to a good start. The kids went to school hugged, happy, and prepared. Lunch presented an additional opportunity. Like most kids, they did not cheer cafeteria food and preferred to brown-bag it. Thus began the lunch bag billboard.

It began innocently enough, printing their name with black marker on the paper sack. Their mom would draw a smiley face on their napkin and write "Hi!" or some other lighthearted words to brighten their day. Then one morning, I drew a cartoon character on the outside of the lunch bag and added some words along with their name in bold letters. Their friends thought that was neat. It didn't take long before colored markers added a special touch to the graphics. Everyday at lunch, kids would stop by their table just to check out the lunch bag billboard. The kids became lunchtime celebrities.

By 1980, with all four children in grade school, drawing lunch bag cartoons became a daily activity. Rising early, I'd have each child's custom-designed tabloid ready by school time. Corny sayings, dumb jokes, holiday themes, current fads, and a variety of caricatures starred on the brown bag canvas. Sometimes, like newspaper comic strips, it took a full week to tell a story. Like old-time serials, kids kept track each day, waiting for the punch line. The illustrated sandwich sacks became keepsakes, as the kids talked about and laughed at a particular drawing. The lunch bag billboard continued until our youngest graduated from eighth grade.

As kids grow up, they develop other interests and parents have to adjust accordingly. The wonder years pass very quickly, leaving mixed emotions in their wake. Watching one's children mature (from kindergarten to junior high, adolescent to young adult), sharing thousands of moments celebrating their childhood, is both satisfying and poignant. Satisfying because they are on course morally, academically, and socially. And poignant because, as parents, we know those moments will never come again.

Quite honestly, I miss those times. Every now and then, in the peaceful quiet of a morning not yet begun, I think about those lunch bags and all they meant to our children. Inside was nourishment for their bodies; the outside nourished their spirit. By now you've probably figured it out: Those brown bags nourished me, too.

Kindergarten

When it came time for me to go to kindergarten, I didn't go. Nevertheless, I've been through kindergarten four times! Let me explain. Like many of you, I was born at a very early age, and started out as child. But perhaps unlike you, I came from the kid factory equipped with asthma, large ears, and an abundance of what is kindly referred to as "baby fat."

As a result of these physical attributes, I was kept indoors on windy days in order to prevent my sail-like ears from giving me whiplash! There also was the danger of being blown over and uncontrollably rolling away. Luckily, as I grew older, my center of gravity located in a more sensible region of my body, and my ears decided I was not an elephant. Unfortunately, by the time these things happened, I was beyond kindergarten age and, upon entering school, found myself in first grade. For the next 27 years, there was an academic void in my education. Not until the first of our four children entered kindergarten was I able to begin filling this chuckhole of ignorance.

My kindergarten "career" began by walking the kids to school whenever I had a day off. Shuffling through dried autumn leaves, we'd happily crunch through these giant cornflakes on the way to the school. When wintertime provided us with an ample supply of "freezing skid stuff," we'd flop flat on the front lawn and make snow angels. As season folded into season, these once-in-a-while school-bound journeys became treasures for the heart.

Soon I was actively involved in the kids' classroom activities. Frequent trips to the store to buy paste and colored paper, an extra set of crayons (for home use only), and some water-soluble markers became a regular part of my evening's schedule. Shortly thereafter, I got my *own* cigar box for *my* supplies, which I kept in *my* desk at home. I was now ready for class.

Kindergarten teachers are very creative and clever. They know how to turn a quiet evening into a scavenger hunt for supplies a 5-year-old needs for the next day's project. When our children were in kindergarten, it seemed they'd come home every afternoon with a "want list" attached to some part of their body. Some of the items listed were: paper plates, Styrofoam cups, half-gallon milk cartons, tissue paper, plastic detergent bottles, yarn, string, sticks of all sizes, egg cartons, and a smock for painting. The rule in kindergarten is: Without a smock, you're not allowed to paint!

Now in all my years of teaching, I never met anyone who actually went out and *bought* their kid a paint smock for kindergarten. This is what usually happened:

> Wife to husband, the morning she remembers the kids needs a smock for school: "Honey, I found this old shirt of yours just hanging in the closet. Do you ever wear this thing?"
> Husband to wife: "Not often."
> Wife to child: "Here's your smock for school!"

Moms are pretty clever, too!

As each of our children took their turn in grade K, I became more and more proficient in making and building the projects. I was quite proud of the fact that I knew how to make a one-hole birdhouse form a milk carton. I've built make-believe stoplights, turned a detergent bottle into a Santa face, fashioned candy canes out of a stick and some red and white tissue paper, and decorated dozens of pumpkin faces. By the time our youngest graduated from cut-and-paste land, my scissors and glue had celebrated every imaginable holiday four times! I even added finger painting to my repertoire of daddy skills.

Today, our kids are all grown up. With high school and college behind them, there's not much need these days for make-believe stoplights or pumpkin faces. And aside from the time a few winters ago when I "spaced out" from the fumes of the snow blower, I haven't flopped flat on the lawn to make snow angels.

I admit I miss those times. Maybe Congress should pass a new law and not let anyone take kindergarten until they're at least 30-something. At that age, hopefully we'd have gotten better at playing fair, taking a nap, and all the rest of the good things one first learns in kindergarten.

Several years ago, I took a graduate course in Early Childhood Education, studying children's speech, language, and play. One of the things the professor taught us was how to paint shamrocks using a green pepper. After slicing through the pepper, she dipped the cut end into a plastic tray of green paint. Then she carefully dabbed the end of the painted pepper on the construction paper several times. It made some neat-looking shamrocks; even the shamrocks with stray pepper seeds stuck to them looked pretty good.

I sat there awestruck as kindergarten flashed before my eyes! The professor looked at me, gestured with her pepper, and asked, "Al, would you like to try this?" My heart was pounding! At that moment, I would have given *anything* to paint with her pepper. Sadly, I shook my head no.

"Why not?" she asked.

"I can't," I answered. "I'm not allowed to paint without my smock!"

Holding Hands

Of all the things we learn in life, one of the most important lessons is to hold hands. Anyone who's been to kindergarten knows the rule by heart: "When you go out, hold hands and stick together." During the school year, we see this rule practiced many times as groups of small children walk along with their hands joined together. Like links in a joyous human chain, they enrich us with their laughter. But for those of us who didn't go to kindergarten, we learned the hand-holding rule just the same; Mom taught us.

Early on, he was told to always hold his mother's hand, especially when crossing streets and stepping up or down curbs. Because of his questionable coordination, his mom held his hand to support and steady his stumble-prone feet. Whenever they went shopping in Chicago, he'd hold her hand tightly for both comfort and security, as he feared becoming lost in such a big city so far from home. He liked holding his mom's hand. Her touch engendered assurance. And even in winter, with his woolen mitten firmly grasping her gloved hand, he felt protected.

Then, in what seemed like a short time, the day came when he no longer needed to hold his mother's hand. Now when they went shopping, he walked proudly by himself, alongside his mom like a grown-up. His mother was pleased at her son's self-reliance and confidence. She smiled to herself; he had learned well.

Once he started third grade, he would not hold hands again until adolescence. When he did, it wouldn't involve his mom or a fear of being lost. What fostered his renewed interest in handholding was an affair of the heart. Now when he held hands, delicious new feelings made their presence known. Even in winter, with her thick woolen mitten gently grasping his gloved hand, he felt her touch. Before too long, he was holding hands on a steady basis with one particular young lady. They shared a mutual affection for each other, and their relationship grew stronger still. To this day, they continue to hold hands.

When they became parents, they, too, taught their children to hold hands, a prerequisite for crossing streets, stepping up or down curbs, and going shopping. Every time a child's mother or father takes them by the hand, they instill a sense of belonging. Such guardianship reinforces the child's worth, strengthens the parental bond, and nourishes the family. Holding hands is therapy for the body, spirit, and soul. Fringe benefits.

He had helped his mother ever since his father had passed away in 1965. As she was now past 80 with troublesome vision, he took her shopping for groceries and other things. He was aware how she held his hand as they crossed streets and stepped up and down curbs. He was there to steady and support her, and she welcomed his touch. He took her hand, carefully guiding her across icy sidewalks and snowy streets. She held his hand tightly, for both comfort and security. Sometimes she held his arm for added balance. Now it was he who gave her assurance and protection. The pupil had become the teacher. On the day she suffered her fatal stroke, he held her hand for the last time.

Some things in life come full circle, reflecting both sameness and change. So it is with holding hands. In the beginning, one hand is strong; the other weak, uncertain. One hand controls, the other dependent. During adolescence and many years thereafter, joined hands become one, sharing strength and confidence from which lifetimes are built. As the circle begins to close, one hand is assuring, protective; the other is frail, fragile, unsteady, and tentative. Yet when joined together—when linked as one an extraordinary transformation occurs. The joined hands convey a commitment, a wordless promise of guardianship. More than that, holding hands is an expression of love.

Over the course of her life, his mom taught him many lessons. One of the most important was to hold hands.

Rites of Passage

Rites of passage are part of every culture. As humans, we note the milestones of life and measure our maturity by an accumulation of these rites, whether they're religious, academic, civic, or social. We celebrate birthdays, baptisms, graduations, engagements, and marriage. As Americans, we proudly acknowledge anniversaries and publicize achievements gained through experience and age. Of all these rites of passage, perhaps the one most looked forward to and treasured by all citizens is the driver's license.

Bestowed while poised on the threshold of adulthood, the driver's license signifies to the maturing adolescent that he or she has been recognized by the state, sanctioned by law, and granted the privilege and responsibility of operating a motor vehicle. The driver's license is the key to the kingdom of independence. In its own way, this license proclaims, "Welcome to the world of grownups!"

From adolescents' point of view, getting a driver's license is the most important thing in life. To them, having a license means expanded freedom, unrestricted mobility, relaxed curfew, added peer status, and fun! To Mom and Dad, it means additional insurance costs, increased liability, big-time worry about their child's safety and well-being, uneasy feelings when their son or daughter is late returning home, and a whole bucketful of general anxiety.

Parents are also concerned whether their carefree adolescent will keep their mind on their driving and choose not to be led into any irresponsible behavior or actions. Privately, they review the hazards and dangers that are part of today's America. Realizing that teenagers are hormone-filled sneakers, more than one parent has offered silent vespers for the safe conduct, passage, and return of their newly-licensed driver. They worry how their treasured offspring will adapt to different road conditions, traffic volumes, and seasonal changes. Each time their kid starts the car, a pensive parental unit silently wishes them good luck and Godspeed.

As parents, we know this is part of the growing-up process. Nevertheless, there is an uneasy apprehension that stays with us until everyone is home safe and sound. It's part of the game. It comes with the territory of raising children. This is major league parenting.

I think back to when I got my license and how exhilarating it was. (Contrary to what my children believed, there *were* cars when I was young.) Back then, my wheels were a used 1954 Oldsmobile four-door sedan, which I purchased from a neighbor. The Rocket 88 was my first car, and it was only slightly smaller than a Shoreline bus. The engineers who designed it were men after my own heart; the vehicle featured room galore for a carload of buddies, yet it was cozy enough for the driver and his best girl. Those were the days before seatbelts, airbags, and crash-absorbing bumpers. The car's main safety feature was a padded dashboard (and the fact that it was built like a tank).

Shortly after I returned from the motor bureau with my prize, my dad quickly put everything into perspective. As I proudly flashed my new license, and beamed appreciatively in front of the highly polished Rocket 88, my father came up to me and asked how the car was running. "Good, Pop, I just had it tuned-up at Mac's." I raised the hood, showing off the V-8, four-barrelled street sled. I boastfully continued, "This car is in top condition, Pop. Everything is right on specs." My dad waited until I finished prattling, and then said, "Just remember, Doc, every part of a car can be safety checked—except the nut behind the wheel!"

"Whad'ya mean?" I asked.

"I mean that it's up to you to keep your mind on your driving at all times," he replied.

I would be reminded of that small bit of paternal wisdom a number of times during my youthful years. Like most moms and dads, mine saw me through a few fender benders and several dings and dents. At the time, however, I didn't realize what effect my "unique" driving habits were having on them. My focus was on me, my car, and my world. But since I've assumed the role of parent, the impact of young driving habits really hit home. I keep returning to the wisdom my dad presented to me in a jocular manner so many years ago. In his own caring way, my father taught me that the greatest automotive safety device is a careful driver. That is why, on the occasion of welcoming a new driver in the family, I present them with this verse:

> The car that I drive can be a weapon or a friend;
> And how I control it will determine my end.
> So if I'm driving for work, or a date,
> I must always remember to concentrate!
> The instant I let my car try and think,
> I'll be injured, or dead—quick as a wink.
> But I'll keep safe and sound,
> When I'm out driving around,

If I remember this simple refrain:
The car that I drive has the power,
But I have the brain!

Innocence's Last Call

She had awakened early, dressed, and went into the kitchen to prepare breakfast. She felt knots in her stomach, signaling feelings she had tried to suppress. She knew that today he would leave her. For more than five years, they had been almost inseparable, sharing each other's company—laughing, loving, and giving one another joy that neither had ever experienced before. Now, by morning's end, that relationship would change forever.

He awoke with surprising energy. He knew that today would be unlike any other day. They had talked about his going and he reluctantly understood that it had to be. Whatever tears there had been the night before had dried. Morning found his blue eyes clear and full of acceptance. She had told him not to worry; things would be okay. Even so, she had searched her heart for courage to sustain them both.

He, too, dressed, and came downstairs like he'd always done, but this morning he sensed a change; things would never be the same again. They happily talked while she served him breakfast, consciously avoiding any mention of the task at hand, lest it bring forth another torrent of tears, amplifying the unexplainable ache and apprehension in their hearts.

He noticed she quickly glanced toward the clock, and managed a weak smile. He knew it was time. He stood up—taller than she ever remembered—and hesitantly walked toward the front door. She touched his shoulder, causing him to pause. Lovingly, she brushed her hands across imaginary creases of his shirt and pretended to straighten his collar. Close to him, she caught his all too familiar scent. Her pulse quickened. As if on cue, he took her hand as their eyes met. He always found comfort in her soft brown eyes. She felt unspeakable emotions as his crystal blue eyes washed over her. Images of him begged for review.

Flashing back, she recalled her feelings when she first saw him—awestruck, overwhelmed. She had never known such happiness; it was love at first sight. She imagined herself as Cinderella and knew that her wish had come true. Now, five years later, as he prepared to break away from her, it was the replay of those memories that filled her eyes with tears. On several occasions, he had talked about her going with him. But, plead as he did for her to do so, she knew it could not be. As painful as it would be, she knew it was best for him to go without her.

He gripped his satchel and stood very still for the briefest of moments. She kissed him gently. He softly said goodbye and bravely walked away. She closed the door quickly, watching him through the small beveled-glass windows to where the bus would stop. Her eyes followed him intently and she wondered about his thoughts. Wiping away her tears, she saw him board the bus that would take her young son to his first day of school.

Scenes similar to the one described above will play out across America as another school year begins. Regardless of whether the student is a novice or seasoned classroom veteran, a myriad of emotions impact the mind, leaving indelible marks on both parent and child.

Years ago, as each of our children entered kindergarten, I never quite felt the emotional wallop experienced by parents—especially moms. As a father, I usually downplayed this first major episode of loosening the apron strings. I couldn't figure out what was so heartrending about a kid starting school, about letting go.

Now I understand. I understand because that question was poignantly answered the Sunday we moved our son John into his college dorm. The realization didn't happen all at once. The feelings came up like a slowly rising tide. Everything prior to departure day was low-key. Packing, last-minute shopping, loading the car—even the early morning drive was uneventful. At the university, the hectic activities of checking in, unpacking, and setting up his new collegiate home did not allow for contemplative thoughts. When things did quiet down and there was time to reflect on the events of the day, long-dormant feelings tugged at the heart for attention.

When children reach college age, parents reluctantly accept the fact that they are no longer the primary focus of their children's lives; that lofty position is usurped by peers, acquaintances, and important adolescent toys. When this passage of priority occurs, this disconnection, this reduction in rank, churns the heart and stirs uncertainty in every parental soul. Usually such shifts of prominence are temporary, a mere signal that the child has ushered in their final phase of adolescence. This is innocence's last call.

By mid-afternoon, the move-in was complete. Our newest collegian would do the final arranging, displaying, and decorating to fit his personal taste later on, after room traffic lessened. As I stood in his room, looking at this almost-grown young man, I remembered that life is a series of beginnings and goodbyes, and no matter the number of our years, we never quite get use to it. Mom's tearful hug spoke for us all. After offering lighthearted words of best wishes, we said our goodbyes and left for home.

Like I said, I could never figure out what was so heartrending about a kid starting school. Now I understand.

No!

One of the very first words we learn as a child is "no." It's the Methuselah of negative responses. Early on, we realize the impact, devastation, and finality this two-letter adverb has on our lives. We also soon discover that "no" has several degrees of meaning, ranging from "No way, not a snowball's chance in hell," to "Well, maybe," and even a cleverly disguised "Yes!" The interpretation depends on the particular issue at hand, circumstance, and participants. The effectiveness of the word "no" depends upon the giver and the receiver involved. The "no" giver is often in a position of power, authority, or defiance.

Some folks find it difficult to say no. (Most of these people have not had children!) Salespeople thrive on those who cannot say no, selling such customers storm windows, clothing, insurance, land, used cars, and gadgets and gimmicks of every kind and type. Human vultures of every persuasion circle the economic skies preying on those too timid to say no, waiting to take advantage of such opportunities. Fortunately, the majority of moms have no such trepidation; "no" is right up near the top of the motherhood vocabulary.

To moms everywhere, "no" is an essential deterrent in the arsenal of parental discipline. It is *the* weapon of choice in the child behavior battle. If moms were paid a dollar each time they said no to their children, banks worldwide would overflow with cash from dollar-rich moms. In all honesty, "no" is also a mother's single most important defense in maintaining her sanity. Children come factory-equipped with thousands of questions about everything. Usually, the little tyke directs these verbal inquiries to mom. After all, until they're old enough for school, mom is a captive audience and easy target: "Mom, can I stay up?" "No!" "Mom, can I play Eskimo in the refrigerator?" "No!" "Mom, can I go for a ride in the dryer?" "No!" "Mom, can I…" "No!"

Pretty soon, mom begins to anticipate the preschooler's questions and cuts right to the answer: "Mom…" "No!" By the time kindergarten begins, a kid has probably heard the word several thousand times. If the kid has a twin, they've heard "no" in stereo! (Boys aren't aware of this when they're young, but hearing the word "no" so frequently prepares them for married life.)

As kids grow older, "no" takes on added importance. There are times when it's tough to say no. In the beginning, young children, for the most part, take a no answer passively, accepting it without a great deal of complaint, save for the "terrible twos." Teenagers, however, actively contest negative decisions. Peer pressure, self-esteem, emotional involvement, social image, and a whole host of factors are at stake in the decision. Parents are sorely tested, trying to find a workable balance and mutual understanding between their adolescent's fledgling independence and their parental concerns.

When their children are teenagers, mom and dad are confronted with challenging issues, some requiring tough no's. Dating, late hours, selection of friends, driving, working, parties, privileges, sleepovers, unsupervised activities, clothes, makeup, behavior, language, grades, alcohol, drugs, videos, movies, music, and dozens of other adolescent activities cause the word "no" to be carefully considered, tempered with common sense, and implemented with fairness; arbitrary refusals no longer serve the purpose. The days of the cut-and-dried response are over. Both sides now negotiate their position, trying to alleviate parental fears without damaging youthful exuberance. One of the toughest things about parenting is deciding how long to hold on and when to let go. Parents realize there are no guarantees, and that some decisions, made with the best of intentions, will come back to haunt their minds for untold days.

Then one day, "no" becomes obsolete. The power is taken out of the word, and it is used primarily in an advisory manner. Both parent and their now adult child share equally in discussion and decision, mutually respectful of the other's position. No longer does the inquisitive innocence of a young child or the contest of will between ancient and adolescent beg for attention. Rather, there's a maturing of spirit, a self-satisfaction for pursuing a noble, honorable course, which prepares the pathway for others who are certain to follow; knowing, too, that the word "no" has served its purpose for another generation.

I Did Nothing

I want to apologize to a little girl I don't even know. Let me explain. One day, around suppertime, my wife and I went grocery shopping. The supermarket was fairly crowded, and basket traffic was heavy in some aisles.

I heard her before I saw her. A small child around 3 years old was sitting in the seat of a grocery cart. She kept saying the word "ticket" in a loud voice, almost crying. Her mother stood in front of the deli counter a few feet away, waiting for the deli-worker to call her number so she could be served. The little girl continued her plea; she wanted to hold her mom's ticket. Mom disregarded her petition, telling her to be quiet. "I have a ticket," waving it in her hand. Mom seemed to be preoccupied with getting her deli order, and wasn't totally tuned in to what her daughter wanted.

The mother, in her mid to late 30s, wore a blue knit dress, nylons, and heels; the kind of attire a working mom might wear in an office. Being the dinner hour, I surmised she'd gotten off work, picked up her child from daycare, and came shopping for a few items. The little girl was clean and nicely dressed. But she continued to fuss about not holding the deli ticket. Mom finished at the counter, wheeled the cart around, and headed down an aisle for other items on her list, paying little or no heed to her daughter's lamentations.

The lady in the blue dress continued to fill her basket with groceries, placing them behind the seated child, and the little girl continued her vociferations, now escalating in both pitch and volume. Mom was clearly becoming irritated, as other shoppers in the aisle looked at the now crying child.

My wife and I were in the same aisle heading in the opposite direction. I was pushing the cart and hesitated a moment because of a mini traffic jam in front of the canned corn. My wife had walked up ahead. As I approached the lady and her sniffling child, the little girl flailed her feet and arms in the air as she sat in the cart's seat. That was the last straw. Immediately, the blue dress became a blur as the lady smacked the child on the side of her face. The child wailed. Mom smacked again; more wailing. A third smack—this one accompanied by mom's verbal reprimand on how to behave.

222

I just stood there as the mother in the blue dress physically disciplined her 3-year-old child, filling the adjacent aisles with loud crying. I wanted to go up to her and say, "Please don't hit that child. If you have to hit someone, hit me—I can handle it." But I didn't. I just stood there. I did nothing. I turned away as I moved my cart past hers and went up the aisle. That woman weighed all of 140 pounds, and I just watched her slap her little kid. Everyone else in the aisle did the same thing—nothing. We went about our tasks, looked the other way, and never said anything.

Maybe she had a tough day at work. Maybe she was upset about the runs in her nylons. Maybe she wasn't feeling well. Maybe, maybe, maybe. All I know is that I had a chance to speak up, to respond to a stranger who was smacking her child, and I did nothing.

That little kid will most likely never read this, but I'm sorry. I apologize for not saying something to your mom. As a parent, I know there are better ways to teach children proper behavior than by hitting them. I'm sorry, too, that your mom doesn't have the tolerance or patience or understanding a child your age requires. You were probably at daycare all day. When your mom picked you up, you wanted her to notice you; you wanted to feel important. You didn't realize your mom was busy with other matters, that your needs would have to wait. You wanted her attention, however, and got it the only way you knew—by exhibiting behavior you knew she'd react to. No one likes to be slapped, but that was the only way mom would give you attention, so you took the slaps. I hope that as you grow up, you learn there are more positive, loving ways to elicit attention. I hope your mom learns that, too.

For the Last Time

◆

(1992)

On Sunday, June 7, the youngest of our four children graduates from high school. As class salutatorian, Dan has given a good account of himself both academically and athletically. In the fall he'll begin his collegiate studies at Indiana University-Bloomington.

As parents, the approaching commencement brings mixed emotions. Not only does this milestone signal new challenges and denote a major passage in life, but it also marks the end of a journey—for both parent and child. It seems only yesterday that we brought the newest member of our family home to meet his sister and brothers. Today he stands on the threshold of adulthood. How quickly time has passed.

The realization that our youngest is no longer a child calls to mind thoughts about growing up. I have often pictured these moments. Now that D-Day ("Diploma Day") is approaching, there's a tender reluctance to accept it. I suspect such hesitance is borne from the realization that more of life has passed than remains, and I'm not quite sure I like that. Parenting has been most enjoyable and I'm not eager to see that task near completion. But children grow up, and life goes on. Rest assured, after graduation there will be new adventures to pursue, and there will be things done for the last time—for both parent and child.

Our youngest son arrived on a warm Tuesday evening in late May 1974. When he decided to make his entrance, he didn't waste any time at all. Luckily, the ship canal bridge was down on the way to the hospital or Dan would have a different first name. Like his sister and brothers, the moment he came into our lives we knew he was special. Before he was 3 years old, he could say "Chicago Cubs." I immediately pronounced him gifted!

In a very short time, Dan became an avid reader. As a preschooler, Dan would peruse the newspaper's sports section, checking on his favorite teams. From little on, he was captivated with team sports and the challenge of competition. This

224

love of athletics led him to begin playing basketball in grade school and all through high school. After his sister introduced him to tennis, he tried out for and made the high school tennis team.

He loves sports. I remember the hours we spent playing catch, shooting baskets, and tossing around the football. It didn't take long before ol' Dad was trying to keep up with him, especially when playing one-on-one. Only my superior use of flagrant fouls enabled me to win an occasional game. When that tactic didn't work, I doctored the score, telling him I was using the metric system. Unfortunately for me, Dan also has a mind for mathematics, and he always corrected my creative totals.

Earlier this year, my wife and I watched him play basketball for the last time. We attended every game—home and away. As parents, we decided early on to support our kids in their class work, athletics, and extracurricular activities. We went to orientations, open houses, plays, banquets, athletic events, and school activities. Together we shared their high school experiences, encouraging and supporting them, and helping when needed. Looking back over those times brings many fond memories. This year, because we've exhausted our supply of high schoolers, carries the added poignancy of being a "for-the-last-time" year.

As a veteran chalkboard jockey, I like commencement. It serves the same purpose as a highway rest area. Commencement is a nice place to pause for a while to check one's progress and contemplate the remainder of the journey. We all need time to reflect on how we're doing; in order to know where we're going, we have to understand where we've been. Commencement does that—for both graduate and parent.

But before diplomas are handed out, officially bringing the high school years to a close, Dad wants to offer his best wishes and appreciation to his youngest son:

Dear Dan:

The day you've worked so hard for, your high school graduation, is almost here. You should be proud of your achievements; Mom and I are. We also want to commend you on the choices you've made thus far. By your performance, you set high standards of ethics, conduct, and character. As your life unfolds, Mom and I are confident you will continue the quest for excellence.

Speaking as your father, I am most proud of you as a person. In an age of lessening morality, substance abuse, and slipshod conduct, you've continued to subscribe to and exhibit positive, constructive values. You are a kind and decent young man, and I admire your qualities of honor and integrity. When given a task, you can always be depended upon and trusted to do an outstanding job. You enrich each assignment by willingly helping others. Not afraid to risk and accept new challenges, I've watched you grow, learn, and live.

Now, in what seems like such a short time, you stand poised to enter the adult world. Soon it will be time to begin the next chapter of your life. Before that page is turned, however, I want to offer my heartiest congratulations for a job well done. I hope each day brings you laughter, love, good health, and good fortune. And I pray that God blesses you and keeps you safe—not for the last time, but forever.

Love,
Dad

Mid-Winter Commencement:
Halfway Toward a Goal

✦

(1992)

There are times when halfway doesn't seem enough. But in the midst of a journey, halfway becomes a significant milestone. For the traveler, halfway marks the midpoint toward an important goal and serves as incentive to continue. As parents, halfway takes on special significance, noting a measure of progress. It stands as a mark of achievement when evaluating headway in regard to long-term commitments such as retiring the mortgage, paying off a car loan, or savoring various stages of a child's development toward independent, self-reliant, on-your-own adult living.

Life affords many opportunities for halfway mileposts to pause and contemplate one's performance. These midway respites serves as "How am I doin'?" rest stops along the way. Parenting provides a veritable franchise of halfway moments. As soon as children arrive, goals are listed, objectives defined, purposes are set forth, and dreams are made.

The birth of a child always engenders feelings of hope and promise. In unexplainable ways, parents can glimpse their child's future, visualizing achievement and success. They wonder, too, what adventures life holds for their newest member of the family, and are prayerful that heaven will guide and protect the "fresh-from-the-factory" tiny person peacefully asleep in the crib.

My wife and I were granted such sneak previews of the future four times. Each child came into our life blessed in mind and body. Throughout their childhood, we worked at providing each one opportunity to become their own person, proudly aware of their unique individuality but cognizant that they were an indispensable, necessary member of our family. Sometimes maintaining the delicate balance between what Mom and Dad perceived as proper and what the child deemed proper collided with considerable impact. And as usually happens when raising kids, both sides learn. It doesn't take long before negotiation and compromise assume critical importance within the family.

At times, it's tough to be consistent, fair, one hundred percent correct, and open-minded. There are moments when parents have to think back to how it was being a kid, and how important things can be during those times. Hopefully, if heaven is kind, mutual feelings of trust, respect, and love will flourish between parent and child. Realistically, though, there are occasions when a kid tries to drive a parent crazy. It is during these times that the parents entertain the possibility of checking the veracity of hospital birth records in search of the answer to the question "Is this kid *really* ours?"

The point of this halfway musing is this: This past December, our oldest son, and second of our four kids, graduated from Purdue University-Calumet. We now have two out of college and two in. When Kevin received his diploma in the mail last week, it signaled the official halfway mark toward a goal—college education for our children. Kevin helped meet some of his expenses by working at various jobs. Mom and Dad helped, too. That was part of the sneak previews in 1970.

Going to school and working part-time has not been easy; there have been difficult moments. But now he has tangible evidence of his efforts, signifying his achievement. For Kevin, the future is now. And as his father, I would be remiss if I did not offer this small note of appreciation:

Dear Kevin:

Congratulations! Mom and I are very proud of you. It's nice to have another college grad to call on for advice. I'm certain you understand why Mom and I screamed "Hallelujah!" at the sight of your diploma, but you may not know why I examined your sheepskin under that special light; I wanted to make sure the ink used to write your name was indelible. You know I don't like surprises.

I want to tell you, too, how impressed I am by the way you met the formidable challenges of college. Although it was not all green lights and blue skies, you persevered and accomplished your goal; that speaks well of your character. Looking back over your formative years, I know there were times of uncertainty. I recall telling you, at age 6, to shape up your behavior or you'd never be 7! Hopefully you knew I was just kidding.

One thing I've tried to instill in all of you is a positive sense of humor. I've also tried to convey the belief that the journey should be as enjoyable as the destination. Laughter nourishes the soul and enriches the spirit. Should you decide to pursue a Master's Degree, Mom and I have scheduled negotiations on Tuesday; make an appointment.

Finally, now that you're a college graduate basking in prideful satisfaction, I want you to know that I only checked the hospital birth records twice. The third time, the line was busy!

Just kidding, son.

Love,
Dad

Changing Times

Acknowledgement of changing times is nothing new. Every generation deals with things that become outdated and obsolete because of technology or modification of lifestyle. After several generations, the gap between what was and what is grows considerably. Explaining mid-twentieth century life to twenty-first century students is a formidable challenge.

Usually such discussions begin with questions about how things were when I was in school: "What was it like back then?" "What'd you do in your spare time?" "Where'd you work in high school?" It's difficult to convey to these modern, up-to-their-ears-in-technology kids a lifestyle they have not experienced. What seems normal and current to me is totally foreign to them. Consider, for example, explaining the job of bowling alley pinsetter. After telling them about lines, double-doubles, flyers, and racks, one kid asked me why they didn't use machines: "Were the machines broke, or what?" It's humbling to tell them that we *were* the machines!

They also can't grasp the concept of life without television. Relating how we sprawled on the parlor rug in front of the radio console, listening to our favorite program, leaves them perplexed. It's hard for them to understand how we could just *listen* to a story. I tell them that if I have a choice between listening to the radio and watching television, I choose the radio. "Why?" they ask. "Because," I say, "the pictures are better!" Don't get me wrong; television is pretty neat, but listening to the radio forces you to use your imagination. Many kids today fail to use their imagination. Because money was tight back then, it took my family a while to get a TV. But even without a television, we bought a then-new product, TV dinners. We'd heat 'em up and eat them in front of the radio. Imagination.

I have tried several times to explain household chores. Before automatic appliances and the advent of permanent press, ironing day followed laundry day at our house. Mom believed every washed item should be wrinkle-free, so Tuesdays after school were designated as "iron-the-clothes-flat" time. She also believed that her children should be skilled in all areas of domestic technology and engineering. The fact that three of her four kids were boys didn't matter one iota. Housework was equal opportunity; there was no gender bias in her house.

We served our ironing apprenticeship by removing creases from towels, sheets, handkerchiefs, washcloths, and pillowcases. Once we passed that "board" exam (and Mom's inspection), we graduated to shirts, trousers, bedspreads, and whatever else had to be de-wrinkled. We were taught how to slightly dampen clothes to eliminate stubborn crinkles. Sprinkling a few drops of water from a partially filled saucepan required deft wrist action. (Later this manipulative dexterity was crucial when throwing a sharp breaking curveball. Coach asked, "How'd you learn to throw a curve like that?" Looking him right in the eye, I replied, "Ironing.")

Often Mom would set up the ironing board in full view of the kitchen. That way, she could continue her culinary duties and monitor our progress, correcting any flaws in our "de-creasing" techniques. Mom thoroughly subscribed to on-the-job training. When I finished relating this information to my students, one kid raised his hand and asked, "What's an iron?"

It's hard to fault kids for not knowing the intricacies of household chores in the 1950s. After all, that's ancient history to them. Just the other day, after a discussion on the causes of World War II, a student asked, "Who won?" Hearing the United States was the victor, he responded, "Cool!"

Kids don't realize how convenient things are today. Back in 1954, as a domesticated adolescent with expertise in laundry, washing dishes, vacuuming, and ironing, Mom decided to add one more skill—sewing. For reasons not fully understood, shirts would be minus buttons after passing through the family laundry and ironing center. Management surmised the missing buttons were the result of reckless ironing, as the appliance collided with the protruding mother-of-pearl. Though we were cautioned to be careful, our shirts continued to lose buttons. My personal theory was that the shirts knew someone other than Mom was ironing, and the buttons decided to make a break for it.

Anyway, by the end of my freshman year in high school, I could mend, hem, patch, and sew with the best. I was careful not to publicize my needle-and-thread talents, however. The last thing I wanted was a picture in the yearbook of me sewing!

I doubt that many kids today mend clothes or sew on missing buttons. Nor do they wash or iron clothes, vacuum floors and carpets, cook meals, or wash dishes. In a way, that's too bad. Years ago, home was the training center where kids learned what it meant to be a family. Doing chores taught valuable lessons, reinforced values, encouraged responsibility, nurtured self-esteem, strengthened one's work ethic, and built character. Admittedly, modern methods are more convenient and make things easier. But there's something about those times that brings me satisfaction and comfort even after all these years. Like I said, times change. I wonder though if it's all for the better.

An Empty Nest—Well, Sort of

In college, I took a sociology course called "Courtship and Marriage." The course focused on the various stages of human relationships, emphasizing significant implications and changes to one's life. One stage, "The Empty Nest," occurs when children leave home and go on their own. At the time, I thought the term "empty nest" was a little odd (leave it to sociologists to come up with clever labels), but as that stage approaches, I suspect it means the "old birds" remain home, while their fledglings fly off to experience life and eventually build their own nest.

When our two youngest children left for college, my wife and I knew we had moved closer to the empty nest. Our oldest daughter was married, and at the time only our oldest son was at home. To be sure, the house was noticeably quieter and suddenly larger. It's hard to believe our kids weren't kids anymore. Time sure flies when you're having a good time.

On the morning after our trip to the university, I was downstairs in the laundry room thinking about this latest passage of life, and how tough it is at times to let go. The reason I was in the laundry room is because that's where I write. I know that might sound strange, so let me explain.

Years ago, when we began remodeling the house, I needed a place to type that wouldn't be inundated with plaster and sawdust. As a teacher preparing course materials, I needed a clean workstation. The laundry room was made to order. I placed my typewriter (these were the days before personal computers) on the table my wife used to fold the laundered clothes, telling her it was only temporary until the remodeling was completed. Twenty years later, I was still using the laundry room. While there were other places I could type, I grew accustomed to the laundry room. Happily, I would type away, serenaded by the pulsating mechanical rhythms of out automatic Maytag. As a tradeoff for utilizing her workspace, I promised to maintain the progress of the laundry and monitor the washer and dryer.

To the right of the typewriter, attached to the wall, is a magnetic bulletin board where I try to keep track of important "stuff." The most important items on the board are not notes but pictures of the kids: snapshots from kindergarten, grade school, winter formals, high school proms, senior year, and a newspaper photo announcing an engagement. I've glanced at those pictures hundreds of times, but in the early morning of the day after we moved our latest collegians into their dorm, I looked at these photographic images and closely examined the faces of our children. I studied their features and privately longed for those days again. How neat it would be to share, once more, the excitement of their childhood.

Each picture triggers remembrances of cherished moments. Automatically, I scan through stored memory, pausing to savor images and events. As I review my collection of Dad's Most Wanted, I find it difficult to grasp the reality of the moment. In what seemed like an instant, the kids have grown up, and stand poised at the threshold of the rest of their lives. I freely admit that I miss their presence.

But all is not wistful melancholy. There are fringe benefits with the reduction of nestlings. Leftovers will once again remain in the refrigerator and not mysteriously disappear to an upstairs bedroom, never to be seen again. The domestic dynamic duo of Maytag and Maytag will get a few days less agitation and tumbling as the elevation of Mount Laundry is reduced. Milk will have the opportunity not to be consumed by its expiration date. When the guys are home, food is on the endangered list. Grocery bills, however, remained about the same because of Mom's frequently mailed "care packages" to campus. That also made the post office happy. Hot water is now abundant, lowering water department and gas company revenues. On the other hand, Ma Bell celebrates the start of college, knowing how collegians love to imitate E.T. by regularly phoning home.

As parents, we were officially sanctioned to wear college sweatshirts and display university decals on family vehicles. We also made a number of trips to campus whenever the kids wanted to come home for a weekend. As it turned out, we were able to see the campus during every season of the year. All in all, not a bad deal.

Sociologists contend that the "empty nest" signals the end of childrearing, and is prelude to the final stage of a relationship. That may be so. Personally, I don't believe our nest will *ever* be empty—not permanently, anyway. For as long as there is food in the refrigerator, efficient laundry service, and plenty of hot water, they'll be back. Sociologists call adult children who return home to live for a period of time "boomerang kids." And speaking like a sociologist, when they return to the nest, chances are they'll find the male nest-keeper in the laundry room wearing a college sweatshirt and a smile as he checks the photos comprising Dad's Most Wanted.

Love and Marriage

✦

(1992)

As parents, we know that one day our children will leave the nest to build their own lives. Hopefully by the time this happens we'll have properly prepared them to effectively meet the many challenges life presents. Thankfully, the transition from dependent child to self-reliant adult is a gradual one—affording both parent and child adequate opportunity to acquire, adjust, and accept these inevitable passages. I mention this because our oldest child, and only daughter, will be married on January 18. Without question, this is a time filled with anticipation, excitement, and best wishes. As father of the bride, allow me a few moments to reflect on this major milestone of life, and perhaps offer just a smidgen of advice to the happy couple, too.

My favorite red-haired girl was born on a snowy Saturday afternoon in early March 1968. From day one, she's enriched and enhanced our life in countless ways. Teaching her, preparing her, and watching her grow into the fine young woman she is today has been a labor of love.

Sometimes it doesn't seem possible that she's getting married already. Just a short time ago I walked with her to kindergarten; together, we shuffled through autumn leaves, chased snowflakes, and felt the warmth of spring sunshine. And was grade school so long ago, when her mom and I helped with posters, charts, and special class projects? I still fondly recall a Styrofoam solar system; the first time Saturn's rings resembled a 45-rpm record. It was our contribution to rock 'n' roll outer space. Then all of a sudden, she was a high school teenager, studying hard in class and involved in clubs and school activities. Whether working with the Drama Club, playing tennis, participating in Student Council, attending National Honor Society events, or planning school dances, she performed her responsibilities with uncommon efficiency and a contagious positive attitude. She was one girl who enjoyed her adolescent years.

No one doubted that she would be successful working her way through college and earning a degree in Communications. Even injuries from a near-fatal auto accident couldn't damage her spirit or deter her from her goal. With heaven's help, she met the challenge, endured the pain, faced the hardship, and came away triumphant—smiling—degree in hand. At commencement that Sunday, I knew this remarkable young lady had the "right stuff" to succeed at whatever she decided to do.

Now, on the threshold of marriage, ol' Dad wants to tell his favorite daughter how proud he is of her. Perhaps the best way to convey these thoughts to her is through a brief letter:

Dear Christine:

I wish there was an easy-to-follow formula that would guarantee a happy marriage. But after more that a quarter century of married life, your mother and I can tell you no such formula exists. Whether a marriage works or not depends wholly on the individuals involved. It requires hard work, dedication, unselfishness, and commitment. I know that doesn't sound very romantic, but that's not the case; for love is the bond that holds it all together. Sometimes love is disguised and not always visible at first glance. But in many subtle ways—caring, touching, listening, speaking—love becomes the unbreakable bond.

Your mother and I have tried to set a consistent example for you and your brothers to follow. I know there are times when we seem old-fashioned and out-of-date. Party animals, we're not; watching corn pop is more exciting. But we decided early on that we would willingly share our lives together, focusing on positive family values given to us by our parents. We made a conscious effort to draw upon the best human qualities and teach them to our children. We believed it was our duty as parents to give each of you a full measure of our energy, time, talent, and love. We taught by word and example. We instilled a love of learning, the necessity for prayer, a sense of family, and the importance of sharing, giving, and helping one another. We also taught you the need for laughter. But most importantly, we gave you sovereignty—the gift to be your own person.

You'll soon discover that marriage requires all of these things and more. Like an exotic fragile flower, marriage needs to be constantly nurtured (paying special attention to matters of the heart) in order for love to thrive and flourish. If properly tended, married life is the most enjoyable and rewarding adventure a man and woman can share. By working together (and together is the key word), you and Andrew will experience many happy years. As poets have written, "It's life's journey to happily-ever-after."

As your father (this is the advice part), I want to give you these small tidbits of counsel. I'd wait until the wedding, but I'll be so dazzling in my Pierre Cardin tux and black patent-leather shoes, I might forget. So here goes:

- Don't worry about things you cannot control.

- Laugh more today than you did yesterday, but not as much as tomorrow.

- Don't ask God to make things easy; pray that He makes them possible.

- Make a positive, constructive difference in the lives you touch.

Know, too, that Mom and I wish you all the best and that we hope each day brings laughter, love, good health, and good fortune. God bless you always.

Love,
Dad

Teaching:
Chalk Dust and Classrooms

Help Mom with the Dishes

Each year, the president awards a crystal apple to this nation's top teacher. Several states and cities honor their best educators in a similar manner. In Chicago, for instance, outstanding teachers are presented with the Golden Apple Award, recognizing individual excellence in the classroom. Reading about such ceremonies gives reason for this particular teacher to reflect on his chosen profession.

As a public high school teacher for almost 40 years, I'm often asked the question "Why do you teach?" My answer has always been the same: I teach because I believe that I can make a positive, constructive difference in the lives of my students. This translates into providing opportunities for students to develop their full potential.

Years ago, the formula for success was rather clear-cut. It included a loving supportive family, a good education, hard work, and being faithful to one's religious and social values. Today, however, the formula for the "good life" isn't as easy to define. Times have changed.

There are three essential elements that hold society together: the family, the church, and the school. In the last 30 years, there's been an unprecedented erosion of these three elements, weakening their individual and collective influence on society. Values once held sacred have been ridiculed or discarded. Nowhere are these changes more evident than in the classroom. To counteract certain corrosive forces, students need to be reminded of their purpose for living. In addition to teaching our students to read, and write, and spell, we must also teach them the sacredness of being alive, and the dignity and wonder of themselves.

As teachers, we try to do this in a variety of ways. Personally, I've set two major teaching goals: first, to make education an enjoyable process (convincing students that education is something we do *for* them and not *to* them), and second, to increase students' personal responsibility (encouraging the growth of their self-worth). Every other aspect of their education is affected by how these two major objectives are attained.

In order for education be effective, one has to be in a relaxed, pleasant frame of mind. No one is able to learn anything positive when angry or upset. So the task at the beginning of each school day is to set the tone of the class, and get students ready to learn!

I begin by writing the "Saying of the Day" on the chalkboard. These are words from poets and statesmen, teachers and kings. They're thoughts about living and life; sayings that I hope will spark students' interest, initiate thinking, release a smile, and serve as an appetizer for the lesson that I've prepared for them. Granted, some of the quotes are corny. Some are jokes so old that you can smell the mold, but in their own way these words call out to each student: Welcome to class!

I make a conscious effort to involve every student in classroom activities, not only by challenging them with questions and quizzes, but also treating them as a person—a very important person. Sometimes I read their T-shirts and sweatshirts, commenting on the rock groups and silk-screened images that serve as their daily announcement of who they are and how they feel. By using the richness of the English language and the flexibility of words, phrases are turned into sounds that encourage smiles.

Creative methods are employed to enhance the transmission of the intangible process we call learning. Each student is personally challenged to capture the characteristics of dignity, pride, tolerance, consideration, cooperation, understanding, and love. The acquisition of these qualities is vital if one is to attain meaningful success. Meeting this challenge requires a personal commitment to all that is good, kind, and decent. The bottom line of this pedagogical pursuit is summed up in the daily reminder I convey to my students at the end of each class: "Help Mom with the dishes."

Upon hearing this "outlandish" request for the first time, many of my teenage scholars look at each other as if to say: "Has Mr. Koch lost his marbles?" "Do the dishes? Is he nuts?" "I don't do dishes! What is he talkin' about?"

I point out to them that "Help Mom with the dishes" doesn't mean they have to actually do the dishes (though I'm sure mom would appreciate it very much). I'm asking them to express their love for someone by doing what is good, kind, and decent. Whether that someone happens to be their mom or dad, brother or sister, or the elderly widow down the street isn't important; what really matters is that they provide a small cup of kindness to enrich the life of another person.

"Help Mom with the dishes" is an attitude I'm asking them to adopt. By doing so, they agree to set aside a small part of their day, a tiny portion of their energies, to express a little kindness for someone. I'm asking them to fill a void left by unkind works or deeds not done, and fill it willingly with the melody of the human spirit. I'm encouraging them to share their positive qualities with each other at the first opportunity, without hesitation or delay.

Because we share a common bond and common purpose, each of us has the opportunity to enrich someone else's life. As young adults, these students can do this quite effectively by setting good examples of moral and social responsibility. Surprisingly, I tell them that they must become a teacher. For whether they realize it or not, we are *all* teachers. We must take the time to *teach* one another, because we *learn* from one another.

Perhaps this is what author Kahlil Gibran meant when he wrote about teachers in his book, *The Prophet*: "The teacher who walks in the shadow of the temple, among his followers, gives not of his wisdom, but rather of his faith and lovingness. If he is indeed wise, he does not bid you enter into the house of his wisdom, but rather leads you to the threshold of your own mind."

This is the focus that has served as a guide for the past four decades. Education involves a partnership of learning. Part of the responsibility within this partnership requires the student to set aside a few moments each day to "Help Mom with the dishes."

Mind-Master

She looked lovingly at her firstborn. He was the "miracle" she had prayed for. Perfectly formed, her son would be strong and wise. While her husband worked, she would prepare the child for living among their people. She was not of high rank and had limited birthright. Her knowledge of home and workplace were acquired through struggle and sacrifice.

Having no family, kind strangers gave her shelter and taught her home skills. She learned well and used these talents to survive. Now with husband and son, things would be different. She promised to teach her infant well. He would be a Mind-Master.

Before her son was old enough to understand, he knew his mother's voice. Each sound was different, and he'd focus on the source. After a while, he'd watch her point to different objects as she made the sounds. Soon he would make similar sounds, and he, too, would point, sometimes touching the object of his vocal noise.

As he grew older, the voice-sounds became familiar. Now, when his mother spoke, he would go to the object without her having to point or prompt. She watched him and smiled. Soon it would be time to teach him the Mind-Master symbols of their people; soon, but not yet. She knew he needed time, attention, and direction. She continued her lessons, and he learned very quickly. Already he could voice-sound pictures of wild beasts and mimic their call. He knew the name-sounds of home things like food and sleep and wash places.

One afternoon, the little boy watched intently as his mother brought a tattered container to the table. Carefully, she untied the string to remove its cover. He could tell by the tone of his mother's voice that something important was about to take place. Inside were the symbols of wisdom. These were the "seeds" of the Mind-Master. "These symbols are very powerful," his mother told him. "They can bring you the treasures of life. When you learn to call these signs by name, I will teach you to make thought-pictures."

The child was wide-eyed as his mother deliberately placed the power symbols on the table, arranging them in the order of fixed custom. In a soft, reassuring voice, she began to teach the lesson of the Mind-Master. Taking his small, delicate hand into hers, she gently placed his hand on the first symbol. Then she took his index finger and, guiding it with her hand, finger-traced the ancient sign, saying its name-sound aloud. She repeated her instruction with each symbol. Trace. Sound. Trace. Sound.

The strange graphic signs and figures were a puzzle to the little boy. Some symbols were composed of interlocked lines of various lengths; others were made up of curved segments and attached by tangents at selected points to straighter portions. One sign was ring-shaped; another snake-like; still another, a cross. He was too young to know about ancient distant ancestors called Hittites, Phoenicians, Indo-Europeans, and Germanic tribes, who first drew and used these signs 3000 years earlier. Nor could he understand ancient people called Greeks and Romans, who altered these signs and changed the sounds in order to record events and share their history. Later, after many years in the Learning Place, he would come to understand the knowledge of his people and the world. But for now, all was hidden in the stars.

When the last power symbol had been finger-traced, and the child's mother had repeated its name-sound, the graphic signs and figures were carefully gathered from the table and placed back in the box. Tomorrow there would be another lesson. Time. Attention. Direction. She would build upon and connect these lessons until her son had captured the image and sound of each power symbol— this was the genesis of light.

Soon he was allowed to open the box and display the signs by himself. He would come to the room and ask his mother for the now familiar emblems. His mother nodded approvingly. Taking the box from the cupboard's shelf, he would go to his room and begin placing them on a small table.

He had been quiet for a while, so she silently moved to the doorway of her son's room and looked in. She stood watching as her son repeated the names of the symbols she had taught him: "A...B...C...D...E..." She smiled proudly. It was time to show him the power of these letters by building words. She would teach him to read and write; to express and communicate his thoughts and feelings. One day he would know the treasures of life. He would become a Mind-Master. The magic had begun.

September New Year

Happy New Year! No, I haven't gone bonkers, and yes, I know what month it is. But for many of us, September is the beginning of a new year. Signaled by the opening of school, we organize our lives by the academic calendar, leaving January 1 to the resolution-makers and serious partygoers.

The new school year begins even while the playboy of the seasons is winking one last time at suntanned faces and falling leaves bid farewell to their branches, having been painted by the flame of an early autumn sun. Emotions run rampant as thousands of children reluctantly set aside the toys of summer and make their way to the schoolhouse door.

For some, the start of school is a continuation, another step toward graduation. For others, it is a beginning, a foundation on which to build and improve the quality of life. But whatever the case, students, parents, teachers, and administrators are all affected by the educational process. This annual assault on ignorance affords one the opportunity to ponder what could be, or what *should* be, in the pedagogical world. And so, before too much chalk dust fills the air, I submit for your consideration, a school-year wish list. I wish:

- Every child came to school well mannered and ready to learn.

- I'd never see another abused child with that helpless, hopeless look in their eyes.

- Everyone in education had a clear value system.

- Students, parents, teachers, and administrators believed that we're all on the *same* side.

- Parents took the time to teach their child how to dress properly for school.

- Students could be convinced that school is something that is done *for* them, not *to* them.

- Students had the strength and courage to reject drugs.

- Every parent loved their child.

- Every child loved his/her parent.
- Every child had a caring, loving home life, with positive role models.
- Every parent would find time for their child.
- Good teachers would not burn out and leave the profession.
- Ineffective, incompetent teachers would get out of education—now!
- Parenting was not an endangered occupation
- Every child came to school well fed and clean.
- Teachers would remember that once upon a time, they were children, too.
- Laughing was a required course.
- Students, parents, teachers, and administrators would overdose on kindness.
- We could make stupidity extinct.
- Each child understood what "Help Mom with the Dishes" is all about.
- Phoniness could be removed from education: phony praise, phony success, and phony importance.
- Administrators would keep in mind that the most important aspect of education involves people, not stacks of paper.
- Everyone understood that teaching and learning is a two-way street.
- Students realized that life is not meant to be fair.
- Children would stop having children.
- We could teach every child the sacredness of being alive.
- Growing older wasn't so scary.
- Children would learn how to behave *before* starting school.
- Parents understood that their involvement in school is crucial to their child's education.
- All teachers liked kids.
- Only the best teachers taught in the elementary grades.
- Children understood how valuable and necessary they are.

- Children were taught that things in life don't always have a happy ending, and that, in spite of their best efforts, they may still fail, but it's nothing to be ashamed of.

- The only days students didn't read were the days they didn't eat.

- Administrators had to return to the classroom to teach kids now and then. A few weeks in the academic trenches works wonders for over-inflated egos.

- We kept in mind that we learn from each other; we are all teachers of human circumstance.

- Kids realized that life comes without a guarantee.

- Common sense wasn't in such short supply in our schools.

- So much food wasn't wasted every day in the cafeteria.

- That upon graduation, every child captured and understood the importance of Trust, Honor, Respect, and Responsibility.

And the biggest wish of all: I wish this list wasn't necessary.

Happy New Year, everyone!

The Gift

Although Christmas is a number of weeks away, it's time for you to receive a present—a very special present. It will arrive fully assembled, is tailored to fit everyone, and can be used any way you choose. It is the gift of gifts, delivered free of charge. Sent direct from heaven's factory by an all-loving Creator, we're presented with the gift of each day—1440 minutes to utilize however we please. These 1440 minutes are justly bestowed; young or old, rich or poor, sage or fool. Each 24 hours is given regardless of race, religion, color, or creed. It doesn't matter if one is a poet, pauper, teacher, or king. Heaven is an equal-opportunity gift-giver.

Each new day comes with unlimited choices as to how this allotment of time can be spent. We can enrich or diminish, share or be self-indulgent, be helpful or hurtful, compassionate or indifferent. We can be a giver or a taker. It is totally our choice. At the end of the day, when we tally our efforts, we're either satisfied or disappointed with how we lived the past 24 hours.

The gift of each day gives us the chance to stand for something, strengthen our character, and shore up our spirit—socially, personally, and morally. Over a lifetime, one is judged by the sum total of their days. As difficult as some days can be, we fully understand heaven's policy: There is no guarantee. We also know that days cannot be saved or sent back. When it comes to life's moments, it's "No deposit, no return." In order to savor past times, moments to remember must first be converted to memories, then stored carefully in our special keeping place.

As humans, we have daily needs. Each of us wants to matter, to belong, and to contribute. We want to care about someone, and have someone care about us. There is within us a strong desire to love and be loved. Still, there is so much to do. Days go by very fast, and as we age, the parade of seasons quickens its cadence. As a kid, days were spent casually; there were so many ahead. Today, each day is treasured like a priceless jewel because the supply is limited.

One day, far beyond the stars, when we are summoned by heaven's record-keeper to review our permanent record, hopefully we'll all be rewarded for using the gift of our days in a positive, constructive manner. In the meantime, it is good to remember:

> Yesterday is history.
> Tomorrow is a mystery.
> Today is a gift, that's why it's called the PRESENT!

Share the gift.

Vacancy of the Heart

It happens every year about this time. In the weeks between spring vacation and the end of school, energy runs low, the mind battles fatigue as frustration levels rise, and the perennial question forges its way to the mind and is given voice: Why do I teach?

When one considers the current state of affairs in public education, it is understandable why the academic doldrums come for their yearly unwelcome visit. After a semester and a half of dealing with all the responsibilities and concerns that affect the educational process, it's amazing that teachers, en masse, don't just throw in the towel and quit.

Maintaining a positive attitude and sustaining the desire to teach is a tribute to incredible human resolve. Hardly a day passes that teachers aren't faced with responsibility for chronically tardy students; negative adolescent attitudes; pregnant teeny-boppers; drugs; alcohol; gangs; disruptive students; rarely-in-attendance youngsters; low student test scores; failing grades; parent conferences; administrative directives; evaluations; exams; committees; in-school and after-school activities; discipline; supervision assignments; schedule changes; curriculum modification; meetings of all kinds; classroom equipment and supplies; budgets; plan books; grade books; field trips; awareness of child abuse; student health and family problems; guarding against student aggression (between students and teacher-targeted violence); general school safety; fire and tornado drills; playground and cafeteria behavior; kids' incomplete classroom assignments and undone homework; verbal and written complaints from anyone about everything; locker problems; missing books; lost articles; formal and informal counseling with students; documentation for every occasion; accurate record-keeping; and a multitude of "little things" that demand attention throughout any given day.

All of this is in addition to the teacher's role of "stand-in" parent, as they try to fill voids in their students' lives left by parents who are either too busy or too stupid to raise their child. It's no wonder teachers are prone to stress, anxiety, cynicism, and sarcasm—or in layman's terms, burnout! In spite of everything, however, most teachers continue to try to make a positive, constructive difference in the lives of their students.

One marvels at the dedication and commitment teachers bring to the classroom. What is the source of this strength? What force drives them to overcome adversity, working around obstacles while leading students to the threshold of their own mind? The answers to these questions are found in the heart of every teacher.

Everyone has a favorite story about school. Perhaps it was a special teacher who helped when things became difficult, or made you feel important by accepting you as a person. I've had several exceptional teachers who made a lasting impression on my life. Without giving away professional secrets, teachers have favorite stories, too.

Over the years, there have been a number of students who touched my life in special ways. They're unforgettable, although probably unaware of their importance to me. They are a source of strength—the reason why I teach. Not all of these memorable students experienced happy endings; some turned quite tragic. But together, their memory keeps me focused on a primary goal. As long as I live, I will never forget the names and faces of these ordinary kids who captured an extraordinary place in my heart.

Teaching is a unique profession. Society expects teachers to perform near-miracles in education, demands excellence, and places responsibilities on teachers that make angels cringe. The public wants exacting results from an inexact science. As family units disintegrate and churches continue to lose their influence, schools have become the glue holding the social structure together. Schools today are viewed as society's fix-it shop. Teachers are called upon and challenged to remedy societal ills that are far beyond their sphere of influence.

Many of the items on the aforementioned "litany of responsibilities" cannot be controlled by either teacher or school. We've been assigned numerous tasks without the authority to carry them out. Despite such uncomfortable circumstances, teachers continue their efforts to make a difference for there are too many children who need the human touch of teaching. There are far too many unhappy faces, searching with empty eyes, waiting for that special teacher to nurture their dreams. It is for these students that we teach. It is for the countless number of youngsters, in spite of all the meaningless busywork, frustration, and fatigue, that we *must* be in the classroom.

Teachers have become the guardians at the gate. There are students waiting for their chance to become. As teachers, we will be there to greet them. Like these students, I wait, too; for there is a vacancy of the heart, waiting to be filled.

To Touch the Stars

It's time to tell you about Jimmy. Especially now that another school year has begun, and teachers need to be reminded of their capacity to touch the stars. At times, I've questioned my effectiveness as a teacher. This soul searching is partly the result of trying to teach kids who often seem unconcerned, detached, negative, and unwilling to learn. Why continue to expend energy on students who show little interest in their education? Admittedly, when everything works, when all the gears mesh and things click into place, teaching is magic! But occasionally, teaching seems as productive as nailing Jell-O to a wall. You hammer away with all your might, but very little sticks. Even so, after almost four decades, there is still more magic than Jell-O, and kids like Jimmy make it worthwhile.

I cannot speak for grammar school or middle school, but in high school, when the counselor comes to your classroom while you're in the middle of a lesson and asks to speak with you privately, you know automatically that someone needs a favor—big time! As I stepped into the hallway, the pedagogical missionary began with: "I have this kid who needs special help..."

I listened as the counselor pleaded his case. Jimmy (not his real name), a troubled 10th-grader, already had a cumulative folder weighing five pounds. His recently failed attempt at self-destruction had only driven him deeper into his shell of isolation and unresponsiveness. Would I accept him in my shop class? Despite being three weeks into the course, I agreed; Jimmy would start tomorrow.

After passively listening to my orientation, Jimmy took a seat in the back row, put his head down, and never said a word. For the next two weeks, the scene was the same. Calling on Jimmy was futile and unproductive. Occasionally, he'd raise his head, peer through the curtain of dark hair which hid his face, mumble some unintelligible response, and re-nestle his head inside folded arms.

Finally I decided enough was enough. I wanted Jimmy to participate in class and I would not take no for an answer. When teaching, I use humor to help make points and convey units of instruction. I decided to focus attention on Jimmy, using humor to initiate conversation. As part of this plan, Jimmy's other teachers agreed to acknowledge him whenever they saw him during the course of the school day. Each time we saw him, we'd say: "Hi, Jim, how ya doin'?" Jim became a designated celebrity. Little by little, teachers noticed improvement in his demeanor.

One day Jimmy found the courage to show me photographs of model airplanes he'd assembled. Other students became interested, and asked to see the pictures. He hesitated only a moment before sharing the photos, describing key points about each model. For the first time, Jimmy was part of the class. Gradually he took part in class activities, discussing assignments, interacting with classmates, and responding to questions. The turning point came when someone said something funny and Jimmy laughed out loud. For the first time in more than 12 weeks, Jimmy shook with laughter. He had broken through his self-imposed barrier of sadness.

The following year, Jim entered a vocational welding training program, and through hard work, excelled in both his academic and technical classes. He continued to improve, and by the end of his senior year, Jim had made great progress, both academically and socially. After high school, Jim planned to work in welding fabrication. The note I enclosed with his graduation card offered congratulations and best wishes. Privately, I wondered about his ability to face the challenges hidden in the future.

Some months later, those concerns were put to rest. Walking through a shopping center parking lot, I heard someone call my name. Turning, I saw a clean-cut young man smiling as he approached me: "How ya doin,' Mr. Koch?" It was Jim. He quickly brought me up to date on his activities, including his welding job at a suburban fabrication factory. "By the way, Mr. Koch, do you still tell those corny jokes?" I pleaded guilty. A moment later, we shook hands, wished each other well, and went about our lives. This once troubled boy, now an adult, celebrated life.

The crux of the story is this: Teachers never really know the extent to which they touch the lives of their students. Each day during the school year, teachers routinely perform their professional duties, giving attention, direction, and purpose to their students. Even students who seem disinterested, detached, and unwilling to learn want teachers to care about them and give them a chance to do better.

As teachers, we occasionally need to be reminded that we are, indeed, special people, granted the privilege and opportunity to enrich and enhance the quality of young lives. By telling Jim's story at the start of a new school year, sharing his academic success and celebrating his triumph over sadness, perhaps we can reaffirm our purpose as teachers; that by making a positive, constructive difference, we embellish the human spirit, and with childlike wonder, touch the stars.

Spring Break

It wasn't too many years ago that college students flocked to Fort Lauderdale, Florida, for their annual spring break. In search of an idyllic week, collegians from across America made this yearly pilgrimage to play in the sand and surf while soaking up warm sunshine and cold beer. Spring vacation became one continuous party. Thousands ate, drank, and slept on the beach under the stars.

But after enduring several tear-the-town-apart disturbances, city officials cracked down on the free-spirited youths. Many out-of-towners were unceremoniously introduced to Fort Lauderdale's judges and jails. As a result of this ruffian exuberance, Fort Lauderdale put their municipal welcome mat in storage. Unperturbed, kids promptly adopted Daytona Beach and resumed the party.

The social impact of spring break during the late '50s and early '60s was so powerful that it produced several books, popular songs, and movies extolling the romantic excitement of this spring phenomena. It was every red-blooded college kid's dream to attend this ritual of overindulgence. And it was every parent's nightmare, knowing their innocent child was among thousands of potentially rowdy, hormone-filled tennis shoes, anxious to take advantage of whatever there was to take advantage of.

It was my luck, however, during the heyday of this foolishness, that I was instead keeping steady company with a Gisholt turret lathe in a steel mill machine shop. While countless vivacious co-eds frolicked in the Florida sun, I had to settle for vicarious thrills of the celluloid type, watching Connie Francis in *Where the Boys Are*. By the time I entered college, commitments and circumstances preempted any thought of a Florida excursion. When spring break arrived, I returned home to the Calumet Region to work as a laborer in the steel mill, cleaning soaking pits and sewers.

When I returned to campus, the dorm echoed with ribald tales of parties, conquests, and consumption. When asked where I spent my vacation, I told the truth: "I spent the better part of every day near a canal, in a 'red-hot' bar!" My dorm mates were *very* impressed. I conveniently neglected to tell them that it was the Indiana Harbor Ship Canal and the 24-inch bar mill sewers!

"Meet any chicks?" was a favorite post-vacation question. "Chicks?" I replied. "None that I remember, but I did encounter some rats!" Most of the guys in my dorm were from towns south of Indianapolis and didn't have a clue as to what I was talking about. They asked if I'd seen any famous celebrities while I was in the 'red-hot' bar. Not in the bar, I said, but one afternoon I saw Connie Francis, Annette Funicello, and Frankie Avalon. What I purposely forgot to add was that I saw them with Dick Clark on *American Bandstand*. The guys were so awed I didn't have the heart to burst their bubble. Even through their Florida tans, you could tell they were green with envy. Too bad they weren't there to see me at the time: I was black with sewer sludge!

I enjoyed several similar spring "vacations," returning to the mill with the faithfulness of Capistrano's swallows. The only birds I ever saw, though, were the resident pigeons that lived high among the steel girders of the building. Actually, I couldn't see any, but I heard them coughing and wheezing. After so many years of breathing iron ore and coke dust, most mill pigeons suffered from emphysema.

After graduation, I traded the campus for the classroom, and my vacation perspective changed dramatically. For a long time, I believed that school vacations were for students, brief respites from tedious scholastic duties. Boy, was I ever wrong! After nearly four decades as a chalkboard apostle, I *know* that holidays, seasonal breaks, and summer vacations are for teachers. This time-off provides an opportunity to recharge the cognitive batteries, unwind taut, overstressed nerves, and tighten loose "neck screws."

Today, I look forward to spring break with as much fervor as I did in college—perhaps more. Now that I'm a veteran educator, I eagerly await the vernal equinox, knowing there will be time to relax and catch up on chores long-delayed. Admittedly, I'm not much of a party animal or traveler. On occasion, I may crank the oldies on the jukebox up a notch, but I rarely venture beyond the front sidewalk. Many teachers head immediately for tropical resorts, warm-weather golf courses, cruises, and popular vacation play lands. I wish them blue skies and green lights. However, I'm content to hang around the house, doing whatever has to be done, enjoying whatever the day brings.

Every now and then, however, I think back to earlier days when spring vacation meant the steel mill, hip boots, sewers, sludge, and coughing birds. While those times are long past, memories stir long-dormant feelings that celebrate youth, commitment, self-reliance, and the season of spring. One might think it odd recalling youthful days spent as a laborer in such an unglamorous industrial setting, far removed from ocean surf, idyllic beaches, and near tropical sun. But by remembering past experiences, we appreciate more fully the delicious endowment of another spring, and savor, in our own way, the sweetness of each day.

Scooter Boards

During my first year as a public school teacher, I taught Industrial Arts at a middle school in suburban Lake County, Indiana. In addition to my regular assignment of six classes, I was also responsible for monitoring the student cafeteria. The principal bestowed this additional task upon me because I'm 6 feet 4 inches tall. He felt that such an imposing stature would thwart any exhibition of mischief by the students (namely, food fights). But like many administrative suppositions, this one also was flawed, as it did not take into account the natural proclivity for nonsense that permeates the mind and body of junior high school pupils. If school administrators expect 400 prepubescent adolescent water bugs to conduct themselves like responsible adults during lunch, they're living in a fantasy world. So before the end of the first grading period, I was scraping assorted gelatins and desserts off various areas of my imposing stature.

There were 34 students in each of my classes. Every student was to experience some hands-on education in Drafting, Metalworking, Welding, and Woodshop. To help supply these 136 students, the principal allotted the shops a total budget of $500. This money was to cover the cost of materials and supplies for the various areas of instruction, bringing each kid's share to $2.45. I was weak-kneed at the thought of such extravagance.

Unfortunately, by the end of the first semester I had depleted the entire budget. And for this blatant display of fiscal irresponsibility, I was called into the principal's office and scolded about my extravagant spending. Because of my financial recklessness, there was no more money available for shop supplies or materials.

"Shop teachers are supposed to be resourceful, creative, and self-reliant," my administrative leader said, rattling off his litany of shop-teacher qualities. "Find a way to make ends meet. Those classes are *your* responsibility. Take care of them." With his final salvo of wisdom echoing in my ears, I returned to my sawdust parlor more broke than the Ten Commandments. What was I to do? Resourceful, creative, self-reliant—those were his words, and as I pondered those administrative gems, I realized what had occurred. My principal, in all his post-graduate sagacity, had just presented me with a blank check to facilitate a solution to my problem. Find a way, he told me. OK, boss, fair enough. So this is what I did.

I went to the Physical Education Department and offered to work on a project they were having a similar problem with. The gym teachers wanted two dozen scooter boards to help with their physical training activities, but they, too, were short of funds. While they had some money, it wasn't enough to buy the scooters. (I should point out that a scooter board is a piece of lumber about 14 inches square with a ball-bearing swivel caster at each corner. Kids lie belly-down on these boards and learn a whole variety of motor skills.)

The P.E. Department had enough for the casters, but not the lumber. I told them to buy the casters and I would supply the wood. The scooter boards would be a perfect project for my woodworking students. Both of us would gain from such a cooperative venture; I would have a project for my students, and P.E. would get their scooter boards.

There was just one slight problem; I didn't have any lumber. I desperately needed lumber, specifically ¾-inch thick lumber. But all was not lost. One shop teacher characteristic my principal neglected to include in his litany was "observant." And I have always been *very* observant. Thus, quite wonderfully, a plan to procure all the lumber I needed coagulated in the boardroom of my mind.

I stayed late after school, and when most everyone had gone home, I made my way to the cafeteria. All those days I had dodged grapes, raisins, and government-surplus peanuts by taking refuge under the cafeteria tables, I'd noticed that they were made of plywood. Succulent, three-quarters-of-an-inch thick plywood! Each cafeteria table measured 3 feet by 6 feet, and there were lots of out-of-service tables stacked against the wall, collecting dust and errant raisins.

I calculated how many tables it would take to make the required scooter boards. At 14 inches square, I could get 10 scooter boards out of one table, so I needed three. And honestly, that's all I *intended* to take. But then I thought about all the neat projects that could be built from ¾-inch plywood, and before I knew what had come over me, three tables became 10. After sliding the tables across the hall and into the now dark woodshop, I returned to the cafeteria and rearranged the tables to cover any indication of my clandestine procurement. The stack along the wall was somewhat lower, but other than that it looked normal.

I went back to the woodshop. I quickly removed all the steel folding legs from the tables, chipped the rock-hard dried wads of gum from underneath, and rip-sawed the tabletops in half lengthwise. In less than an hour, I had a storage room full of ¾-inch plywood planks, each 6 feet long and a tad under 18 inches wide. I stored all the metal hardware from the legs in the loft above the shop. (I would later use this metal for my welding class; I was also frugal.) I gave the shop a quick broom and went home.

There's not much more to tell. The scooter boards came out just fine. The kids enjoyed making them, and we even displayed a couple in the showcase by the principal's office. A week later, the principal came by and thanked me for providing the Physical Education Department with scooter boards. A month after that, I received a letter of appreciation from the school board.

I only taught there one year, but I could have stayed on. I figured there were enough cafeteria tables for at least three years, barring an increase in enrollment. But I decided that given the price of plywood, and my creativity and resourcefulness, the kids would've been eating their lunches on the floor!

Time-Capsule Letter

Teachers won't readily admit this, but when their teaching days are over, and all the chalk dust has settled behind the closed door of their classroom, they'd like to be remembered by their students. No other profession engenders such a desire. Although teachers share only a brief amount of time in a student's life, somehow these pedagogical encounters leave indelible marks and make lasting impressions. Without question, teachers touch lives in memorable ways.

Everyone remembers a favorite teacher and how he or she made a positive, constructive difference in their life. From kindergarten through high school, we collect remembrances of specialness, caring, patience, and understanding from gifted educators who helped us learn lessons, develop skills, master concepts, strengthen confidence and enhance self esteem. Every day in classrooms throughout this country, teachers provide sustenance to students via supportive smiles, encouraging words, and a willingness to help them succeed.

The process of how ordinary school days become treasured memories is not fully understood. At the time they occur, most folks are not aware how meaningful particular people, places, and events will become. As students, we were often preoccupied with a particular assignment that demanded our full attention. Much later, when times-past mingle with maturity, experience, and reverie, we realize those ordinary, everyday happenings were transformed into moments to remember.

In August 1968 as a rookie teacher beginning his second year, I not only wanted to effectively teach my students, but also make their year special. I had accepted a position to teach Vocational Machine Shop with the Fayette County School Corporation in Connersville, Indiana. Machine Shop is not the most glamorous curriculum offering, but my class of seniors was enthusiastic, cooperative, and eager to learn. Being a job-training program, my students were in class for three consecutive hours. At the completion of their training, they were to have mastered entry-level skills in machine trades. By the time graduation drew near, they'd surpassed all my expectations. Their camaraderie, unity, and machine skills had achieved high levels of proficiency and excellence.

A week before graduation, I called the seniors into my classroom and announced an optional assignment. In addition to their final exam, I asked them to write a letter to themselves. The information sheet I handed out explained that this letter should contain three parts: Part 1 was an overview of their current circumstances (family, hobbies, school activities—things like that); Part 2 was what they planned to do in the next five years; and Part 3 was reserved for their long-range goals—hopes and dreams of what they'd like to be doing in 10 years. They could also add photos and notes from family, girlfriends, or classmates.

The letter was due their last day of school. I supplied the necessary envelopes and told them to self-address the envelope and indicate on the back if they wanted their "time capsule" letter returned in five or 10 years. They were to turn in their letter sealed. I would pay all postage costs and promised their letter would be mailed as they'd specified. Every senior prepared a letter. Surprisingly, every one was turned in on time, addressed and sealed. A few opted for the five-year return; most, however, chose the 10-year option.

I mailed the first letters back in May 1974. Almost every year after that, I returned time-capsule letters to former students. Due to the mobility of families, some required considerable searching. Almost every letter, as promised, has been returned. One young man was killed while serving in the Armed Forces. I contacted his mom, explained the letter, and mailed it to her. I ended my time-capsule letter assignment in May 1992, and mailed the last batch in 2002.

In the 24 years students wrote personal letters to themselves, a number remained undelivered. Privacy laws, government regulations, and numerous name changes have thwarted my efforts to keep the promise I made to these students. Hopefully, the Internet will provide the avenue for these letters to be delivered. Thus, the quest continues.

Like I said, most teachers would like to be remembered. Over a career, there are countless hours and ordinary days that hopefully will become moments to remember for students when the classroom door is closed for the last time. But that is for later. Already another school year has begun. Teachers of all grade levels will try their best to make an important difference in the life of every student. Perhaps one day, they, too, will be remembered. For now, there is work to be done; there are lessons to teach, skills to develop, and concepts to master. Somewhere, a teacher will call seniors to the classroom and ask them to write a letter to themselves. Then, in what seems like a moment, their special letters will be returned.

Back to School

Back to school. That particular phrase has been part of my life almost every year since first grade. As this is being written, I'm at the midpoint of my 38th year as a teacher. For nearly four decades, the scent of chalk dust and hearing the excitement of children's voices have drawn me back to the classroom. When I started school in 1946, the academic year began the day after Labor Day. Now the scholastic New Year begins around the middle of August. And whether teacher or student, the new school year offers an identical opportunity: a clean slate, a new beginning, a renewal, a continuation of the educational process.

As a parochial grade school student, summer seemed endless. June to September seemed like forever, as if there were three months of Saturdays all in a row. As soon as the nuns left the Sacred Heart School for their Mother House, Saint Mary of the Woods in Terre Haute, Indiana, the lot next to the convent became a softball field. It became a summertime ritual. Our only concern was beating out a slow roller before the ball was in the pitcher's hands. In late August, the nuns would return from their summer respite. An occupied convent meant an end to singles and doubles and game-winning homeruns; the game was called on account of Providence and too many back-to-school habits.

As one grows older, the passage of time accelerates. One day you're a freshman in high school; the next day, you turn around and it's 1958, you're a graduating senior, and high school is over. The following September offers choices: college, work, or military service. I chose the factory, signing on as an apprentice machinist—four more years in the classroom. Back-to-school had become a way of life.

Like vacation slides in a carousel, summers flash by. In a wink, six years passed. Now a trade journeyman, an opportunity to become a teacher was too good to pass up. Back-to-school begins once again on a college campus in Terre Haute, Indiana, and Indiana State University becomes my Mother House.

During the next four years, studies occupied all seasons. Then at last, a day that once seemed so far in the future—a goal that seemed unattainable, the impossible dream—arrived: Commencement. The following September, I would once again be back to school, this time not as student but as teacher.

At the start of each school year, I cannot help but recall my personal collection of first days of school. Like faded photographs, some images are blurred while others remain in sharp focus, unaffected by the passage of time.

Remembrance of a fearful, apprehensive little boy, filled with excitement and expectation as he holds his mother's hand tight, trying to be brave on his very first day of school. All the back-to-school days of his grammar school years are inextricably bonded together, laced with scenes depicting one's struggles for knowledge, self discipline, adherence to rules and religious teachings, courage, and survival.

Such images are in contrast to memories of high school. As an adolescent, back-to-school was a summer highlight; I couldn't wait for school to begin. High school meant new classes, Friday night football games, sock hops, and time spent with classmates. During those four years, one edged closer to adulthood and planned for the future.

When back-to-school time arrived while a factory apprentice and collegian, it was used to mark important milestones toward a goal. When coursework was completed and the degree conferred, I savored a sense of accomplishment and satisfaction.

Since becoming a teacher, back-to-school has taken on a different perspective and meaning. Each year welcomes new freshman and returning upperclassmen. Each student comes to school with their own hopes and dreams. Some have special needs, some are fragile, and some arrive with a bruised spirit. Each one wants to fit in, belong, be noticed, valued, appreciated, and feel important.

Every child deserves the opportunity to learn and grow, the chance to develop individual talents, skills, abilities, and gifts to the fullest. That's part of the back-to-school agreement. As educators and parents, we owe our children a full measure of the process of education and more. Most kids remember the first and last days of school. Teachers and parents have the responsibility to make all the days in between beneficial, enjoyable, and memorable.

Hopefully, if teaching and parenting and learning mesh together in just the right way, today's kids will one day recall with fond remembrance their back-to-school days, as I do.

Sometimes, a Free Lunch

We learn early that there is no free lunch. Somethin' for nothin' there ain't. And for the most part this is true. But once upon a time, several years ago, I was the recipient of a free lunch.

On most school days, I ate lunch in the teacher's cafeteria. Once in a while though, I'd forego the school's exquisite cuisine and eat out. One warm, sun-drenched spring day, with landscapes celebrating their annual season's greening, I decided to spend my lunch hour enjoying a tranquil meal at a local eatery.

After satisfying my hunger pains with palate-pleasing morsels, I relaxed and waited for the waitress to bring the check. Soon time was growing short, and no one came. The lady who had served at my table was busy taking care of other customers. I tried to catch her attention, but had no luck.

Knowing I had to be back at school within the next few minutes, I went to the cashier and told her I had not received my bill. She looked at me and said, "Your lunch has been paid for." Bewildered, I looked about the restaurant trying to identify my benefactor. There was not one familiar face among the luncheon crowd. The cashier noticed my quizzical expression and nodded in the direction of one of the waitresses. "She paid for your lunch."

I looked toward where the waitresses picked up their orders. I saw her, but I did not recognize this waitress, a lady in her late 40s. She looked up, acknowledged my gaze and smiled, and began walking over to where I stood.

I thought she had me confused with someone else. At the time, I was teaching metalworking and drafting classes at Thornton Fractional North High School in Calumet City, Illinois. Being a shop teacher is not all that glamorous. While other teachers dispense knowledge about mathematics, science, history, and English, shop teachers are working feverishly to prevent a worldwide shortage of birdhouses and napkin holders. Admittedly, most of us look precious in our shop apron, but I didn't think that warranted a free lunch.

My benefactor was nearing the cashier. Gesturing with her hand, she motioned for me to take a seat in a vacant booth. I was puzzled. "Mr. Koch," she began, "I know you have to hurry, so I'll just take a minute. I've wanted to thank you for what you did. I meant to write or call, but…" her words trailed off softly.

266

Pausing for just a moment, she then brought me up to date on her son. Now I remembered.

As a high school student, her son was a troubled young man. Withdrawn, sullen, disconnected from the mainstream of adolescent activities, Jim (not his real name) was on the brink of self-destruction. His academic performance was dismal. He showed little or no interest in anything. His negative attitude amplified his low self-esteem. His classroom behavior consisted of sitting in the back row, head bowed, oblivious to whatever was going on. He was a lost teenager, silently crying out for help.

His school counselor scheduled him for my metalworking class, hoping the less restrictive environment would spark his interest and encourage him to participate and interact with fellow students. In his regular classes, Jim rarely spoke. At the outset, he was non-communicative in my class as well. Although he turned in written assignments, his participation in shop work was minimal; while other students worked on their swag lamp project, Jim remained seated in the classroom.

One day I decided enough was enough. I slammed a book on the desk so loudly that Jim raised his head to see what happened. I seized the moment. "Jim," I said, "I've had it. I cannot allow you to constantly disrupt this class with your laughter. What's your problem?"

Jim looked at me with his sad eyes. "I haven't said a word."

"That's exactly the problem," I replied. "I've given you my cleverest lines and corniest jokes, and you don't even bat an eye." Jim looked at me, and for the first time, cracked a smile. Little by little, he took tentative steps away from the darkness. He got involved in the project, shared photos of his model airplanes with his peers, and never looked back. He discovered that he liked welding and completed his lamp before Christmas vacation.

A few days before school was dismissed for winter break, I jokingly said to Jim, in front of the class, "Don't spend more than fifty bucks on my Christmas present." His eyes lit up and he shot back: "No problem, Mr. Koch, I ain't gettin' you nuttin'." His classmates laughed uncontrollably. For the first time, Jim left the classroom smiling as his classmates cheered him on. I mailed him a Christmas card and wished him a Happy New Year.

By the end of the semester, Jim was a changed kid. He had become more outgoing and talkative, and readily helped others in the class complete their projects. As the school year drew to a close in June, Jim had decided to become a welder. He completed the two-year training program with honors. After graduation, he was hired by a large manufacturing firm. A year later, we ran into each other in a mall parking lot and he filled me in on how things were going.

Being a teacher isn't always easy. There are days when one wonders if it's worth all the effort. And then there are those times when a grateful mom expresses her appreciation to a teacher for helping her son rediscover the value and treasure of his self-worth and recapture the sacredness and joy of life. Sometimes there *is* a free lunch.

First Valentine

There are times when you do things for one reason, but affect others in ways you never imagined. A simple act of goodness takes root where least expected and bears surprising fruit. When frustration and anger are present, understanding and helpfulness can revitalize the human spirit. A case in point is what happened to one boy in the early 1970s. To protect his privacy, I'll call him Dennis.

Dennis was a new student in our district since the previous September. After the divorce of his parents, he'd moved up north from Florida with his mother. He was a troubled youth: angry, quick-tempered, always ready for confrontation. Just 15 years old, he was big for his age, and his size served to intimidate students less formidable in stature.

I met Dennis for the first time when he arrived in my second semester metalworking class. Uncooperative and belligerent, Dennis made his presence known immediately by bullying another student to give up a seat in the back row. The next day, a new seating chart had Dennis in a front row seat, close to my desk. His permanent scowl communicated his feelings; he was not a happy camper.

He rarely came to class prepared. Pencils were lost, and his book misplaced or in a friend's locker. Rather than play his game, I provided pencils and a spare copy of the text. A few days later, it became obvious why Dennis always "lost" his book. Though he was a sophomore, he could barely read at the fourth-grade level. Much of his anger and misbehavior was designed to cover up and deflect from his academic deficiencies.

To his credit, Dennis was mechanically inclined. When it came to metalwork and welding exercises, Dennis was one of my top students. Still, he wouldn't start his project. So one day after class, I asked him why. With eyes lowered, he told me he couldn't read a ruler; he couldn't measure. "I'm not very good at reading, either," he said, looking at me through tear-filled eyes.

I had assumed that because Dennis was a transfer student, he'd mastered basic shop prerequisites. Obviously, there was work to be done. After a few measurement lessons, Dennis began his project. At first, he came to me when confronted by difficult words, but soon his classmates were assisting him. By the fourth week of the spring semester, Dennis was improving steadily.

One of the school clubs was selling Valentine's Day treats to raise funds. For a dollar, one could send a valentine to someone else in the school. I decided to mail a valentine to each student in my metalworking class. Each one had a corny joke or pun, and I thought the kids would get a kick out of receiving a valentine this way.

To say the least, the valentines were a big hit. I heard corny jokes until spring vacation. Unexpectedly, Dennis transferred to another school and didn't return the Monday following Valentine's Day. School resumed, and I forgot about Dennis.

Four years later, shortly before the end of the school year, a young man stopped in for a visit. It was Dennis. Not only had he graduated from high school, he was currently living in Michigan, where he was attending college. His mother had purchased a small home near the campus, so he was able to forego dormitory life. I was amazed at how this young man had changed: athletically trim, full of self-confidence, and beaming. His smile would have ripened a truck-load of bananas. We had a delightful visit. Then he paused and said, "I really came here to thank you."

"For what?" I asked. "You were here less than a year."

"That's true, Mr. Koch, but in those few months, you taught me how to measure. And you taught me to believe in myself. And that valentine—that was the first valentine anyone had ever sent me. I still have it."

We shook hands and Dennis said he'd keep in touch. "By the way," I inquired as we walked toward the door, "what's your major? What are your plans?"

Dennis smiled. "Elementary education, Mr. Koch. I want to teach kids how to read."

More than 30 years ago, valentines were sent to a group of ordinary kids; a simple act of goodness that bore fruit in ways never imagined.

Calendar Contemplations

Calendar Contemplations

Can you believe it? Are those numbers correct—2005? You've got to be kidding! The twenty-first century is already a preschooler! Where have those years gone? The new calendar isn't so new anymore.

I remember asking my mom, shortly after we moved into Grandma's house, if it would always be 1947. (Even at an early age, it was obvious I wasn't Nobel Prize material.) Mom patiently explained how the year number changed every January 1.

"How come?" I asked.

"Because," she explained, "it's the way we keep track of things and plan for the future."

Sure enough, when the first of January rolled around, the new calendar given to customers of the State Bank of Whiting read 1948.

The calendar was prominently displayed in the kitchen, hung on the wall by the sink. I soon realized that calendars were essential domestic bulletin boards, noting special events, holidays, birthdays, and reminders of things to do. Calendars of yesteryear (at least those from banks and businesses) had big squares outlined in black for each day. Important stuff was written inside these squares, like: "Pay gas & light," "Mortgage payment due!" "Payday," "Doctor appt.," "Hospitalization & Life Ins.—pay," "So-and-So's birthday."

Another calendar, hung in Mom and Dad's bedroom, was from church. It had all the feast days and holy days of obligation printed in red. This calendar also had squares for each day but the boxes were much smaller than the ones from the bank. Each parish calendar noted fast days with a printed fish inside the square, along with Mass vestment colors of the day. Little space was left in the box for notes. Because everyone knew church law and understood the rulebook, reminders weren't necessary. Beneath the name of the particular parish was the local funeral home that underwrote the cost of the calendar. Churches and funeral homes—a formidable combination, to say the least.

I vividly remember 1948 because of my oldest brother's passion for baseball. That year, the Cleveland Indians (led by player-manager Lou Boudreau, Bob Feller, Joe Gordon, and company) won it all. At the time, my brother was a high school freshman, and I tried to imagine the year 1954, when I, too, would be in high school. That's how it all started, figuring what year this or that would happen. Whenever milestones were calculated—finishing grade school, high school graduation, completion of an apprenticeship, college commencement—the years seemed so far away.

When I was 7, I couldn't imagine being in high school. Then time unexpectedly accelerated. In what seemed like a moment, I was a freshman one day and a graduating senior the next. All of a sudden I was 21, working in the steel mill. The ink on my journeyman's card had barely dried when I found myself in college, preparing to be a teacher. A year later, I got married. And then, after 160 weekends working labor in the mill and traveling highways, I completed the requirements for a teaching degree. From classroom to factory, factory to campus, campus to classroom, I was engaged in a continual process to learn, grow, and live.

Calendar after calendar—pinned to walls, hung on doors, set on desks, kept in wallets—day upon day upon day passed. Fully occupied with teaching, parenting, remodeling a house, post-graduate education, caring for parents—commitments, responsibilities—ordinary day-to-day living and extraordinary obligations. Scores of calendars soak up time like thirsty sponges. Days rush along, blending together. Hours, minutes, and seconds speed at mind-boggling velocity. Weeks pass so quickly that calendars are checked for verification. Months fly by like flash cards in a grammar school drill. Days, weeks, months, years, and decades accumulate in the past like souvenirs from treasured places. Events come and go—anniversaries, birthdays, holidays, weekends—faster and faster. Time flies by at the speed of life.

The kids are now grown—college, work, marriage. My wife and I add "Grandparent" to our personal resumes. My teaching career spans nearly four decades. Mark the calendar—changes, adjustments, passages. When? Where? What about the good ol' days? Gone! Memories—pictures in scrapbooks, old calendars—are saved and savored. Regrets? None!

Welcome to the next calendar. I don't intend to waste a minute. The best is yet to come!

Dawn

Dawn signals the birth of a new day. Without a whisper, the last vestige of night-time's darkness is dissolved by the emerging rays of our faithful daystar. Dawn is daytime's wake-up call. It's breakfast-is-served for the early bird. Dawn is a special assembly of moments, arranged to reflect light like the facets of a diamond. Dawn is a daily opportunity to invest the day's 1440 minutes to bankroll productive activity. The dawn of day offers tranquility, meditation, contemplation, and prayerful petition.

Dawn's peaceful stillness encourages exercise for the mind. Like an understanding friend, dawn welcomes reflective thought while one quietly savors a cup of freshly brewed coffee. In undisturbed privacy, we treasure past milestones, inventory the present, and ponder the future. No other part of the day allows for such contemplation of the human spirit. Dawn is God's gift to refresh the earth and ourselves.

Dawn's arrival depends upon the season at hand. Summer's version is an early riser, eager to get started. Like an impetuous child, dawn shoves shadows aside, lighting landscapes for die-hard golfers, determined fishermen, and exuberant larks. Cleverly, dawn supplies more light with less heat, enabling the pursuit of outdoor activities without soaking participants with perspiration.

Summer's dawn incites songbirds to rehearse their evening concert. It coaxes dew to sparkle like crystals, before releasing its nourishing moisture. Dawn in summer is seductive, tantalizing all living things with a promise of precocious behavior, teasing everyone and everything with its not-quite-ready-for-prime-time attitude. Dawn winks at the day ahead as if to say, "Let's play!"

In winter, dawn keeps the covers pulled up until the last possible moment, taunting alarm clocks and daring darkness to stay overtime. Only at the last minute does dawn allow its light to overtake the stars, brightening the frozen horizon like a reluctant schoolboy whose homework assignment isn't done. Hesitantly, solitary rays of morning sun poke through leaden skies, conveying what everyone already knows: Dawn has set the thermostat way down! It's dawn's way of balancing the books for summer's extravagance.

Still, dawn in winter bears magical qualities. Alone in the dark-before-dawn kitchen, cozily wrapped in a favorite down-filled quilt, one witnesses a wispy plume of steam from a boiling teapot, signaling that it's ready to perform duty on the teabag that waits in the cup. Alone, but not lonely, thoughts are allowed to mix and mingle, like children on a playground.

The bits and pieces of a lifetime—images, memories, events, experiences, hopes, and dreams—come together for an instant. Some thoughts you try to hold in your mind, but they're too elusive; they escape, leaving an unexplainable ache. Other thoughts beg for attention. Like trying to keep your tongue off a broken tooth, it's not possible. Only after acknowledging their presence do these unwanted thoughts withdraw. Sitting by the window in the opaque light of a frozen winter's morn, you find solace in the knowledge that the shadowy places within will be held in check like the night, as dawn brings its welcomed glow.

Dawn is never solitary. Regardless of season, dawn never arrives unattended. At various times throughout the year, it pals around with familiar acquaintances. When conditions are just right, dawn invites a couple of clouds to see everything at ground level. Looking at fog-shrouded neighborhoods, surrounded by muted sounds and diffused light, one has a feeling of serenity. For a few delicious hours, gray becomes nature's color of choice. To those of us who feature similar shades of hair color, we feel like an honored guest in this monochromatic tableau.

Rising early in order to enjoy a warm spring dawn is worth a king's ransom. Equally precious is to encounter a crisp autumn dawn amid a carpet of fallen leaves, while fall's creatures chorus nature's bounty.

Dawn is a beginning—another chance to do better. Dawn is prelude to the sunset. It's the day's appetizer, an invitation to do one's best. Regardless of our station in life, dawn is bestowed on us all. Those brief, fleeting moments are presented to us for whatever use we make of them. In an almost mystical way, dawn reminds us of our beginning—our origin. It encourages us to use the day wisely and prepares us for the sunset and inevitable darkness that follows. Dawn is our reward for making it safety through the night. Get up early now and then, and collect your reward.

Rain

I love rain. Regardless of the season, rain serves as refreshment for all living things. One pleasure of spring is listening to the sound of a gentle rain and savoring its fragrance. Watching leaves flutter joyously from each drop, as plants and trees quench their need for moisture, makes one feel privileged to be part of the scene. Feelings of tranquil isolation and cozy solitude touch the heart when it rains, as life pauses to wait out nature's shower. During a rain, there is time to reflect upon the peaceful stillness, deliciously interrupted by the muted patter of jeweled droplets as they land on random targets of nature and man.

Sitting outside, sheltered from the rain, enjoying a freshly brewed cup of coffee, there is an unexplainable serenity. The early morning leaden gray skies blanket the landscape, causing one to huddle close and cup hands around the warm coffee mug. Everything is wet with rain: plants, trees, houses, verdant lawns, and sedans still snoozing on driveways. Rain soothes the soul and calms the spirit. It's nature's baptism, renewing promise, offering hope, and cleansing the good earth.

As little kids, we used to sit looking through a rain-pelted window. We'd watch the tiny rivulets plinko their way down the glass to the sill, changing familiar objects to watery blurs. On the screened porch, we'd sit close to the sash and feel the cool damp mist as wind-driven rain filtered its way through the screens' mesh, leaving goosebumps and shivers on the rain watchers.

While in grammar school, I walked home in the rain many times, usually dallying along the way, puddle-splashing and absorbing water like a thirsty sponge. Raincoats and umbrellas weren't for me, so I was soaked by the time I arrived home. Aware of my duck-like affection for rain, Mom greeted me at the door with a towel and maternal scolding. Even though I incurred her disfavor, I knew that when she handed me the towel, everything was okay. Changing into well-worn play clothes while soggy corduroys drip-dried by the boiler in the basement engendered warm feelings of home that are difficult to explain.

During high school, rainy days had moods of their own, as changeable in temperament as adolescents. Each rainfall had its own personality. After all these years, memories of walking uptown with classmates after a rain-soaked football game on a warm autumn evening are still vivid. With thoughts focused on more important matters, we hardly noticed the rain.

But rain has not always meant pleasant memories. Some of the most difficult moments have been shared with rain. The night I received word that my father died, it was raining. Driving home from Indiana State University's campus in Terre Haute, alone with my thoughts, I was aware of the wipers sweeping across the windshield. I was aware, too, of moisture-filled eyes blurring my vision into the night; rain from the heart.

Twenty-five years later, at the hospital by Mom's bedside in Intensive Care, I watched machines monitor her final hours. Surrounded by family, she was peacefully leaving this life. A steady August rain showered the windows. I caught myself watching raindrops collect on the glass like giant tears before flowing away from view. Through the gray dusk of that Friday evening, prayerful words are remembered. Mom always thought of rain as a heavenly blessing. This night, heaven blessed her one last time.

There are times, however, when rain is inconvenient, even a nuisance. When accompanied by its rowdy companions—lightning, thunder, and wind—rain can be downright threatening. To enthusiastic Little Leaguers, rain meant no ball game. Extra bicycle trips to check the field at Standard Diamonds didn't hasten infield drying. Sitting on the bench in full uniform, the kid plays the game in his head. He goes 3 for 4, makes several outstanding defensive plays, and scores the winning run. He pedals home in victory. His flannel uniform, drenched from the early summer downpour, sags on his small frame. He doesn't mind. Stuffed inside his saturated jersey, his fielder's mitt is protected from the rain. He is already thinking about the next game.

Rain is a healer, a natural therapeutic. Is there a more comforting, restful sound than rain dancing on a roof? The raindrop ballet encourages an extra 40 winks and entices pillows to be softer. Rain is nature's permit for a lazy day.

On some very early summer mornings, when moisture-filled clouds are showering the landscape, I drive to Whiting Park and watch it rain. Willow trees bow in appreciation and delicate flowers deftly catch nourishing droplets, while plantings throughout celebrate the liquid banquet. The only sound is the rhythmic cascade of falling water. Lake Michigan's surf quietly applauds the latest delivery of fresh moisture. Even the songbirds are silent, choosing not to sing in the shower.

Alone, but not lonely, there is a feeling of contentment and repose. There is also a sense of oneness with nature, of bearing witness to the renewal of promises made long ago. I love rain.

Sunday

Sunday, the day of the sun, is the first day of the week and the Christian Sabbath. It has a pulse and pace unlike any other day of the week. It is a day of rest, prayer, play, or toil. Sunday is for family or a time for personal solitude. Sunday is for all seasons, readily adapting its song to enrich the melody of the human soul.

Sunday is church bells and hearing the Good News. Sunday is shined shoes, combed hair, and neatly pressed clothes. Sunday is joyous noise, singing songs of salvation. Sunday is Gospel and quiet hymns. Sunday is collection plates and fidgety little boys in dress shirts and neckties. Sunday is sleeping in and unheeded alarm clocks. Sunday is freshly brewed coffee, the sports section, wheat toast with jam, and orange juice. Sunday is unhurried hot showers that only end when the water heater sends its chilly reminder. Sunday is playfully wrestling with kids on the bed. Sunday is staggering barefoot over cold floors to let out the dog. Sunday is prime time snuggle-together-fest.

Sunday is trying to discover the paperboy's newest landing site, hoping you can reach the newspaper without using equipment from the garage. Sunday is an 8:00 AM tee time and being golf-ready at 5:30. Sunday is quiet streets and shuttered stores, all-night diners and donut shops. Sunday is jogging while keeping rhythm to ear-fed Walkman and iPod tunes. Sunday is ice cream cones and sundaes covered with chocolate that call your name. Sunday is sharing togetherness, holding hands with a special someone, speaking by touch through love lit eyes. Sunday is family dinner, grace before meals, home-cooked delights, conversation, and laughter. Sunday is children giggling at their favorite newspaper comics and television cartoons. Sunday is helping mom with the dishes.

Sunday is spring bonnets and print dresses with ribbons for the hair. Sunday is flower buds teasing the senses with seasonal promise. Sunday is washing the family limousine— scrubbing wheels, polishing bumpers, and cleaning windows—knowing your actions will encourage rain. Sunday is shopping, invading neighborhood malls, challenging one's willpower and the bankcard's limit. Sunday is answering rote questions: Paper or plastic? Credit or debit?

Sunday is watching TV, dressed like "Who cares?", snacking through programs, and diet promises. Sunday is giving the La-Z-Boy recliner a serious road

279

test, curled up inside a cozy comforter with a favorite book. Sunday is bathrobe and housedress, slippers, and bare feet. Sunday is a hot cup of soothing tea savored while reading the papers. Sunday is naptime; delicious snoozes coaxed by soft music from CDs or FM radio.

Sunday is taking a drive, checking out flea markets, garage sales, and other bargain sites. Sunday is kids playing sandlot baseball, playground basketball, touch football, and hockey on frozen lagoons and lakes. Sunday is hangin' with the guys, cruisin' with the top down, hittin' the beach, the slopes, or a 16-inch softball.

Sunday is being young or old, or any age in between. Sunday is the weekly free day. Sunday is take-your-college-kid-back-to-campus day, the trunk loaded with enough food to feed a small European country. Sunday is apartment cleaning, grocery shopping, Laundromat visiting, and catching up on everything that couldn't be done during the week. Sunday is working in the yard, tending the garden, mowing the lawn, raking leaves, and sweeping frozen crystals from already icy steps. Sunday is feeding the gulls by the lake. Sunday is a visit to the cemetery, remembering.

Sunday is strolling through leafy autumn carpets of sun-painted cornflakes, celebrating the bounty of a summer passed. Sunday is football, baseball, basketball, and the *Wide World of Sports*. Sunday is an alphabet of choices: NFL, NHL, MLB, NBA, NCAA, CBS, NBC, ABC, CNN, or ESPN; countless channels to surf and savor via satellite and cable. Sunday is Saturday night's best friend, providing starry-eyed lovers extra hours past midnight with moments to remember. Sunday is setting the clock back in October and springing ahead in April. Sunday is a synonym for "Take a break!"

Sunday offers time to reflect on times gone by and family and friends who've passed on. Sunday is all-night radio, as thousands across America listen to voices, programs, and music that filled youthful days. For a few brief hours, just east of midnight of a brand-new Sunday, it's yesterday once more.

Sunday is early Mass, a second collection, and an after-church bake sale. Sunday is visiting friends. Sunday is family albums and stories about Uncle Joe and Aunt Mary. Sunday is the laughter of children.

Sunday is tranquility, time alone with one's thoughts. Sunday is a fresh start for a new supply of weekdays. Sunday is hope, renewal, opportunity, kindness, and peace. I like Sunday.

August

Already the days are noticeably shorter. Too quickly, the long daylight hours of June and July have been tucked away for another year, challenging August to cram its annual allotment of summertime into limited hours. The challenge is willingly accepted. August is the playboy of the seasons—summer's trump card. In August, the sun turns up the heat a few more notches, broiling sidewalks, drying lawns, and toasting suntanned faces to a darker shade. As unpredictable as the Cubs' relief pitching, August features surprise thunderstorms that suspend picnics, halt outdoor chores, and disrupt a much-needed late-inning rally at Wrigley Field.

Summer saves all of its extra humidity for August. Generously, like an intoxicated tycoon, August dispenses soggy, saturated air at will, wilting hairdos, wrinkling suits, and eroding tolerance—fraying temperature-sensitive nerves. August is the host month for the year's annual wheeze-and-sneeze olympics, as plants of every persuasion gleefully release their bounty of pollen. Land-locked citizens procure copious amounts of Kleenex and hankies in an attempt to stem the flood of draining sinuses. So often are handkerchiefs and tissue in evidence, it appears that the natives are under a flag of surrender.

August is equal opportunity aggravation. Our eighth month also generates mixed reviews for its summertime efforts. While the simmering late-summer sun bakes highways, overheating car and driver alike, sun bunnies and bronzed beach boys celebrate sand and surf. August can be tranquil or turmoil. On any given day, one must be wary of its changeable personality. August is summer's impersonation of Dr. Jekyll and Mr. Hyde.

If there are dog days in August—sapping strength from all who labor in its heat—then August nights are reserved for those seeking respite from those labors. When evening arrives, August puts on its best behavior. Like a politician currying favor, August provides caressing breezes and star-filled skies and dazzles the landscape with incandescent moonlight. August encourages lovers to share magic moments. August knows romance.

There are occasions, though, when August forgets. Several times during its 31-day engagement, August neglects to lower nighttime temperatures, causing untold discomfort to both man and beast. When that happens, citizens retreat indoors where purring air-conditioners compensate for the oversight, leaving the sultry outside to wildlife more accustomed to such fare. Power companies love August.

August is summer's last hurrah before the season's holiday finale, Labor Day. By this time, August has become a conflict of interest. On one hand, kids strive to stretch out each remaining day of vacation; on the other, moms scurry store-to-store readying their children for the opening day of school. Almost imperceptibly, changes occur. Put away for another season are beach towels, bathing suits, and suntan oils. In their place come haircuts, daily showers, clean clothes, brushed teeth, and school. And as with every passage in life, there remains a sweet sadness poignantly tugging at the heart.

Memories of Augusts past fill scrapbook pages that only the heart is able to see. Carefree times at playground and parks, shagging fly balls at Standard Diamonds hit so high it was like following a white dot across a cloudless blue sky. Hours spent sitting on the curb at the end of Oliver Street (the absolute limit of permitted distance from home for a second-grader), waving to the engineer as the train roared along the Pennsylvania tracks, whistle sounding, smoke billowing, and cinders from the engine filling the sky. Sneaking chunks of crystal clear ice from the ice wagon with neighborhood buddies, while the deliveryman toted the tong-held block of ice on his shoulder to his customer's second-floor flat.

A whole host of August forget-me-nots flood the mind. Hanging around with friends doin' nuttin'. Riding bikes rigged with baseball cards clipped to the frame, motorboating down the street. Dropping a bobber in Wolf Lake one last time before school ends fishing season. Cruising along in the '60 Olds with the top down and radio turned way up! Memories of drive-in restaurants, drive-in movies, pizzas, White Castle Slyders, and beer. Beginning work at the steel mill, leaving for college, class reunions, and the rainy Friday evening Mom died.

Augusts past, filled with beginnings and endings, and all things in between. August engenders admiration, reverence, respect, melancholy, eminence, and awe. August is a month for all seasons of the heart.

September

If a year has such a thing as middle age, then September qualifies. No other month comes along with such an inventory of seasonal goodies. September is also a month with an attitude. It is both an ending and beginning. Labor Day officially closes out summer vacation and leads the way back to school. For countless students, September is the start of a new year—a clean slate. It is the calendar's "All is forgiven" greeting card for kids who need another chance to learn, grow, and live. September is prelude to autumn, when leaves begin their annual journey from branch to lawn. Like an elegant movie star, September's dawn takes longer to present her radiance, making the early bird wish he had a flashlight.

September is apron string-loosening month, as teary-eyed moms send little ones off to their first day of school. September is collegians back on campus—attending classes (hopefully), adjusting to dorm food (supplemented by fast food runs), and pursuing extra-curricular activities that keep regiments of guardian angles working overtime. September is stocking up on allergy pills and Kleenex. It is summer's last call for suntan lotion and beach blanket bingo.

September is when the sun previews its fall colors and shows off its new wardrobe in rainbows, leaves, and early autumn sunsets. September is one long football weekend with a few baseball games in between. It is Friday night after-the-game sock hops where teenagers fill high school scrapbooks with moments to remember. September is sigh-of-relief time for moms, as kids return to classrooms. September means routine schedules, alarm clocks, and get-your-act-together plans.

September brings an end to summer reruns, both on television and at home. The new season means early get-ups. September is morning traffic jams in the bathroom, chaos in the kitchen: "Where's my lunch?" "I can't find my books!" "Did anyone see my other shoe?" Clock radios are scolded for disrupting sleepy human units who cannot believe it's time to wake up. September is the year's way of telling everyone that summer camp is over! September weekdays take their sweet time moving along; its weekends seem so far away, yet fly by when they arrive.

September splashes colors around like a playful child finger-painting. For 30 delicious days, the calendar slips into casual clothes and settles back, putting the year on cruise control and gliding into autumn. September is contented. It wears a smile that could ripen bananas. It signals mums to begin their parade of blossoms, decorating landscapes. September calls bees to their annual convention, buzzing natives at every opportunity, causing arms to flail, newspapers to swing, and sales of Raid to skyrocket!

September is one last time around with the lawn mower, a victory lap for a race that resumes in the spring. September is "Wait'll next year" for "Honey-do" projects not begun. September is Maybe Month: "Maybe I'll clean the garage, and maybe I won't," "Maybe I'll paint the railing, or maybe I'll wait 'til spring!" Spring wins.

September is grandparents watching their grandchildren so working parents can get ahead. September is dad playing catch with his son, neighborhood kids shooting baskets, and sandlot football on Sunday with the guys. September is looking at vacation photos, summertime snapshots, and videos from family weddings and class reunions.

September is remembering parents, classmates, and friends. September is savoring summers past: drive-in movies, convertibles, cruisin', and Bobby Beach. September is birthdays, anniversaries, football homecomings, and a happily-ever-after first date. September is the lead chapter of everyone's yearbook. September is mirth and melancholy. It is being alone in the night, gazing at stars, and being awed at the vastness of space. September is walking in the moonlight, holding hands with a special someone. September is peaceful easy feelings, porch swings, lawn chairs, and being near those you love.

September is more than a collection of days. "September can be an attitude, or an age, or a wistful reality." September is a song. September is mischievous; it winks teasingly one last time at suntanned faces as they march to school, unable to join in September's fun and games. September is warm rain and cool evening breezes. September is like a faithful friend; the welcome mat is always on display, fresh coffee is brewing, and if you're late, September will leave a light on for you.

September knows beginnings, endings, and everything in between. Most of all, September knows a year is a long time and that there needs to be a respite—an oasis—along the way. September decided to be the calendar's rest stop—part Disneyland, part National Park, and part meadow by a quiet stream. Enjoy September.

Autumn Serenade

Once again it's time. Autumn is in full splendor, and for those who cherish fall days, the seasonal banquet is ready. Almost every afternoon the letter "V" fills the sky as geese fly south, jubilantly celebrating another bountiful summer. Their wings sweep majestically across the face of the harvest moon. Clouds tag along like fluffy pillows, enticing the skyward travelers to enjoy a well-deserved rest.

Along roadways, trees display their elegant opulence, radiant in crimson, saffron, bronze, apricot, and gold. Sunlight shines translucent through gossamer leaves, highlighting their delicate lattice. Carpets of grass cover landscapes with various shades of green. Verdant conifers deepen their autumnal tunics, flaunting rich tones of regal emerald. Like throw rugs randomly tossed about a meadow, patches of russet-colored turf offers bounty to ground squirrels scurrying about, gathering dried foliage for their winter burrow.

Precocious breezes coax leaves to take flight. Spinning, tumbling, floating, swirling, cascading from branches like giant cornflakes. Encouraged by playful gusts, the once green leaves of summer perform their aerial acrobatics choreographed to a symphony of seasonal sights and sounds. No Broadway show ever had a better finale. Only after the last leaf has fallen can trees showcase the majestic character of their natural architecture. High above—visible for the first time— the nesting places of summer songbirds and tree squirrels are closed for the season.

Rural streams and small rivers take on added prominence as sport-minded leaves windsurf together, leisurely flowing along to a gathering place not yet determined. Lakes and ponds become parking lots for waterfowl as they grab a little R&R on the way to warmer climes. Coffee-colored cattails sway gently amid tall swamp grasses, saluting the passing season and welcoming the next.

Creatures of air, water, and land know that this is a time of transition, change, and preparation. With nature calling the signals, they know there are things that must be attended to. As soon as autumn arrives, the sun begins to tuck itself in a little earlier each day. Twilight gets top billing as darkness arrives sooner than an unwanted relative. Until winter arrives, there will be more shadow than light.

Some may not appreciate the additional nighttime hours, knowing the cold cannot be far behind. But this time of year encourages a slower, more deliberate pace; an easing back of life's throttle. Autumn is an ideal time to reflect and review. This serenade of days provides moments to remember—a tranquil pause before gearing up for year-end holidays. Autumn is the sweet-sad season of the heart.

Waking up long before sunrise in late October, thoughts of seasons past come by for a visit. As if watching a movie, random scenes from childhood, adolescence, and adulthood fill the mind. Each one takes turns filling the heart with remembrance and poignant thoughts. One by one, the sights and sounds and scents of autumn arrive.

How easy it is to recall the perfume of burning leaves and carved pumpkins, walking with friends to a Friday night football game, seeing classmates' faces clearly almost a half-century after graduation. Why do certain images retain their sharpness? Ordinary events have become treasures of the heart: walking uptown as a youngster to buy the latest hit 45 record; a high school assembly; Mom reading the *Chicago Daily News* on the front porch while I folded papers for my route; shoveling a winter's supply of coal; our senior class hayride; Dad working the main desk at the Community Center; playing the jukebox at the Oil Can; playing snooker at Nick's; watching *American Bandstand*, sprawled on the rug in front of the TV; walking your kids to kindergarten, shuffling through fallen leaves that crunch like giant cornflakes.

In a flash of memory, I'm having homemade soup at Mom's; going to our son John's school play; shooting baskets with our youngest son, Dan; playing catch with my dad; serving as DJ at our daughter Christine's after-prom party; enjoying drive-in movies in October (just right for blankets and hot cocoa); grocery shopping with Mom (never a dull moment); driving home weekends from college; serving early Mass for Father D.; Whiting's Halloween Parade and stage show, with kids guessing the number of pumpkins seeds for a $5 prize (big-time stuff in the '50s).

Like eager inductees, snippets of memory wait their turn to participate in this autumn serenade. It's getting light now; soon a new day will begin. Quietly without protest, the memories slip back to their keeping place. Once again it's time. Autumn is in full splendor. The seasonal banquet is now being served.

October's Gift

October is near the top of my favorite months. Others have written that October is the "sweet-sad" time of year. They'll get no quarrel from me. During its allotment of calendar days, every season of the year stops by October for a brief visit, leaving samples to savor.

Some October days are summer-like, using the sun's warmth to coax leaves into showing off the brilliance of their fall colors. On other days, October hunkers down, churning everything in its path with chilly, rambunctious winds. Such pre-winter forays signal a change in uniform for all living things. Leaves bid farewell to branches while small animals rapidly thicken their fur coats to help defeat winter's oncoming cold. As humans, we, too, heed October's signs. Sweaters and windbreakers, storm windows, and antifreeze become priority items.

Many folks travel considerable distances to photograph fall colors, nature's annual kaleidoscope presentation. These filmed treasures are later enjoyed at home during winter's bleak, frigid days. Just as certain creatures search out and store food for sustenance through winter, pictures of autumnal splendor remind us of seasons past, embellishing memorable events in our lives. These recorded images also serve as nourishment until another spring arrives to replenish our spirit.

October is a time for weekend football games, homecomings, and special moments under the light of a harvest moon. It's an ageless time for anyone and everyone who sincerely believes in the magical Great Pumpkin, the permanence of tree-carved initials, and romantics holding hands.

October is a time for taking quiet walks where the only sounds are supplied by gossiping squirrels playing tag around fallen leaves. This is the season when cool October rains wash the remaining sunshine from summer's foliage. Chrysanthemums huddle like football players, deciding their next play. Dressed in their team colors, they thrive in October's chill. Blossoms of crimson, ivory, and saffron applaud the senses, conducting a symphony for the eyes. Amid plants already burnished by October's rationed sunlight, mums rejoice, flaunting their harvest rainbow.

This is the time of year when the sun turns in a little earlier each day, when gray becomes a favorite cloud color, and the accompanying mist-like rain sends rippling shivers down backbones. It is also a season of farewell. Watch as geese fly south, proudly displaying their in-flight 'V' sign for victory, saluting the triumph and bounty of another summer.

Contemplate October. Remember youthful times: the golden days of Indian Summer, the perfume of burning leaves, the stillness of early morning fog, dazzling crisp afternoons, evenings for cuddling, nights for snuggling—time to nurture dreams.

This is a month for all seasons. It fills us with melancholy joy, like seeing a long-together couple holding hands; knowing that after so many years, gentleness and understanding is more valued than passion. We sense their love; the sharing, the giving, and the acceptance that make up a lifetime.

Within us, we carry special feelings for this time of year. We host festivals to celebrate autumn, commemorate holidays, follow age-old traditions, and express general appreciation for this "sweet-sad" season. It is also a time to bestow gifts. This may sound odd, considering the traditional season of giving is still weeks away, but autumn has riches that beg to be shared.

On a delicious fall afternoon several years ago, I went to Whiting Park and scooped up a couple of bags of dried leaves. Using my hand as a rake, I gathered willow and oak, elm and maple. I added birch leaves from my backyard to top off my leafy autumn recipe. I wanted to share the season with friends and classmates who live in other parts of the country.

So I mailed each of them a package of leaves from their hometown, gathered from the park where together we shared carefree times of youth. I enclosed a note explaining the contents to dispel concerns that someone had sent them a bird's nest. I encouraged them to feel and crunch and toss their leaves skyward, perhaps even barbecue just enough to sample their fragrance. I closed my note with: "Not only are these leaves part of your hometown's autumn—they are a part of us."

Now it's your turn. This season's supply of autumn leaves is already in abundance. Have your own personal Octoberfest. Set aside a few moments with someone special. Take a long, quiet walk, hold hands, and feast upon this seasonal banquet. This is October's gift. Enjoy.

Jewels of Autumn

Everyone is familiar with the adage "You can't get something for nothing." Luckily for us, October doesn't know about this and puts on its annual display of autumn jewels. After enduring a full solstice of July's ego, August's arrogance, and September's sophistication, October arrives just in time to tidy up after summer's exuberance, redecorating the landscape for the banquet called autumn.

Using sunshine like a master artist, October delicately paints leaves in amber, scarlet, saffron, and gold. Late-blooming flowers willingly offer fragile blossoms to October's gentle touch, eager to contribute their colors and show off perennial skills while serving as honor guards to fall's parade.

Like handholding romantics, trees slow dance with courting winds trying to coax gem-colored leaves from their branches. In quiet whispers, falling leaves carpet grassy knolls, woodland paths, and well-manicured lawns. A bounty of mature acorns tempts squirrels to give up playful antics and sample oaken treats. Blue jays trumpet their presence, announcing territorial imperative in no uncertain terms.

As if on cue, conifers assume elegant stature, aware that their season of prominence is fast approaching. Spruce and pine watch as their deciduous cousins shed a full growing season of foliage, becoming lattice-like against the azure October sky.

Sounds of autumn accent quiet early mornings as wildlife prepares for winter. Along lakeshores, diminutive waves advance and retreat, rippling through bulrush and marsh grasses. Cattails salute this sweet-sad season like dancing cigars, swaying their cylindrical flowered heads in rhythm with the moving water.

Across the land, orchards and fields present their bounty. Crops are gathered, hay is put up, apples are picked, and pumpkins are selected for carving the jack-o-lanterns of Halloween. October's celestial nightlight illuminates the landscape, leaving enough shadow for dreamers and lovers to plan happily-ever-afters.

Under the glow of a harvest moon, hayrides and home team victories encourage snapshots to capture moments that fill scrapbooks. After a hard day at school, kids shuffle through bronzed oak leaves, crunching and laughing as they amiably jostle one another on the way home. Cool breezes summon sweatshirts and sweaters from closets and bureau drawers. Below slate-gray October clouds, rain descends on all living things, persuading shivering creatures everywhere to seek shelter and warmth.

Small streams and energetic brooks welcome the flotilla of discarded leaves that sails and surfs in harmony with the current, bumping against stones or becoming entangled on partly submerged branches. Momentarily, they are captured, held, and then released to continue a journey of no particular consequence. Though each leaf seems to act randomly, collectively these remnants of autumn follow a plan designed eons before starlight.

On special fall mornings, the sky glows with muted hues of pink, blue, and mother of pearl as heaven prepares for a new dawn. Delicate fog-like mist hovers at ground level before dissolving into dew. Each day, nighttime extends its domain over autumn. Evenings arrive sooner than supper, impatient for sunlight to vacate the premises. Porch lights, streetlights, and headlight beams stave off darkness, assisting travelers along their way.

October is forever changing, but always remains the same. Like a living kaleidoscope, autumn presents a banquet for our senses. For both the casual or discerning observer, the end-of-the-year equinox provides an opportunity for contemplation, reflection, and reaffirmation of our purpose and place on this earth. By the time the last leaf signals the advent of winter, the jewels of autumn have been put away for another year. October is the guardian at the gate, the caretaker of those times that help us understand the changing seasons and passages in our own life.

November

By any standard, November is not a very attractive month. In fact, there are times when November could use a press agent to punch up its image. Dispensing its allotment of days in cold, gloomy, sun-stingy wrappings does little to enhance November's stature. If it weren't for Thanksgiving and Veterans Day, November would be hard pressed to justify membership in the month club. Unlike its calendar colleagues, November is not a top choice of poets or songwriters. Like an eccentric relative, November goes its own way and does its own thing, marching to the beat of a different drum.

November is not pretentious; what you see is what you get. Long ago it was decided to accept November's straightforward, no-nonsense approach. November's primary job is to prepare us for winter—in whatever fashion it sees fit. Without exception, November comes prepared. Attired in its favorite late-autumn colors of gray and brown, November sets about the task of removing remaining leaves from branches by vigorously blow-drying resident elm, maple, birch, and oak trees. A few stubborn chrysanthemums challenge November's authority before finally packing it in for the winter.

When moisture is on the late-autumn menu, November supplies its own special recipe, believing rain is best when delivered chilled. In fact, all of the month's main weather courses are served cold. Occasionally, November prepares a holiday entrée of "freezing skid stuff," blanketing the landscape with white crystal flakes. Such events warrant immediate attention. A few extraordinary moments during an ordinary month causes work to be put on hold, while natives savor the unexpected but welcome wintry preview.

Almost bare branches form intricate latticework against leaden gray skies. Like finely crafted lace, the now leafless trees take on unaccustomed delicacy, swaying majestically in concert with November's icy wind. Playful winter gusts momentarily change the doily-like patterns, as if an unseen kaleidoscope sweeps the horizon.

November teasingly allows brief respites from the biting cold, sometimes inviting balmy breezes and bright sunshine in for a visit. Then, right in the middle of light coats and no scarves, the sun takes a hike, the wind picks up, and temperatures plummet, creating an epidemic of head colds. One can't help but wonder if November has stock in the aspirin and chicken soup business.

For countless turkeys, however, November is anything but a party. For them, it's bottom-line time, roasting-pan city. If they had a voice in the matter, they'd probably promote seafood. But November is quite gifted, and knows a good meal when it sees one. The only thing missing is a good song. Since Thanksgiving tunes seem to be in short supply, perhaps the following will suffice. You'll have to furnish the melody:

> Let's give thanks for all our blessings,
> All the living years.
> Let's recall all the moments,
> Every happiness and tear.
>
> At tables brimmed with harvest bounty,
> With loved ones, family, and friends,
> We share the goodness of this land
> Through prayer and touching hands.
>
> For health and laughter, love, and all that,
> Be thankful your petitions were heard.
> But, most of all, be most grateful
> You're not the roasted ol' bird!
>
> Happy Thanksgiving, everyone!

December

After 11 months of preparation, the calendar's annual year-end bonanza arrives full of anticipation and promise. No other month carries us along with such frenzy and excitement as does December. For 31 glorious days, people everywhere recharge their batteries and retune their circuits, allowing kindness, compassion, generosity, and goodwill to have free reign of the human spirit. All around, one truly feels the exuberance of the season.

December is woolen hats and knitted mittens, decorated stores, and evergreen trees. December's early darkness welcomes the kaleidoscope of seasonal colored lights as porches and rooftops take on unaccustomed prominence, glowing like electric rainbows; glittering, shimmering, and twinkling greetings to passers-by. December comes wrapped in blankets of gift paper, adorned with ribbon, hiding treasures and tokens of love. December forgives budgets and waistlines, knowing full well that both will expand.

December is snow shovels and window scrapers, aching backs and sore muscles. December is holiday school assemblies, Christmas vacation, basketball games, and high school sock hops. December is office parties and late-hour excuses, traffic-jammed highways, and tow-away snow zones. December is Santa Claus with flying, sleigh-pulling reindeer—one with a bright red nose. December is children, bursting at the seams with excitement; bubbling, joyful laughing all the way.

December is cold: the onslaught of winter, ice-skating ponds and sled-slick hills. December is shopping for groceries, bargains, and gifts tagged "From Santa." December is tinsel and ornaments and popcorn on a string. December is parades, mistletoe and merriment, carols and hymns, and songs celebrating Christmas.

December is fireplaces, fresh buttered popcorn, and love-lighted eyes. December is frozen toes and frosty noses. December is a Nativity scene and midnight Mass. December is walking hand-in-hand with someone special; window shopping, stargazing, and building dreams. December is hot chocolate and fruitcake, homemade bread and nut roll. December is grab bags and surprises, Christmas cards, and long overdue phone calls.

December is shivering in the car until the heater kicks in and icicles at rest along a roof's edge. December is baking cookies and roast duck, snack trays and board games. December is *It's a Wonderful Life* and *Going My Way*. December is holiday specials on TV and preempted programs. December is "White Christmas" and "The Little Drummer Boy." December is Advent and Christmas Eve.

December is melancholy and childhood memories. December is family and love for one another. December is buying a Christmas tree and searching for toy sales. December is friends, present and past. December is eggnog and strudel. December is photographs in the family album, favorite songs on the radio, cozy comforters, and down-filled pillows. December is childhood with sugar plum dreams and loving hugs.

December is silver bells and sleigh rides. December is crystal-clear moonlight and bone-chilling wind. December is inventory time, New Year's resolution time. December is memories of faces and places and times of our life. December is remembering Mom and Dad, brothers and sisters, hanging stockings, and opening gifts while still dressed in pj's.

December is being a grade school choirboy, decorating the family tree, and sitting alone in the darkened parlor watching tinsel light-dance the shadows. December is prayer to the Christ Child. December is the Festival of Lights, Hanukkah, and the menorah. December is "Peace on Earth, Good Will Toward Men." December is the Christmas Star, the Three Wise Men, Joseph, Mary, and the Prince of Peace.

December is sharing, giving, belonging, listening, and helping. December is children singing "Silent Night." December is Bethlehem, no room at the inn, a manger, and Baby Jesus. December is welcoming college students home for the holidays. December is an opportunity to rekindle friendships, dispel ill feelings, and let your heart shine. December is the Christmas angel trumpeting the Good News!

December is quiet reflection and tranquil meditation. December is solitary, time for being alone with one's thoughts. December is crowds; hustling, bustling throngs of Santa's helpers. December is snowfall, snowballs, and drifts just right for kids to make snow angels.

December is youthful and energetic, caroling with the neighbors, brightening the spirit of shut-ins. December is Christmas Day and New Year's Eve. December is "Jingle Bells" and a snowman named Frosty. December is freshly scrubbed children peacefully asleep in their beds. December is wide-eyed kids on Christmas morning. December is family and loved ones. December is you and I, its promise bestowed upon all. December is neat. Enjoy.

Snow

The weatherman's annual white sale arrived Saturday, flake by flake. When it ended, 5 1/2 inches of partly cloudy covered the landscape. Snow is the only substance that creates a variety of moods, triggers long-dormant memories, and teases the senses with delicious emotions. When accompanied by friendly winter breezes, or in partnership with cold cruel winds, snow takes on Jekyll and Hyde personalities. On those occasions when snowflakes fall in silence, unattended by wind, the feather-light frozen crystals quietly descend in pristine solitude, cloaking everything and everyone in wintry white blankets of peaceful tranquility.

For mysterious reasons, falling snow activates memory's replay. Instantaneously, poignant scenes from bygone times fill the mind's screen. Each episode recalls a specific time and place, illuminating experiences shared with family and friends. It's odd how one's perception of snow changes as one ages. As children, snow is a prayed-for event, a heavenly toy offering an unlimited supply of pretend and play. The deeper, wetter, and heavier the snow is, the better!

Think as a child for a moment and remember the youthful exhilaration felt while building snow forts in vacant neighborhood lots and defending them against an imagined enemy. Recall the uniform of long-ago winters: mended woolen mittens, patched corduroys, scratchy scarves, and snug, knitted hats. Call to mind the occasional scolding received for coming home snow-covered and soaked; Mom didn't always fully grasp the hands-on engineering necessary for building snow forts. A few days later, sore muscles reminded a kid of the Herculean effort spent rolling and stacking humongous snowballs into the snowman now serving as frozen sentry in the front yard. Purloined items of Dad's old clothing, a few donated lumps of coal, and a single carrot rescued from chicken soup personalized the character of the rotund, kid-crafted sculpture.

Adolescence cast snow in a different light. Instead of an element for play, snow is viewed more romantically, as a vehicle to enrich and enhance the teen years. Without doubt, there are frequent snowball attacks; but these antics are employed as attention-getters, a way to be noticed by peers. Snow offers timid teenage boys the chance to be chivalrous without being self-conscious; helping your girlfriend navigate a snow-slick street or lending her steady support through knee-deep snowdrifts were good reasons to hold hands. Sharing an evening of ice-skating fun at the Whiting Park Lagoon provided teenagers the opportunity to form friendships, to belong, and to share experiences which, in later years, turned into treasured remembrances.

As we mature, snow assumes an unfavorable status, becoming an unwanted wintertime nuisance. Once working in the real world, it doesn't take long for snow to be labeled useless! Snow means there are walkways and driveways to be shoveled, steps to sweep clean, and salt-coated highways that corrode the family car. Snow discourages travel, snarls traffic, and is prime cause of spinouts and dented fenders. It's a foregone conclusion that falling snow causes many people to meet by accident. The "freezing skid stuff" loads up wipers, clogs washer jets, and reduces visibility. Driving becomes a hazardous, nerve-fraying challenge. Snow makes parking lots nearly impossible to navigate and parking spaces almost extinct!

Nevertheless, new fallen snow has a way of uplifting spirits and bringing unaccustomed elegance to landscapes of every description. I still vividly recall winter's artwork among steel mill furnaces. Uncountable snowflakes, cascading in a frigid shower from lead-colored skies, fought for landing sites amid the soot and soil of steelmaking. By shift's end, blankets of white adorned rooftops and railings, roadways and walkways. For the briefest of moments, the mill took on a subdued, almost cozy appearance. Workers changing shifts bore witness to the transformation and smiled. Voices joked about the weather, anticipating a blizzard. Several snowballs took flight as the 10-year-old boy within all men was let out to play.

I remember, too, the quiet trip home through heavy wet snow as my '54 Oldsmobile sedan lumbered its way through unplowed streets. No need of Rocket 88 power that night. Instead, I enjoyed a cautious unhurried ride, with wipers and radio keeping time to Charley Rich's "Lonely Weekends."

On many occasions, while traveling the highways as a college student, I watched the countryside fill with snow as the landscape changed into its winter outfit. One had the feeling of being part of a Currier & Ives picture that had come to life. Winter birds, livestock, and resident vegetation wore the white mantel of crystallized ice. Green boughs of conifers and bare-branch deciduous trees welcomed the season by willingly stretching limbs, all eager to capture the snow-soft flakes.

As a homeowner, it's easy to complain about snow and view its arrival with disdain and cynicism. It means snow blower and shovel, sweeping porches and steps, and muscle aches and pains. Then, almost on cue, the senses click on, attuned to the sight and sound and fragrance of a wintertime snowstorm. Like

Disney magic, a gentle, unseen force tugs as memories, images, and feelings of yesteryear nudge their way into head and heart, nourishing the spirit. A baseball-sized snowball is packed and sent zinging smack into the trunk of the backyard birch tree. The impact shatters it into glistening sunlit diamonds. And for a few fleeting moments, that 10-year-old boy, now tucked inside a senior citizen, is let out to play. Tell me snow isn't magic.

Seasonal Snacks

Winter's Fringe Benefits

As winter firms up its grasp on the landscape and all living things defend against harsh winds and numbing cold, the lengthy nights that accompany the season provide opportunity for reverie and remembrance to those securely sheltered from wintry elements.

For reasons not revealed, sun-starved frozen January days serve as a catalyst that awakens long-dormant memories of times past. Like dear friends, images appear unexpectedly but are always welcome. Each mental photo complements the quiet darkness that embraces the wee small hours of a morning awaiting the dawn.

Somehow, in a wonderfully mysterious process, bits and pieces of a lifetime randomly appear, filling the mind-screen with people, places, and events. Unannounced and triggered by subconscious prompts, sights and sounds combine with familiar faces, replaying— for an audience of one—the times of your life. Alone, but not lonely, a peaceful inner solitude beckons thoughts of yesteryear to be companion to the present. Together like friendly classmates, they invite the host to revisit memorable moments of personal experience.

Image clarity rivals current video technology, with razor-sharp pictures and sound. Within this virtual reality of the mind, every sensory circuit is attuned and focused as a symphony of ideation and imagination evokes feelings of melancholy and longing. Searching special keeping places within the memory bank, the host initiates a scan of possible recollections for review. Like an old-fashioned jukebox at lightning-quick speed, thought codes are entered and subject matter chosen; in an instant, memory playback begins.

Regardless of whether recall is consciously or subconsciously activated, quality and substance are never compromised. Amazingly, age seems to enhance and enrich stored memories. Childhood reminiscences become more detailed as one moves on in years. Ordinary day-to-day happenings are more prized. The good ol' days are cherished for giving meaning to life. Memories of what we did and the way we were serve as reference to experiences that shaped who and what we are.

Lying awake, snuggled cozily in a down comforter, thoughts about friends and family, places and events, tough times, and personal triumphs compete for onscreen replay. Sometimes I think about the years I worked in the steel mill. Though three decades have passed since I clocked out for the last time, memories of early morning bus rides, coworkers, shift work, apprentice school, and a thousand ordinary moments more valuable than diamonds remain vivid and alive.

Sometimes I recall kid stuff, like delivering newspapers on my Cleveland Avenue route for the Whiting News Company; the many carefree afternoons spent fishing at Wolf Lake with friends, trying to entice elusive bluegills to feast on baited hooks at the end of an old bamboo pole; the penalty for being the smallest brother when it was time to fill the coal bin for winter, stationed in the coal bin with rake and shovel, leveling out each load my Dad and brothers delivered through the coal chute, and adding boards across the bin's doorway as the level in the bin increased; my days as a Little Leaguer at the Standard Diamonds' field of dreams; setting pins at the Community Center; serving early Mass for Father Daniels at Sacred Heart Church; or roughhousing with a dog named Sam. Kid stuff, but experiences that helped make a man.

In the middle of the night, when the only sounds are a faithful furnace delivering a fresh supply of heated air, the steady tick-tock of the grandfather clock, and random creaks from well-worn floors, I recall high school classmates, teenage foolishness, and adolescent adventures that still radiate warmth for the heart. Every once in a while I remember, in a special way, family and friends who have passed on. They are forever alive. All the times we shared together engender thankfulness that they touched my life.

Musings and memories are fringe benefits of winter. The extended hours of darkness afford each of us time to reflect, remember, and savor thoughts that we were often too busy to enjoy at the time they occurred. In the peaceful darkness before dawn, take your memories from their special keeping place and give them voice. Some may bring sorrow and sadness; others, laughter and smiles. Occasionally, we need to visit the past. Like photographs in a scrapbook, our memories serve as reference to whom and what we are. Relish winter.

The Cold Season

I don't especially like the cold. I prefer warmer temperatures. I'm at the age when I get chilled standing too close to the frozen food section in grocery stores. At its present setting, my body thermostat can handle about 15 minutes of coldness before triggering a goosebump alert.

It wasn't always like this. Once upon a time, I relished cold weather. As a kid, I couldn't wait for winter's snow. As soon as the last autumn leaf was raked and bagged, I'd start planning for wintertime fun. When I was a teenager, I was impervious to cold weather. Rarely did I zip up or button my coat, and I never wore a hat—greasers didn't want a hat messing up their DA. In the '50s, guys would load up with Vitalis or Wildroot, comb it in, and be ready for whatever social occasion came along. I can't speak for those lads, but the stuff I used—Charles Antell's Formula No. 9—set up pretty firm in cold weather. Even icy, off-the-lake blasts couldn't mess it up. It was like wearing a lanolin helmet, so who needed a hat?

Galoshes were out, too. No self-respecting teenage hunk was about to wear galoshes to the Friday night sock hop. We had an image to maintain: open coat, loosely tied scarf, well-oiled hair, and rabbit fur gloves—definitely no boots. As for being cold, that wasn't on the program. Besides, male adolescent hormones rate high in BTU potential, so the onset of cold weather lowered the ignition point, keeping scores of teenage boys from spontaneous combustion.

In high school, one of winter's most anticipated events was ice-skating at the Whiting Park Lagoon. During the summer, the lagoon was home to tennis and softball. In winter, the entire area was flooded, frozen, and transformed into a skater's paradise. Once the ice was ready, the warming house next to the lagoon was opened for skaters to enjoy. A fire in the big iron stove warmed cold feet, frozen toes, and dried clothing wet from snow and ice. The bare wood floor, saturated by melted snow, gave off fine wisps of steam as heat from the iron stove met the moisture of the soaked lumber.

Most of us don't remember days; we remember moments, small snippets of a lifetime that imprint our mind and remain vivid through the years. Some of these moments are of winter evenings, filled with youthful images of days gone by; of classmates and friends who shared carefree moments on a frozen lagoon; the remembrance of athletic skill and limitless energy; and one particular evening when all the pieces of the mosaic came together, transforming the ordinary to extraordinary.

Those moments passed by too quickly. And with the passage of time came changes. As the parade of seasons continues, winter no longer beckons the spirit with the same enthusiasm it did in younger years. Ice skates were long ago sold at a garage sale. Frozen lagoons await the blades of a new generation. And we who shared those times reflect upon them in the comfort of our home by a kitchen table, over a hot cup of tea.

The kitchen clock reads 3:40 AM. I've been up since 2:00 AM, trying to get the upper hand on a cold that has robbed me of sleep for the better part of three nights. I'm heating chicken noodle soup on the stove. Not so much out of hunger, but that my medication must be taken with food. The capsules my doctor prescribed are big enough to require license plates, so I've chosen a noodle chaser. I'm supposed to take all the pills, finishing the bottle over the next few days. I count the capsules. I don't know if I can handle 20 cans of soup.

I turn on the radio and dial up an early morning voice, just loud enough to hear. In between spoonfuls of soup, the weather report says the wind chill index is minus 36 degrees. In the coziness of the warm kitchen, just thinking about the cold makes me shiver. I drift along mental pathways, remembering winters past: midnight shifts at the steel mill; late-night journeys over frozen highways; shoveling snow before dawn; cars that wouldn't start; walking home from Indiana Harbor after the 4:00 to 12:00 shift; playing hockey on Wolf Lake with my buddies from Inland Steel; and ice-skating at Whiting Park with my classmates. Bits and pieces of life. Wintertime.

In the darkened kitchen (illuminated only by the appliances' digital clocks), I finish the soup, take the medication, and quietly listen to the night sounds of our house as it confronts the frigid blast of winter. Soon it will be time to begin another day. Leaving the house, my scarf will be snug, my parka zipped up as high as it will go, my wool cap will cover my head and then some, and I'll even put on my Totes. Why not? After all, image isn't all it's cracked up to be. And besides, I no longer use Formula No. 9, and it is the cold season.

Signs of Spring

The signs are everywhere. Winter has finally packed it in for another year. According to the calendar, it officially ended on March 21, though winter couldn't resist a few nasty last-minute swipes. Now all that unpleasantness is a fast-fading memory. In its place is a new season, and a new beginning. Spring has arrived! The vernal equinox, a delicious and wonderful commencement of nature's promise has made its annual appearance.

Once again, Mother Earth's pledge of renewal to all living creatures and things flourishes with fresh energy and vigor. After a few warm days, the landscape erupts in newness. Everywhere one looks, the eye sees an awakening. Dormant foliage, no longer suppressed by winter's chill, emerges from its keeping place to greet a warming sun.

Spring is heaven's promise of a new season after autumn's last leaf was covered with snow. Spring is fulfillment of Earth's contract with the solar system. Spring is reaffirmation of God's love for a planet's people that, at times, test his supreme patience. But in spite of insensitivity to the environment; disregard for the atmosphere; disruption of wildlife habitats; ambivalence to common ecosystems; arrogance and self-importance; and all manners of human disrespect, spring returns to offer another opportunity to make things better. Spring is another chance to begin anew. The season of spring is love that few can understand.

Once the weather turns warm, all signs of spring parade for attention. Eager to enjoy the additional daylight, we "spring forward" one hour, adjusting clocks to extend sunlight further into evening's timeslot. This daylight-saving time is filled with every activity imaginable.

As if on cue, baby carriages and strollers appear uptown as young moms proudly present the newest member of their family. Little Leaguers and sandlot stars walk with bats resting on young shoulders, gloves hooked on the wrist of their free hand as they make their way to the field of dreams; jaws filled with bubble gum, they're tomorrow's promise. On neighborhood streets, tricycles, bicycles, Rollerblades, and skateboards roll and glide young pilots to no particular destination. Sidewalks become chalked game boards and concrete canvases as young children display both athletic and artistic ability.

Uniforms of the season are shirtsleeves, shorts, and sneakers; if you're really cool, a cap—worn backwards, of course. Winter clothes are sent to be dry-cleaned. Closets are cleaned along with the rest of the house. Windows are washed, patios swept, rugs shampooed, and floors waxed as winter's grime gives way to the season of cleanliness.

The quiet of an early spring morning is disturbed by flocks of returning geese, gossiping about their vacation as they display the formation of their favorite alphabetical letter. At ground level, there are garage sales galore, backyard barbecues, and restful moments on the porch swing.

Springtime is hardware store heaven as homeowners sweep, scrape, sand, paint, and fix up their domestic castle. More creative householders bypass the do-it-yourself scene by handing their spouse the Yellow Pages as they head to the golf course to conquer challenging sand traps and putting greens. "Gone Fishing" becomes the plan of the day.

Spring cures cabin fever. Residents kept indoors by winter weather welcome the warmth. Once more they begin preparing gardens, develop weed attack strategies, initiate lawn care, and wash the car. Spring signals transition: from storm windows to screens, from furnace to air-conditioner, from snow blower storage to lawn mower debut.

Spring brings weather with an attitude. Some days are cloudy and sunless. Other days roar in with strong winds, cold rain, and a few snow flurries for garnish. Just when one stops to check the calendar, bright blue skies arrive with a warm, gentle breeze. As expected, April showers visit regularly, providing raindrops playful opportunities on windowpanes. Sidewalk puddles ripple from the wind like fluid mirrors, as a few hearty songbirds sing in the springtime shower.

In high school classrooms, teenagers afflicted with spring fever try to snooze their way through class, saving their energy and enthusiasm for the important stuff after school. Thoughts turn to formals, tuxedos, limos, and the prom.

Throughout the community, sights and sounds announce the season. Playgrounds and schoolyards resound with the voices and laughter of children. Along Main Street and at shopping centers, parking spaces are in short supply. Parks have greened, flower buds eagerly soak up nourishment from the sun, and wildlife scurries about. The season of spring is universal; one size fits all. It's spring—enjoy!

Halloween

Years ago, Halloween was a big deal in my hometown of Whiting, Indiana. Festivities began with an early evening parade down 119th Street and culminated with a rally at the Whiting Community Center.

Parade participants assembled on Community Court, in front of the Center. By 6:30 PM, hundreds of costumed youngsters eagerly awaited the signal to begin. Local police and fire department units added to the evening's excitement as the procession of goblins, ghosts, and characters of every persuasion displayed their disguises through downtown Whiting. Accompanying the youngest masked trick-or-treaters were scores of moms and dads, older brothers and sisters in tow. The annual Whiting Halloween parade was truly a family affair.

Along the parade route, judges selected individuals for the costume contest by handing out cards to present at the post-parade rally in the Community Center's auditorium. Prizes were awarded in several boy and girl age group categories. Admission to the rally was free, and upon entering, each child was given a numbered ticket. That way, every kid from the community had a chance to win a prize. A favorite award was two free passes to the Hoosier Theater.

Traditionally, the post-parade celebration featured several events. Because contestants were chosen at random to participate, each kid looked at their ticket stub and listened while Andy Yanas, the Center's manager, called out numbers as he pulled them from a drum. There was a cider-drinking contest, where super-thirsty kids guzzled apple cider until filled to the gills. Next was the cracker-eating-and-whistling contest; each contestant was provided with a substantial supply of saltine crackers to eat and swallow before attempting to whistle. The first clear whistle won. Andy also served as judge, and to the best of my recollection, no one ever argued with the judge!

As soon as stray cracker crumbs were swept away, large galvanized laundry tubs filled with cold water were moved on stage. A dozen apples bobbed in each tub. With four kids to a tub, the object was for one of the sharp-toothed youngsters to take a bite out of the chilled Washington Red Delicious. At the sound of Andy's whistle, heads and faces hit the water, trying to capture the elusive bobbing fruit. In their quest to win, heads would occasionally collide, bouncing around more than the apples. By this time, the entire audience was in a frenzy!

The grand finale was the costume contest. Contestants would line up on the stage and one of the judge's helpers would hold their hand over each contestant's head; this was the signal for the crowd to cheer. The loudest cheer was named the winner. If there was a close call, a cheer-off was held. By then, the kid-filled auditorium was really rocking. Just before the crowd reached its point of exhaustion, Judge Yanas made his decision. The winner was awarded free tickets to the Hoosier Theater, along with a certificate and a $5.00 prize. Back in the early '50s, $5 was heavy, heavy money; it was real foldin' dough.

After the rally, most kids headed home, the result of a clever promotion set up by Whiting officials. As a way to encourage kids to be off the streets, thwarting their proclivity for mischief, the Community Center sponsored a pumpkin-seed-guessing contest. A week before Halloween, kids would register their guess of the number of seeds inside a large pumpkin on display at the Center's front desk. First prize was also $5.00, but the winner had to be home to receive the phone call at 9:30 PM. Halloween contest winners were then featured in the next issue of *The Times Grafic*, Whiting's hometown newspaper, complete with story and pictures. To a kid, having a picture in the local paper was a big deal, and those that won thoroughly enjoyed their brief moment in the celebrity spotlight. That didn't mean that every kid went home. Enough trick-or-treaters roamed around town, activating resident doorbells and making stray cats nervous, to make things interesting. But overall, the youthful silliness was tolerable.

Today, Halloween engenders caution. Children are now carefully monitored as they trick-or-treat through familiar neighborhoods to keep them from harm. Trick-or-treat time is scheduled during daylight or dusk hours to guard against darkness-generated mishap. In some cities, curfews are put in place for the duration of Halloween in an attempt to reduce lawlessness and violence. And some towns restrict sales of spray paint and alcohol until after Halloween.

Too many misguided citizens use Halloween as license for arson, destruction of property, disobedience, and civil disorder. For some twisted reason, they put civilized behavior on hold until their destructive behavior runs its course. Perhaps these maladjusted individuals could be taken to a fast-food restaurant and forced to bob for french fries!

It's too bad we can't return to less complicated times. Maybe kids today wouldn't be interested in this stuff, but I suspect a lot of adult-kids would once again enjoy swigging cider, whistling through crackers, and bobbing for applies (no dentures, please!). As for prizes, free passes to the Hoosier aren't the draw they once were, and Hot Dog Louie's chili is no longer on the menu, but how about a sack full of White Castle Slyders with extra onion and pickle (and a gift box of Rolaids)? This may never happen, but just in case, I'm going to check out some costumes. Catch you later.

Thanksgiving

With the annual Thanksgiving holiday upon us, I thought it would be a good time to reflect on this past year and extend a personal note of appreciation as we celebrate our nation's bounty. Still, when one considers the turmoil and problems throughout the world—including the United States—any celebration of bounty seems hollow, blemished with human suffering.

In our country, tough economic times, unemployment, job insecurity, rising healthcare costs, escalating insurance premiums, unstable energy supplies, homelessness, dysfunctional families, unwanted and abused children, illegal drug use, AIDS, political corruption, poverty, rampant social and domestic violence, the war on terror, disillusionment with government, displacement, and weather-related destruction—in addition to a marked erosion of national character—portend "unthankfulness."

Disturbingly, most agree that this is just the tip of the iceberg. Yet as a nation, we officially set aside time to mark a day of thanksgiving. Why? Because by doing so, by celebrating this national day of thanks, we replenish and nourish our national spirit, thus reaffirming the legacy of America's founders. When we acknowledge the plentiful goodness and fruitful blessings of this land, we validate the values and qualities that give us strength, sustenance, and purpose; we refill our hearts with compassion, gratitude, and uncommon empathy.

Each Thanksgiving, countless citizens spend the holiday helping the less fortunate, bringing comfort to muted lives and dispelling shadows that beat down and bruise the human spirit. These ordinary Americans work in extraordinary ways, sharing their blessings with those in need. The vast majority of Americans, however, will mark this special day by gathering with friends and family, enjoying the traditional turkey dinner in the comfort of their home.

Because of heaven's kindness, my family has been abundantly blessed with laughter, love, good health, and good fortune. There is much to be thankful for:

- Our family, our home, and all the happiness that brings
- Having a clean bed in which to sleep

- A warm house in winter, a cool house in summer, and all those comfortable days in between

- The support of loved ones; knowing that I'm not alone, that I can always count on them

- The healing sound of laughter

- All the gadgets and gizmos that make modern living easier

- Farmers who work the soil and all who harvest the bounty that fills our table

- The collective creative genius of America: inventors, engineers, builders, technicians, and all special people whose vision of a better world benefits us all

- The comfort and familiarity of home and hometown, and the sense of belonging

- Family, friends, and classmates who helped me over the rough spots while growing up

- My parents, who taught their children how to work, how to pray, and how to live positive, constructive lives

- America's Founding Fathers, whose genius is evident in the Declaration of Independence, the Constitution, and the Bill of Rights

- The countless pioneers of every generation, whose courage helped build America; they, too, share our thanksgiving

- The opportunity each day to improve our circumstance.

- The ultimate gift that America presents to her citizens: sovereignty.

When Thanksgiving Day arrives, take a few moments, and in your own words—in your own way—give thanks for the blessings of our land and this past year. Cherish the moments, treasure your loved ones, and share a cup of kindness with someone. Many people are struggling to survive. Help those you can, pray for those in need, and give heartfelt thanks for heaven's kindness.

May this Thanksgiving bring you peace, health, and bounty. Happy Thanksgiving!

A Special Letter to Santa

Dear Santa:

Even though I haven't written to you in a long time, I hope you will do your best to fill my Christmas wish list. Maybe you thought I'd stopped writing to you because I was upset about the Christmas you didn't stop by my house with a lot of toys when I was a little boy. I'm not. Mom told me many times how busy you are on Christmas Eve, and that some children need you more than others. She told me, too, that when you're not able to stop by, you leave a special gift with the Christmas Angel to place in our hearts. Thanks, Santa. I've treasured those presents most of all.

Though I'm now a senior citizen, I trust I'm not too old to send in my letter, and I hope it's not too late. I know you'll do everything you can to fill my requests. To help you out a little bit, I'd better bring you up to date on some things. When I first wrote to you, I was short and chubby—a mop head with brown hair. Today you might not know me. I'm a little taller, considerably more than chubby, and my brown mop head has become a sparsely seeded test site for Grecian Formula. Only the Lone Ranger has more silver than me. Nevertheless, I'm confident that you'll be able to recognize me. So, Santa, here is what I'd like for Christmas:

- I'd like to be 10 years old again—just for a couple of hours. Summertime would be preferable, during Little League season. And Santa, could you fix it so I'd get a hit?

- I'd like to take my dad to a White Sox game; they were his favorite team. Box seats behind the Sox's dugout, and have the White Sox win the game. Pop would really like that!

- I'd like to spend a little time back in high school with the whole gang—nothing extravagant, mind you—just a day here and there: Go to a football game on Friday, a dance on Saturday; maybe spend a couple of periods in Taylor's Spanish class, Ulrich's English class, or McClure's Machine Shop class, or…well, you get the idea. Surprise me!

312

- I'd like to meet my wife again for the first time, and enjoy all those moments once more.

- I'd like to take Mom grocery shopping one more time. Her item analysis and pricing comparisons were delightful!

- I'd like a chance to go back and clean up some messes I made while growing up. And perhaps I could use your special eraser to remove some of the misspoken words and boneheaded deeds that are on my permanent record.

- I'd like to spend a summer's day as a young kid, fishing at Wolf Lake. If that isn't possible, change seasons, and substitute one of the hockey games I played there with boyhood friends. And this time, Santa, is it okay if I score a goal?

- I'd like to go back to seventh grade, long enough to sing "Silent Night" at midnight Mass on Christmas Eve with the boys' choir at Sacred Heart Church.

- And as long as we're in the area, Santa, I'd like to serve a Latin Mass for Father Daniels.

- I'd like to spend time with some very special people who aren't here anymore, and tell them how much they've meant to me.

Just in case you're not able to fill my wish list, Santa, kindly pass my name along to the Christmas Angel for one of those special presents. Please be sure to mention my current address; remember, I moved since the last time I wrote to you.

Well, Santa, thanks for reading my letter. I'll see to it that milk and cookies are placed by the tree. Merry Christmas!

Sincerely,
Al

Christmas Treasure

Tucked away in attics throughout America (for those fortunate to have an attic) is the surplus of living: seasonal decorations, knickknacks wrapped in old newspapers, books, household records, heirlooms, and outgrown toys and other kid things. The attic offers a convenient resting place for stuff too valuable to throw away, too useful to sell at a garage sale, and too sentimental to part with. Like cellars of yesteryear, attics provide handy storage—a catchall for whatever. In no time at all, the attic becomes a family's time capsule.

In our attic, dozens of boxes of various sizes fill the space between floor and rafter. Each box, printed with black felt-tip marker, identifies ownership and contents. There are, however, several boxes with no identification. Even so, my family knows that these well-used, dog-eared, kinda-beat-up cardboard cartons contain my stuff. Without tag or title, it's understood these corrugated treasure chests are mine.

Around this time each year, I go into the attic, open one particular box, place the contents on the plywood floor and, in the unheated attic, take inventory. The items within this paper vault have little or no cash value. Assorted papers, special letters, keepsake birthday greetings, long-ago graduation cards, get-well wishes from colleagues when illness forced an extended respite from teaching, and a variety of cards from family, friends, and loved ones fill the major portion of the box. But near the bottom in one corner are the "diamonds." Still wrapped in festive Christmas paper and tied with narrow red ribbon are several small packages marked "For Santa."

I carefully remove them from the security of the paper strongbox, and hold them in my hand—touching, feeling their shape and texture—as my eyes, once again, savor the feast of childhood past. Sitting alone in the quiet of a December chilled attic, I recall the images and voices of earlier days, when our children were quite young and filled the season of Christmas with their excitement and wonder. Illuminated in the bare-bulb lighted enclosure, amid the boxed inventory of our family, the remembered magic of a special Christmas beckons the heart.

With Christmas but a few days away, our children were full of joyous anticipation. They constantly checked the tree's ornaments and lights, touching tinsel and needled branches, asking questions about Christmas and Santa Claus. They listened in awed silence to the story of the First Christmas. Surrounded by family in a warm secure home, perhaps they did not fully understand the plight of Joseph and Mary that long ago night in Bethlehem, but they knew they were loved and cared for like the soon-to-be-born child Jesus.

We also read *The Night Before Christmas* to them, that ageless account of St. Nick's visit to all good boys and girls. With Christmas just around the corner, there wasn't any doubt—when it came to Santa Claus, they believed! Days before, each of our four children selected a favorite stocking to hang where Santa would be sure to find it. With their letters to Santa's North Pole headquarters already mailed, all was ready for the Night of Nights.

For parents with young children, Christmas is magic. Without question, it's the high point of parenting. Sharing their childlike wonder, seeing the look of expectation in their eyes, giving freely a full measure of genuine love and goodness fills the heart with the happiness and joy of angels.

By Christmas Eve at bedtime, everything was in place. Stockings were hanging by the tree, waiting to be filled. Near the stockings on a table was a tray with several cookies and a glass of cold milk. After baths, evening prayers, a bedtime story, and goodnight kisses, we tucked them in bed. As I walked into the front room, I noticed something on the cookie tray: three small gift-wrapped packages with red ribbon. Underneath was a note addressed to Santa.

As one of Santa's helpers, I carefully picked up the note and read the words. It was from our daughter, Christine: "Dear Santa, here are some pieces of wood for you to take back to the North Pole to make toys for next year. Thanks for coming. I hope you like chocolate chip cookies. Merry Christmas."

Early Christmas morning, four wide-eyed children in pajamas surveyed the Currier & Ives-like scene. Presents were piled under the tree, stockings bulged with goodies, and an empty glass was all that remained on the tray. Obviously, Santa had enjoyed his late night-snack and had taken the wrapped pieces of wood back to his North Pole workshop.

Actually, that's not exactly true. Oh, Santa enjoyed the cookies and milk all right, but he caught me peeking by the door. Calling me over to the tree, he handed the small packages to me, along with my daughter's note. Then he reached inside his big red parka and gave me the letters the kids had sent him. With a twinkle in his eye, he said, "You keep these. They're Christmas treasures." Then he was gone. I did as Santa asked, and kept them in a special place.

Today our children are all grown up; as far as I know, they haven't written to Santa for some time, nor have they gift-wrapped wood for his workshop. But each year, the treasures of Christmas past awaken magical moments, and once more the wonder of childhood touches the heart.

Little Star

Long, long ago, when the heavens were being assembled, the Starmaker called upon his angels to arrange the galaxies and assign the various solar systems. The angels had an almost limitless inventory of stars from which to choose. Nevertheless, competition to select the finest stars was formidable, as each angel wanted their assigned portion of the heavens to shine more brightly than any other. Such rivalry made the Starmaker smile. Unbeknownst to his angels, he kept a single star in reserve for a special assignment, and now the time had come.

All the chosen stars boasted about their position and power. Proud to be the center of solar systems, each one burned intensely, providing eons of life-giving warmth and light. Soon the heavens were ablaze with billions and billions of stars, gathered in clustered arrays, pinwheel spirals, and disc-shaped bowls, while others were randomly scattered about like celestial gems twinkling in the night.

Now the Starmaker went to the special keeping place of the single star. With a loving smile, He beckoned the Little Star to come forward. The Little Star was timid. Unlike solar system-sized stars, this star's light was delicate and fragile. Rather than a full corona, the Little Star focused its energy in a laser-like shaft of blue-white light. The Little Star understood why the angels had left him behind; heaven needed to be flooded with light, and his single ray of starlight was not suited for the vastness of the universe.

"I'm giving you a special assignment," the Starmaker said.

"But my light is not strong enough to light any part of heaven," the Little Star protested.

"On the contrary, Little Star, your light will be more powerful than all the others, for it will shine brightly in hearts and souls everywhere," the Starmaker said reassuringly. "I have chosen you to be the star of Bethlehem, the single light announcing the birth of Jesus. You will become the Christmas Star, light of lights. You will guide shepherds and Magi to the manger. Your brightness will announce 'Peace on Earth, Good Will Toward Men.' The warmth of your fire will nourish those in need, give hope to those who despair, strengthen those weary in spirit, and heal the brokenhearted. You, Little Star, will be the brightest star in all of heaven!"

And so it came to pass in the town of Bethlehem, amid straw in a manger upon a barren dirt floor, a child was born unto the world—the Prince of Peace. As Joseph looked upon his wife Mary and their newborn son, an all-encompassing love touched their hearts. High above, the light from a brightly shining star washed the manger in gentle warmth. As the Starmaker promised, the Little Star served as a beacon for shepherds and Magi, and became the brightest star in all of heaven.

May the Light of Christmas nourish you and your loved ones, now and always.

Once Upon a Christmas

Once upon a time, long, long ago, at an oasis several miles from a desert town called Sidon, a slave girl gave birth to a baby boy. The boy's father was a nomad merchant who traveled from settlement to settlement, oasis to oasis, with any convenient caravan. When he saw his newborn son was disfigured, he disavowed any kinship or responsibility, cursing both child and mother and abandoning them both.

Awaking to find the caravan and the baby's father gone, the boy's mother was left alone to care for her child. For a while she stayed at the oasis, working long hours sewing and mending blankets and robes for meager scraps of food. She soon realized, however, that both of them could not survive on what little nourishment she provided. In desperation, she convinced a couple who had stopped at the oasis on their way to Tyre to take her child. Apprehensively, the wife cradled the baby in her arms. She noticed his malformed leg and disfigured mouth. "What is his name?" she asked. With tear-filled downcast eyes, the baby's mother whispered, "Joseus."

The couple took Joseus to Tyre, but left after a few months to live in the town of Nazareth. In Nazareth, the boy was teased and ridiculed. His withered left leg gave him an awkward gait and his harelip, a grotesque smile. The couple had been married more than 10 years. Even though they were of some wealth, their marriage had not been blessed with a child. Then unexpectedly, she became pregnant. Joseus was now an embarrassment. Initially, they accepted the child out of pity. But after several years of caring for the slave-girl's illegitimate son, and with their first child on the way, Joseus had become a liability, both socially and financially. So one day, without warning, the couple sold Joseus to nomads on their way to Ramalla.

Ramalla was a dark, foreboding place. After his arrival there, Joseus was bought and sold three times. Now 8 years old, he was conscripted by a camel trader to clean livestock pens and stables. Joseus worked long, hard hours. His compensation included discarded clothing and leftover food scraps. Sometimes his hunger would be so great that he'd poach animal food from the barn's feeding

319

bins. More often than not, Joseus went to sleep hungry and slept on hay alongside the animals.

One evening, he overheard his master's plan to sell him. Filled with fear, Joseus fled first to Jerusalem. Then after begging for alms in the streets there, he made his way to Bethlehem. Joseus was now 12 years of age.

By chance, he found work at an inn. In the adjacent stable, he cared for both the innkeeper's and travelers' livestock. Occasionally, his duties included sweeping the storeroom and entryway clean. For his daily toil, Joseus earned two small coins. Alone, late at night in the inn's storeroom, seated at a bare wooden table, he supped. In the corner was a straw mat on which he slept.

It had been an unusually busy day. Travelers from near and far had filled every vacant room. Throughout the day, Joseus had limped up and down narrow stairs, assisting patrons with their satchels and belongings. The knee of his withered leg throbbed and ached. He heard taunts from unkind customers who mocked his features and speech. By nightfall, he was exhausted, too tired to attend to the inn's livestock. He sank spent to his mat, and in spite of a blinding headache, fell fast asleep. Almost immediately, the innkeeper kicked him awake. "Go put clean hay about the stable. I told a couple they could spend the night there. The inn is full."

Joseus dragged himself to the stable. As quickly as his fatigued, aching body allowed, he placed new straw and fresh hay in a manger that was near the center of the stable. He was struggling to keep his balance with a large bale when a kind voice filled his ears: "This will do fine, son."

Joseus turned and looked into the gentle eyes of a man leading a donkey. Seated on the beast of burden was a beautiful young woman, great with child. Carefully, the husband helped her down. With unimaginable peacefulness, the mother-to-be reclined on the straw blanket next to the manger. Joseus heard the husband's prayerful whisper: "The time is at hand."

For what seemed like only a moment, Joseus turned away. When his eyes fell back upon the lady, he was awestruck! There, lying in the manger, wrapped in swaddling clothes, was a newborn baby boy. An all-encompassing love filled the stable. The boy's mother beckoned Joseus to come close to the manger. Gently, she took her son's tiny hand and touched Joseus' face. She smiled and cradled her son close to her bosom. Joseus withdrew to a corner of the stable. Using his hands as a rake, he made a haphazard bed of straw and fell fast asleep.

Sometime during the night, Joseus was made whole. He awoke to find his withered leg fully developed and strong. His reflection in a trough of water was that of a handsome young man with near-perfect features. He felt unrestrained forgiveness and unfathomable love. He bore no anger to those who had been so unkind to him. For the first time in his life, he was at peace. From that moment, Joseus promised to serve others with kindness, goodness, decency, and love.

In the silent night of an inn's stable, the gift of the First Christmas was bestowed upon a disfigured stable boy. Today, more than 2000 years later, the gift of the First Christmas is given to us—the gift of his love. May the gift of Christmas enrich and nourish all our days. Merry Christmas, everyone.

Christmas Remembered

Why do we remember certain times? Every now and then during the course of one's lifetime, we experience events imprinted so indelibly on our mind that they stay fresh and vibrant throughout the course of our lives. And no matter the number of our years, these memories remain as vivid and as new as if they'd happened yesterday. This is how it is with the season of Christmas. Let me tell you about one in particular.

The year was 1946, and money was scarce. I remember waking up that Christmas morning and going into the parlor to see if Santa Claus had stopped by. It had been a tough year for our family. A near fatal illness had struck my baby sister, and the medical bills incurred during her treatment had drained the meager savings my parents had managed to tuck away. New clothes were out of the question, so everything I wore was either mended up or a hand-me-down from an older brother.

The four-room garage flat where the six of us lived was crowded and cramped. But now at Christmas, it seemed empty because there weren't any ornaments, lights, or tree. Soup had become the main staple of our diet; meat was a commodity that only occasionally visited our dinner table. Countless times I watched my mother lovingly mold the dough that she made into noodles for the soup. Beef bones, along with chicken parts that Colonel Sanders would have rejected, were used as stock for the broth. A few sliced carrots were added to garnish the liquid meal.

The night before Christmas was always special. We were allowed to stay up until 9:00 PM, a full hour past our usual bedtime. Just before we climbed into our beds, we would kneel at the bedside to say our evening prayers. Either Mom or Dad would kneel alongside us and guide us through the words that they'd taught us. Tonight we prayed with Dad.

And tonight, because it was Christmas Eve, a special story was read. After we'd pulled up the covers, the small bed lamp would remain on, offering enough light for Mom or Dad to read by. This night, Mom read the story of the First Christmas to us. As I lay in my warm bed, loved and cared for, listening to the plight of Mary and Joseph, I tried to understand why they weren't allowed to enter the inn. Knowing how cold it was outside my bedroom window, I shivered just thinking about Mary and Joseph having to sleep in a manger on beds of cold straw. I knew I wouldn't have liked being outside in the darkness with nowhere to go and with no one to take care of me.

I pulled the covers tight under my chin. Somewhere between the birth of Jesus and the arrival of the Wise Men, I drifted off to sleep. Mom's voice had a soothing, gentle quality, and I fell asleep many times listening to that sound. I often had the feeling that someone hugged me as I slept. Then in what seemed like an instant, I was awakened simultaneously by my brother shaking the bed and Bing Crosby's voice coming out of the Crosley radio in the kitchen.

I ran to where I had pinned my stocking by the front door, so Santa would be sure to find it. Sure enough, inside that mended old sock were an orange and one red apple. The single gift left by Santa was a Monopoly game that my two older brothers and I were to share. I can still see the smiles and appreciative looks on my brothers' faces as we unfolded the game board and set up the pieces.

That was a long time ago. I don't see my siblings very often these days, and we find it difficult to get together and visit as a family. Until Mom passed away in 1990, she made soup. She still added sliced carrots, but would use the more "respectable" parts of the chicken for her soup; store-bought, they came in a bag. Dad died in 1965. He's been gone 40 years, and I still miss him. I tell you this because it's Christmas, and these memories are part of Christmas. As I grow older, the parade of seasons seems to quicken, and I wonder what times my children will keep for their memories; I wonder what treasures they will keep for their hearts.

As I said, money was scarce in 1946. It was the sparsest Christmas we ever shared as a family, but it's the one I remember most. It was the best Christmas, the best one of all.

A Tree for Christmas

As the Christmas season shifts into high gear, the annual task of buying a Christmas tree assumes top priority. Many people solve the dilemma of searching for the perfect tree by purchasing an artificial one. Though they look remarkably realistic, I prefer a real, grown-in-the-ground tree. Even news of pine beetle infestations has not deterred my desire for the real thing. I'm willing to put up with the additional visiting wildlife rather than have a phony tree.

I've made this choice based on solid, practical reasoning. I'm well aware that artificial trees have some positive features: flame-retardant, non-allergenic, symmetrically balanced, non-fading colors, easy to assemble, disassemble and store. I know, too, that artificial trees are more economical and cost-effective, and can last a lifetime without dropping a single needle. Some trees are accessorized with pine-scenting aerosols to give the tree an "authentic pine-forest fragrance." I know all that. But even so, I prefer real to fake.

The major reason for my allegiance to natural Christmas trees is how the phony trees are made. Some branches for artificial trees are manufactured using the same machines that make household brushes. To produce yuletide boughs, only the color of the bristle material is changed. After assembly, it may look like a Christmas tree, but to tech-smart consumers, the product is nothing more than a 6-foot-tall green brush on a stand. It just isn't the same, trying to light and decorate a gigantic brush.

Besides, tree hunting is a joyful yuletide tradition. Checking out fir trees on cold December days is what it's all about. If the tree shopper is lucky, a snowstorm will serve as companion while the search for the perfect tree continues from lot to lot.

In earlier years, my annual Christmas tree search included taking along the kids. As teenagers, they had determined their assistance was required because of a certain tree I once bought unchaperoned. After methodically scrutinizing my prized conifer, they agreed that Dad was never to buy another Christmas tree unless one of them was present. They teased me about buying a deformed tree, but I said it had character. I had to agree, though; by any arboretum standard, that particular tree was definitely unique.

For years, whenever it was Christmas-tree-buying time, we'd go to a dozen places and look at trees. Day, night, cold, wind, sleet, snow—it didn't make any difference; we were on a mission and would not be deterred by the elements. At each lot, we'd check for bare spots, needle size, bushiness, straightness, height, freshness, and finally, price. Before making our choice, several unsuspecting evergreens had received a thorough physical exam. Finally, we'd select the perfect tree and take it home.

Then one year, in a moment of reckless abandon, we bought a tree on the spur of the moment. My wife and I had gone shopping that Saturday morning, but had not planned on buying a tree. However, while driving past a shopping center on the way home, we noticed Christmas trees being sold by a local charity organization as a fundraiser.

I parked the pick-up and we took a quick scan of the available trees, all priced at $20 each. Looking further, I noticed a lone tree leaning against a parking lot light pole. At first glance, it looked good. It was the right height, bushy and full, smelled fresh, and had the preferred needles—but no price. On closer inspection, I realized why it had been separated from the rest; the trunk was gnarled and bent in two places, and was out of plumb in three different directions. No matter how one tried, the tree stood crooked. I asked the guy in charge about the tree. "We put it over there because it's deformed," he said.

"How much?" I asked, holding up the pine-green pretzel.

"You want that one? It's crooked!"

"Yep. How much for this crooked tree?"

The guy behind the card table said, "Make me an offer."

"Eight bucks."

"Eight?"

"Listen," I said, "no one will buy this crooked tree, and it'll wind up on the scrap heap. I think this little gem deserves a chance to be a Christmas tree. How 'bout it? Eight bucks."

"Sold!"

Well, the pine-green pretzel worked out just fine, even though it took three support wires tacked to the windowsill to keep it vertical. Once fully trimmed and decorated, it was a terrific Christmas tree. As the kids placed lights and hung ornaments, they were extra careful not to disturb its delicate balance. While decorating, though, they questioned the wisdom of the tree buyer. But in the end, I was right.

Christmas is a time to share and build moments and memories with those you care for and love the most. The unwanted bent and crooked fir tree I brought home became more than a celebrity that Christmas. It symbolized what we all want—an opportunity to show our best. And if someone will look past our flaws, give a little support, and have faith in our potential, we, too, can become quite special. Try and get that from an artificial tree!

New Year's Resolutions: A Proposal

In a few days, another year will be history. As usual, year-end parties will help close out the old and usher in the new. Amid the musical strains of "Auld Lang Syne," millions of resolutions will be made. But in spite of one's best intentions, most of these New Year's promises will fall by the wayside and wither before the end of the first month. Commitments to lose weight, stop smoking, exercise regularly, and cut back on alcohol are the resolutions most frequently made. But unless one is part of a group with similar goals, we tend to "fudge" on our commitment. When part of a group, the resolve to achieve a goal is stronger. Perhaps that is what we need to do on a national basis.

As a nation, we should resolve to accomplish something each year. Throughout the United States, citizens could select and subscribe to "The National New Year's Resolution Coalition." If there truly is strength in numbers, think how strong the commitment to achieve a goal would be when supported by almost 300 million Americans!

History has shown that when we put our collective energies into a project, we are highly successful. Every day we witness groups working together to achieve a common goal. If such commitment can be accomplished on a local level, why not nationwide? Why can't we, as a nation, select one or more of our major problems and decide to solve it? Many people are content to wait for the government to solve these problems. All too often we forget that we are the government, and therefore we must be the problem-solvers.

Granted, there are problems facing our country which seem insurmountable, unsolvable. But by working together—focused, in every positive, constructive way—even these problems can be solved. Imagine the possibilities. What would happen if on January 1, we made the following commitments as a nation, and resolved to:

- Offer kindness instead of meanness.
- Respect and protect the dignity and sacredness of life, from the unborn to the most elderly.

- Put down the gun.
- Make children our most important priority.
- Place quality ahead of quantity.
- Share instead of grab.
- Give instead of take.
- Heal instead of hurt.
- Pray instead of curse.
- Help instead of hinder.
- Build instead of destroy.
- Teach instead of torment.
- Love instead of hate.
- Trust instead of distrust.
- Honor instead of dishonor.
- Respect instead of disrespect.
- Help Mom with the dishes!

Soon another New Year will be presented to the world. Once again, we have an opportunity to make things better. In addition to losing weight, giving up cigarettes, exercising, and cutting back on booze, perhaps some of the resolutions listed above will be considered, too. Happy New Year, everyone.

Koch's Choice

Bulletproof Fudge

My wife and I were married on June 19, 1965. In 2005, we celebrated our 40th anniversary. In this day and age, such a milestone is no small achievement. Somehow during the past four decades, we've managed to nurture and sustain the essential ingredients for a successful marriage: trust, honor, respect, unselfishness, humor, and love. Admittedly, things are better that I deserve, and I've never had a better time. Perhaps this is one of the benefits of building and sharing a lifetime together. I hope so.

As newlyweds we made a promise to love and honor each other, for better or for worse, in sickness and in health, for richer or for poorer. We added one more: To always choose laughter over tears when things don't turn out as planned. Early in our marriage, this additional vow was put to the test. Case in point: the bulletproof fudge.

According to the directions on the box, making fudge is easy—foolproof, even. Encouraged by those words from the manufacturer, my young bride decided to make a batch. The box continued: "In a heavy gauge saucepan, combine 7 oz. of marshmallow cream, 1 ½ cups of sugar, 2/3 cup of evaporated milk, ¼ cup of butter, and ¼ teaspoon of salt. While stirring constantly, bring this mixture to a full, rolling boil. Let it boil for about five minutes, stirring constantly. Then, after removing it from the heat, add in 1 cup of semisweet chocolate and 2 cups of milk chocolate. At this point, add a cup of chopped walnuts, a teaspoon of vanilla, and blend it all together. Lastly, pour this delicious-smelling mixture into a baking pan, and let chill until firm." Nothing to it. Piece of cake. (I mean fudge.)

To this very day, my wife contends she followed the recipe correctly. But for reasons unknown, the ingredients refused to cooperate. Later that evening, my wife went to prepare the fudge for serving by cutting it into small squares, like the picture on the box. Hearing her summons, I went into the kitchen.

"Whad'ya need?" I inquired.

"I can't get the fudge out of the pan—and that was a gift from my mother. It's my best Pyrex baking dish!"

I tried. The knife never made a mark. The fudge wouldn't budge. This is ridiculous, I thought. How do you get stuck fudge out of a glass dish?

As husband and "king of the castle," I immediately took command of the situation. After all, I was a high school graduate, a card-carrying machinist, and an avid reader of *Popular Mechanics*; this problem was right up my technical alley.

I turned the dish upside down and gently tapped the glass bottom. Nothing. I ran warm tap water over the bottom surface, and then tapped. Nothing. I tried to slide the blade of a knife along the outside edge of the solid chocolate. Nothing. Finally I decided to soak the Pyrex dish in hot water in the basement laundry tub. Nothing. That did it! No more Mr. Nice Guy. This was war! And in war you're forced to make tough decisions. My wife decided that the Pyrex Mommy-gift had to be saved; the fudge was expendable!

I came up with a plan to drown the fudge. I filled the laundry tub with enough hot water to more than cover the glass dish. For the next two days it sat submerged—and defied me. Two-and-a-half pounds of coalesced fudge remained arrogantly constipated, stubbornly clinging to its glass fortress.

Then on the third day (sounds almost biblical, doesn't it?) the fudge rose from its watery grave. A solid monolithic slab of fused chocolate floated to the surface. I was ecstatic! I had gained the "inevitable triumph"!

Now that the Pyrex dish had been rescued, what to do with the tombstone of crystallized fudge? I discovered that it wouldn't warp, crack, split, break, or bend. It was also impervious to power tools. Because municipal laws barred testing with firearms or explosives, I had to assume it was bulletproof!

Not wanting to waste good ingredients, we placed the epoxy-like fudge where the neighborhood wildlife could enjoy a sweet-tooth snack. We watched rib-tickling comedy as birds pecked and hammered away with their beaks trying to chip off a flake of the succulent mixture. Nothing. Bewildered birds squawked their frustration, circled, dove, attacked, and were knocked senseless. Brown and gray squirrels broke teeth in a gnawing frenzy, attempting to free the walnut morsels trapped in the rock-hard chocolate. Dogs, cats, and creatures of all descriptions tried to unlock the vault of sweetness—still nothing.

Finally a scruffy, street-smart mongrel with a cast-iron stomach and an abundance of scavenging experience had the answer. Using his tongue as a rasp, he licked his way to glucose ecstasy. It took him the better part of a month to wear a hole through the slab of fudge. But as each day ended, we'd watch a very weary mutt stroll away from the tasty treasure with a contented look on his face. What started out as a stovetop disaster turned into a laugh riot!

During 40 years of marriage, a couple shares all the emotions and experiences of life. It's this sharing that bonds a couple together. Today our marriage is as solid and sweet as that bulletproof fudge. Sometimes when we're walking and holding hands, my wife will catch me smiling or laughing. She looks at me and asks: "What's so funny?" I take a long look in her eyes and answer, "Fudge."

My Favorite Things

In the movie *The Sound of Music*, there's a song entitled "My Favorite Things." Each of us has a personal list of favorite things that brings us pleasure whenever they're encountered or remembered. Over the years, I've added to my list, each additional entry enriching the sweetness that floods the mind at their recall. Most have become treasured memories, welcomed like good friends:

- The sweet-sad season of autumn, when the leaves of summer show off new fall colors
- The aroma of freshly ground coffee
- The lonesome voice of a steam locomotive's whistle in the night
- The carefree clapping of a wooden screen door, applauding another summer
- Picturing my Mom in the kitchen making noodles for her homemade soup
- The smell of freshly laundered clothes hanging outside to dry
- The captivating incense of burning autumn leaves
- The contagious laughter of children
- Baking homemade bread (Is there a more tantalizing bouquet?)
- The gentle, restful cascade of warm spring rain on the rooftop
- Old people smiling, radiantly aglow like human sunsets
- Silently falling snow
- A choir of children singing "Silent Night"
- Church bells rejoicing on Sunday morning
- My wife's special fudge (the non-bulletproof kind)
- The delicious sound of popcorn popping, and how succulent it tastes when buttered

- Holding hands while walking with my wife
- The magic of blossoming spring flowers
- Watching children on their first day of school, poised on the threshold of wonder
- The fragrance of a just-mowed lawn
- The comforting, relaxing, "home sweet home" essence of coffee brewing in the morning
- The magic of Christmas Eve
- Listening to the summertime song of the red-winged blackbird
- Walking barefoot on the beach, feeling the cool, wet sand beneath your feet
- Watching cotton candy clouds lazily puff up a bright blue sky
- The hopeful, peaceful message of Christmas
- Looking at stars with childlike wonder
- The last day of school before summer vacation
- Feeding the ravenous gulls by the lake
- Remembering summer nights, convertibles, and drive-in movies
- Mom's fresh, just-out-of the-oven, homemade apple pie
- Holding your child's hand as you walk with them to school, church, or uptown
- Ice skating on the lagoon at Whiting Park
- Savoring the lakeshore's gymnastics when the wind is up
- Shopping for a Christmas tree with your teenage kids
- Hot summer days
- Remembering fun times as a teenager, setting pins at Whiting Community Center
- Listening to favorite tunes on the radio that make it yesterday once more
- Savoring long ago summer nights when best friends went cruisin' to drive-in restaurants, teasing carhops and collecting souvenirs
- My wedding day

- Crisp, windy fall mornings
- Being there when your children are born
- The way late-afternoon sunlight washes walls with shadows
- People watching
- Winning the Bob Collins/WGN Pop Quiz in 1988
- Quiet, tranquil meditation in the wee small hours of the morning
- Becoming a teacher
- Relaxing under a friendly shade tree on a hot summer afternoon with a serious supply of iced tea
- Being a parent
- Having a front row seat on a screened porch, listening to the late-night sounds of nature's springtime symphony
- Remembering shopping with Mom—groceries and tap shoes
- Being a husband
- Talking with friends
- Having little kids in the house and being their hero (This doesn't last too long, but when they hug you and say, "Thanks, Dad," it doesn't get any better.)
- Remembering the first date with my wife
- Receiving cards and letters from friends
- Remembering Bobby Beach, moonlight, and watching submarine races
- A dazzling sunrise, announcing the dawn of a new day
- Thinking about friends I don't see very often
- Remembering loved ones who have passed on

That's enough for now. I'll save the rest for another time. You can do that with favorite things; they keep their freshness for a long time. Have you looked over your list of favorite things lately?

Promises to Keep:
A Story of Friendship

"Friend" may not be the most popular word in the English language, but it's right up there with mom, dad, family, and love. These words define the substance of human relationships. Early on, we're encouraged to cultivate friendship. As humans, there is a basic need to bond, identify, trust, and share experiences with people outside one's family. Friendship becomes an extension of what and who we are, affecting both the fabric and texture of our life.

People first meet as strangers. But through some delightful emotional process, certain strangers become dear friends. Regardless of age or station in life, seeds of friendship can take root at any time. Children befriend one another at school, forming cooperative relationships during learning tasks and play activities. Such social encounters are refined, embellished, and treasured as one matures.

Emotions and mutual need often play key roles in selecting candidates for friendship. Rarely, however, does one consciously design a plan to become friends. Part of the richness of friendship is its happenstance, its randomness, its pure unpredictability. Some contend a majority of relationships are based on propinquity. Perhaps so, but other factors must be present, in just the right amount and mix, to provide a favorable environment and atmosphere for friendships to grow and flourish.

Nowhere is there more fertile ground for friendship than high school. Within that four-year span, strangers arrive as freshmen, become classmates, and ultimately graduate as lifelong friends. In June 1958, the 85 seniors at Whiting High School prepared for commencement. Then, tragically, less than a week before graduation, one of our classmates unexpectedly suffered a fatal heart attack. He was a decent young man, a beloved classmate, and a good friend. Only moments earlier, at Whiting Park, we teased him about his car and challenged him to play softball at our senior class picnic. He readily accepted; as soon as he dropped off his Dad's car, he'd return.

A short time later, we heard the terrible news. Everything stopped. Like fragile glass dropped on granite, the day shattered. Almost immediately, stunned classmates left the park in small groups, in pairs, and alone.

My walk home was solemn and solitary. Though it was a warm and cloudless May afternoon, I shivered. Nothing seemed real; my shocked senses were numbed. When you're 17, you believe you're invincible. Disease, illness, and death are things that happen to others, not teenagers. Facing the finality of our loss, we knew childhood was over. This tragedy was our wakeup call to adulthood.

A few days before graduation, still deeply affected by the events of the preceding days, I looked up at the star-filled night sky and wondered about life's meaning. I thought about my classmates, all the good times we had shared in high school, and the uncertainty of future days. I recalled moments of friendship, the closeness one felt as a class, and how valuable their gift of friendship had become.

I realized then, what I must do. I promised never to let a day end without offering a prayer for my classmates, asking that heaven's peace, protection, and love be granted to each of them. This promise would be a memorial to our classmate called home in the spring of his life. This promise would be a legacy to friendship.

As the Class of 1958 prepared to graduate that first Wednesday in June, each of us knew we would encounter difficult times as our lives unfolded. A personal decision was made not to dwell on sadness or sorrow; but to make laughter, kindness, and goodness lifelong companions, drawing sustenance and strength from family, faith, and friends.

It has been 48 years since that personal commitment was made under a star-filled sky, and with few exceptions, that promise has been kept. Over the years, difficult and trying times have occasionally interrupted the normal day-to-day tranquility of life; but thanks to heaven's generosity, there has always been more light than shadow. As the years accumulate, one treasures the friendships nurtured over a lifetime even more.

Throughout one's life, the circle of friends grows; so, too, does the commitment. The scope of the promise has expanded to include family, friends, and departed loved ones. Each morning becomes a daily remembrance and appreciation for those who touched my life and willingly presented their gift of friendship. Because of their kindness, there are promises to keep.

Vacuuming the Road of Fame

As the late Andy Warhol once said, "In the future, everyone will be world-famous for 15 minutes." My brief time in the spotlight passed much too quickly to be showcased on any television show or newscast. Instead, I am left with the memories of those fleeting, golden moments from the spring of '82 when I dazzled countless millions during a radio broadcast over a clear-channel station.

Several years ago, the late Bob Collins ("Uncle Bobby") hosted a top-rated show from 7:00 to 9:00 PM on WGN-AM in Chicago. One of the features of his show was "The Tyrone F. Gindleman, Don't-Call-Us-We'll-Call-You Radio Amateur Hour." Listeners were asked to call WGN and audition an act. If selected, they would be called back to perform their audio talent over the airwaves. The chosen contestants were awarded dinner for two at one of Chicago's finest restaurants. All in all a pretty good deal for the "TFGDCUWCYRAH" participants.

My particular talent specialty at the time was playing "God Bless America" using a rubber glove inflated by a vacuum cleaner. Some may wonder why an allegedly sane, college-educated person would jump at the chance to make a nationwide fool of himself on big-time, major-market radio. The answer is quite simple: I'm into cheap thrills! Bob's producer, Mickey, obviously felt the same way, because I was selected as the closing act of the show.

While waiting for my turn to perform, I practiced in the laundry room with glove and vacuum. Several times I encountered what they refer to in radioland as "technical difficulties." Actually, to put it bluntly, rehearsals were a disaster. First, I forgot to switch the Electrolux from intake to output and the machine sucked up my rubber glove—fingers and all. I watched in awe as the vulcanized right hand disappeared down the vortex throat of the wand, lodging in the flexible hose. A stuck rubber glove inside the hose of a running vacuum cleaner makes a strange sound as the machine tries its best to digest it.

It took a while to fish out the mangled glove with a wire coat hanger. Perturbed? A little, but the show had to go on. The second rehearsal was an even bigger fiasco. I remembered to set the machine on blow and, unlike the first time, secured the rubber glove to the wand with duct tape; however, I forgot to punch pinholes in the fingers to release the pressure. Consequently, when I fired up the vacuum, the pink rubber glove inflated too fast. It resembled the business end of an upside-down milk cow with a terrible rash.

Before I could react and hit the off switch, the bloated glove exploded and darn near tore my head off. (I remember asking myself if I really wanted a free dinner this badly.) Remnants of the rubber glove were all over the place. I found the shriveled thumb stuck to the side of the washing machine, like the grotesque remnant of a hitchhiker who got smacked by a speeding Maytag. My professional advice to any amateur who attempts this highly technical stunt: Keep your mouth shut at all times! Having pieces of rubber glove stuck between your teeth is not a pretty sight.

It was less than two minutes to my on-air performance, and I was down to my last pair of rubber gloves. Shrapnel from two pairs of gloves littered the laundry room and back staircase. This was it; no more practice. The curtain was about to rise, and hopefully, so would my rubber glove.

Carefully, I taped a glove to the wand. And just as carefully, I made the precision punctures in the end of each supple latex digit. For reasons only showbiz artists and professional performers will understand, as I envisioned the rubber gauntlet beginning to expand, pulsating gently from the electromagnetic throbbing of the vacuum's powerful motor, I fought the urge to become emotionally involved.

The seconds were ticking down. Over the telephone, I heard the voice of the show's producer say: "You're on!" I listened as Bob Collins offered this introduction: "And now, ladies and gentlemen, we have come to what they call, in France, the piece de resistance, the crème de la crème, and like that. For those of you who speak French, you, of course, know what I'm saying. Ladies and gentlemen, please welcome to the stage and spotlight of the 'Tyrone F. Gindleman, Don't-Call-Us-We'll-Call-You Radio Amateur Hour'—Big Al. Good evening, Al."

"Hello, Uncle Bobby."

"How are you, sir?"

"Strange."

"I can believe that without a whole lot of difficulty. Al, I have been waiting all evening since Mickey told me about the talent you auditioned with. I have been waiting to hear your particular act. Would you care to 'splain to the boys and girls what it is that you do?"

I briefly explained my expertise and outlined the technical procedure required for my performance. I continued to build the suspense. Unable to contain his excitement any longer, Uncle Bobby said, "I can't wait anymore. Al, would you inflate your glove for the audience, please?"

I did. Immediately, the glove inflated and exploded with a 50,000-watt bang!

"Al, what happened?" Collins asked.

I mumbled some clever phrases about a slight problem, apologized, and taped on my last rubber glove. This time I made the finger holes bigger.

"I'm all set, Uncle Bobby. This may sound a little different, though; I've never played the left thumb before."

This time, it worked! With the vacuum motor whining at maximum speed and the bulbous glove fully deployed, I began to manipulate the puffed-up digits with the dexterity of a veteran dairy farmer. The melody got lost somewhere along the way, and instead of "God Bless America," listeners were treated to a screeching rubberized version of "Jingle Bells."

I turned off the vacuum and ended with the stereophonic sound of the deflating glove's whoopee cushion-like flatulence. Through his laughter, Uncle Bobby asked if I had hurt myself. I told him no, but it was enjoyable.

All told, my claim to fame lasted about three minutes. If Mr. Warhol was correct, I still have another 12 minutes coming. Even so, I think I'll take a pass. Being a star is not easy. Three minutes in the limelight was enough for me. I won my free dinner, and I proved to WGN's listeners that I'm much more than just another pretty face.

I'll end with this bit of advice to all of those potential showbiz stars waiting in the wings to take their shot at fame. Rubber gloves do not make good dental floss!

Passages

Captured in the parade of seasons,
We march along,
Following summer's carefree cadence,
Heeding autumn's muted call.
Mingled among lockers and yearbooks,
Friends and faces that make up a life,
Grasping at a forever spring
We know cannot last.
September will offer sweet sadness and song,
Holding off the night.
Sadly, December—
When life's sparkle and melody are forever stilled—
Leaves behind remembered symphonies of human song.
Still, summer is the essence of youth.
The perfume that carries its fragrance
Makes those of us who are ancient,
Believe once again in that magical time of the young.

Laughing Sheep

This is a true story. I must warn you, however, that I make up some of my true stories. Now that I've stated my disclaimer, let me tell you about laughing sheep.

I taught Industrial Arts Metalworking for many years. During the course of instruction, as technical processes and tools were introduced to the class, students would ask questions as to their origin and development. After listening to the same questions over and over again, and sensing a need to supplement the dull, technical information by spicing things up with a little humor, I began fabricating creative tall-tale responses to their queries. One such annual inquiry was the source of steel wool: "Mr. Koch, where does steel wool come from?"

I briefly looked into the beaming face of the student who asked the question. With a straight face, I answered, "Steel wool comes from a special breed of sheep." I saw looks of startled disbelief. I knew I had the full attention of the class. It was time to tell them the "rest of the story."

Once upon a time, many years ago, there was a special breed of sheep that lived in South Dakota. These sheep were raised for their unique wool. Genetically, because of excessively high iron in their system, these sheep produced steel wool. And because this metallic hair resulted in a heavier bodyweight, these sheep required extra special care and tending.

The few sheepherders raising these animals were licensed under federal law. Sworn under oath, they were mandated to protect these sheep from life-threatening hazards and injuries. In short, the farmers had pledged to keep these sheep out of the rain. Should these iron-saturated mutton-munchers get wet, they would, in a matter of minutes, rust to death.

Unfortunately, fate was not kind to these sheep. With the ranchers out of town attending the annual Steel Wool Growers Association meeting in Indianapolis, Indiana, the unexpected happened. Severe thunderstorms deluged the entire countryside. Sadly, the majority of the steel wool-bearing sheep had been left out on the open range unprotected. As sheep after sheep was soaked by the heavy rains, thousands succumbed to Iron Oxide Corrosive Syndrome. Aerial photographs taken after the storm showed pathetic, reddish-brown blotches against the green meadow—the only remaining physical evidence of the now-dissolved flock.

The steel wool industry was nearly wiped out! But as bad as things appeared to be, all was not lost. Luckily, several breeding pairs of steel-wool sheep had survived the storms. Fearing the sheep's possible extinction, the federal government immediately placed the breed on its endangered species list, and took deliberate measures to restore this vitally important livestock.

Subsequent studies by the U.S. Department of Agriculture revealed the surviving sheep suffered from deep depression. (Under the circumstances, it was quite understandable.) The symptoms included cloudy eyes, listlessness, and—forgive me—sheepishness. Although massive doses of a potent iron tonic were administered, the depression was so immobilizing that the sheep couldn't summon enough energy to point north.

As a last resort, sheep scientists recommended a geographical change. They proposed rebuilding the flock by relocating them to a dry, rain-free part of the country. By moving the flock, the scientists hoped that the sheep would overcome their mutton malaise, thriving and breeding to produce enough steel wool to relieve a growing worldwide shortage. A perfect location was found on the southern portion of the West Coast. And like it says in the textbook on American Government, the rest is history.

Not only did the flock thrive and drastically increase its numbers, and not only was the steel wool industry saved from economic ruin, but the sheep overcame their depression. Once the sheep had rid themselves of mutton malaise, they became happy animals. The more time the sheep spent in the hot, dry climate of their new West Coast home, the happier they became. Soon they were laughing: "BA-HA, BA-HA, BA-HA." Hundreds of thousands of happy, laughing sheep could be heard all across the land: "BA-HA, BA-HA, BA-HA."

The nearby residents thought of these gleeful ewes and rams as a good luck sign. Somehow the citizens knew that better times were just around the corner. To recognize their impending good fortune, the city fathers decided to name the land after the laughing sheep. And so they did.

That was a long time ago. Even so, to this day, the land is still known by the name it was given because of the laughing sheep. I know you've heard of this place. It's called "BA-HA," California!

To Protect the Brain

This is a partially true story. You decide which part. There are several important milestones in life. Depending upon one's gender, these episodes either enrich and enhance your life or they leave an indelible, black-and-blue mark right where you live. A select few become nightmares. By age 13, I was thoroughly bruised. In the midst of adolescent evolution, I was terrified by acne, was under constant attack from assorted hormones, owned a mouthful of cavities, and possessed little or no athletic ability. It was with some apprehension, therefore, that I entered the realm of high school freshman in September 1954. But even with this pubescent litany of unwanted biological shenanigans, all was not dark clouds and gloom.

In preparation for this momentous event, my parents had provided me with eight years of Catholic education. During those formative years, I memorized all the questions and answers in the *Baltimore Catechism*, digested a full menu of knuckle sandwiches served up with relish by Sister Bruiser, and learned how to play Bingo in Latin. Most importantly, however, I learned how to protect the most important part of the body—my brain. From first grade on, my mother and father always told me, "Feed your mind, protect your brain. It is the most important part of your body." Again and again, I heard this refrain: "Feed your mind, protect your brain." And so, with this slogan of salvation ringing in my ears, I entered high school.

Things went surprisingly well the first week until that fateful day in gym class. This is the class where you have to put on a baggy gym suit that makes you look like an advertisement for a skeleton convention. It was here, while pondering my image as a living X-ray in gym shoes, that I came upon a giant pothole on the adolescent highway of life—and fell in!

After taking attendance, our gym teacher, Mr. Fitness, gave us this instructional mandate: "Each of you is to have an athletic supporter with you by Monday." Collectively, the class grunted an acknowledgement and we were dismissed to the locker room. Coming from a Catholic grade school where there was no gym class, many of the words and terms I was now hearing were foreign to me. Also, I was too naïve and self-conscious to admit my ignorance by asking questions.

As a way of resolving my cognitive shortcomings, I made the acquaintance of a fellow gym-mate, a public school veteran and street-smart kid nicknamed Stroker. (And no, I'm not going to tell you why they called him Stroker.)

Lucky for me, Stroker didn't live too far from my house, so we were able to walk much of the way home together. "What did you think about today's gym class?" I asked nonchalantly.

"Piece of cake," he replied. Stroker's confidence and self-assurance was enviable. "Where you goin' for your athletic supporter?"

My defense mechanisms were up and working. "Oh, I don't know. Where you goin' for yours?" I learned that technique in parochial grade school when about to get nailed by a nun's guided muscle; answer her question with a question of your own. That always threw them off balance. It was a matter of survival.

Stroker spit on the sidewalk, then spoke. "I think I'll go to Neal Price."

Neal Price was the guy who owned the local Firestone store, a business home to appliances, records, cameras, TVs, and sporting goods. Leave it to Stroker to go to the best. Neil was an excellent choice; he'd make a terrific athletic supporter. I didn't want to be a copycat, so I figured it was up to me to find someone else. As soon as I got home from school, I changed clothes and went uptown.

The only guy I really knew well enough to ask was Dave the druggist. The pressure was on. I had to ask Dave before one of the other guys got to him. I took a deep breath, walked in the drugstore, and casually sat down on a stool in front of the soda fountain where Dave was tending bar. Lucy usually took care of the fountain and Dave the pharmacy, but Lucy was away from the store, so Dave did double duty.

"Give me the usual," I said.

"One small cherry Coke, comin' right up," Dave answered as he pumped in the syrup. "Anything else?"

"Matter of fact, Dave, I need a favor." I tried to act confident and businesslike, but inside I was as nervous as a bride.

"If I can help, kid, sure. What is it?"

"I need you to be my athletic booster for gym class." I spoke rapidly, not knowing for sure if I had used the right words.

"A booster for gym class? Something new—I never heard of such a thing." I didn't realize it at the time, but Dave looked very puzzled.

"I guess so. Coach told us about it today in gym class." I tried to sound as official as I could.

"When do you need me?" Dave asked.

"Monday. I have gym in the afternoon, so could you be there about 1:30?" I took another long draw on my cherry Coke.

"Monday at 1:30. You got it."

Dave had no sooner finished his words before I was off the stool and out the door. I did it! I got my athletic booster on the first try. Stroker went to Neal Price and I corralled Dave the druggist!

In gym class on Monday, we lined up alphabetically and waited as Coach called names and checked something in his grade book. Most of the guys were carrying a little orange box. I had this strange feeling something was wrong, but I couldn't put my finger on it. Suddenly, I heard my name being called.

"Here, sir," I responded.

"Do you have your athletic supporter with you?" asked Mr. Fitness.

"I think so, sir," I replied, frantically looking around. In the far corner of the gymnasium I saw Dave. "Yes, sir, I do." My voice rang with freshman authority.

"Well, show it to me," said our guru of physical fitness.

"He's right over there," I replied.

"Who is?" asked Coach, beginning to sound agitated.

"The athletic supporter, er, booster you told us to have," my voice squeaking like a trapped rodent. At this point, I became aware of snickering and laughter.

The model of Physical Education walked over to where Dave the druggist was standing and said something we couldn't hear. Dave shrugged his shoulders, turned, and left the gym. I could sense a storm brewing. Coach aimed his fiery eyes toward me and bellowed, "COME OVER HERE!"

I started to shake. "Yesssssir?"

He moved over to an old canvas duffel bag lying on the gym floor. Shifting to one side, and with one large sweeping motion of his massive hairy right arm, reached down and opened the drawstrings. Immediately I detected a gamy odor reminiscent of a fungus that had become good friends with my feet a year earlier. He plunged his hand deep inside and after a brief, Braille-like search, pulled out the most grotesque-looking piece of rubberized fabric I'd ever seen. Throwing it at me, he screamed: "You have less than two minutes to get into the locker room, put this on, and get back here in line! Do you understand?" He was livid.

"Understand," I lied.

"Hold it, genius," he barked. "Do you know how to put that on?"

"Nnnoooooo, sir, not exactly." I was near panic, and wanted to disappear.

"That protects the most important part of your body, Tarzan—the most important part of your body!" By now his veins were an inch outside his neck, and he was purple with rage as he roared and passed gas at the same time.

It was at that moment that I remembered what I had been taught all those years about protecting my brain. I ran to the locker room at the speed of light. Working in frenzy against the time limit imposed by the bellowing gasbag in gym shoes, I struggled frantically trying to get my arms through those small openings. With a final slingshot snap, I forced my arms through, adjusted the remaining fabric on top my head, and got that sucker on. I flew up the stairs and made it in line with only seconds to spare. Proudly, I stood before the class with my brain fully protected.

I heard the alarm go off. I awoke sweating, shaking, heart pounding. Sitting up, I felt the top of my head to prove it was only a nightmare. Bedclothes were tossed and tangled, and I couldn't find my pillow. On my dresser was the small orange box that contained my athletic supporter. It was Monday. I had to get ready for school—and gym class.

Travelin' Old 63

For the better part of my undergraduate years, from September 1964 to June 1968, I drove the highways between Whiting and the Terre Haute campus of Indiana State University. Returning home each weekend to work as a laborer at Inland Steel, I became quite familiar with the roadways and byways along the route. As soon as class ended on Friday afternoon, I'd fire up my '62 Oldsmobile Starfire and head for home.

These were the years before four-lane interstates and limited-access superhighways allowed for smooth, nonstop travel. As it was, the two-lane roadway wound its way like an undulating, free-flowing ribbon of asphalt, impeding motorists with sharp curves, hilly terrain, and an occasional pothole. Passing was permitted in limited designated zones, and drivers often found themselves bringing up the rear in a semi-truck conga line of traffic. When inclement weather and seasonal changes were brought to bear, motorists had to exercise extra caution and reduce speed, adding stress and time to their journey.

The routes available to Terre Haute were limited. U.S. 41 was the roadway of choice, heading south from Hammond to Kentland. It offered four-lane efficiency, if one discounted the more than 40 signal lights and the congestion of urbanized industrial traffic. Just south of Kentland, U.S. 41 resumed two-lane status, winding through places like Earl Park, Boswell, and Attica. About six miles south of Boswell, at Carbondale, Indiana, State Road 63 begins westward. Like U.S. 41, Indiana 63 was an asphalt two-lane road. But unlike its more popular neighbor, Old 63 had much less traffic, fewer trucks, and bypassed many of the small towns that bordered U.S. 41.

Less than a month of driving back and forth to Terre Haute had my patience wearing thin. I mentioned this to my former high school Machine Shop teacher, George McClure (an alumnus of Indiana State and native of Clinton, Indiana), who suggested I give Route 63 a try. I felt like the traveler in Robert Frost's "The Road Not Taken": 'Two roads diverged in a wood, and I—I took the one less traveled by, and that has made all the difference.'

My first experience driving on Old 63 was a trip home in early October. Conditioned to the frantic pace of U.S. 41, this road offered a tranquil, unhurried journey. Crossing the well-worn wooden bridge over the Wabash River into Clinton, Old 63 served as the town's main street, and afforded motorists a leisurely view of local merchants. The municipal tour ended at the graveyard on the city's outskirts.

Unfamiliar names and highway markers would soon become as well known as my hometown communities: rural metropolises named Hillside, Montezuma, Newport, Cayuga, Perryville, Jessie, Covington, and West Lebanon; intersections of U.S. 35, Indiana 71, 234, 32, U.S. 136, and a final crossroads at Indiana Route 28, before Old 63 ended by merging with U.S. 41.

Cruising along, windows down, the sights and rural autumnal fragrances blended with melodies from the radio. The late summer sun, generous with its warmth, washed the countryside with color and shadow as road and driver ducked in and out of areas shaded by verdant forest. To a city guy accustomed to industrial landscapes, the unfolding rural panorama was exhilarating!

Past the gravel runways of the Clinton Airport to where U.S. 36 intersected with Old 63, a short section of divided highway led to Newport. Driving down the steep hill just past Newport, the highway unrolled like an arrow-straight ribbon, bordered on either side by harvested cornfields. Off in the distance, a lone deer dined on remnants. Nearly hidden from view, a rustic covered bridge beckoned travelers to investigate a quiet country road.

In those days, Old 63 undulated like a benevolent roller coaster. Like a child who couldn't make up his mind, the road narrowed and widened, forcing a driver's common sense to kick-in and reduce speed. Mile upon mile of fence line disciplined fields and encouraged livestock to keep off the road, out of harm's way.

Once past the S-curved intersection near Covington, Old 63 wound its way along the rim of an ancient floodplain, making its way toward West Lebanon. An occasional cabin fronted the roadside and farms dotted the landscape. At one small weathered wooden house, an elderly man eagerly waved to me as I rolled past. Dressed in overalls, he watched traffic while relaxing on his open porch swing. I always waved back.

Over the next several years, I took the opportunity to stop at country stores, rural diners, and roadside service stations. During those brief visits, stories and tidbits about life would be shared with storekeepers, waitresses, and gas station operators. Some made lasting impressions while others have dissolved like watercolors in the rain.

I think often about the old railroader who sat on a wooden crate near the corner of the fence line just outside Newport. The closest building was several hundred yards away, yet he'd walk across the grassy fields to be alone and watch passing traffic. He always waved hello. I always greeted him with a wave and a smile. I recall, too, young children on a playground next to an old red brick schoolhouse in West Lebanon and the shuttered public library a few doors away. That scene conveyed a melancholy ache and unexplainable sadness.

I would travel Old 63 in all seasons, at all times of day and night, alone or with companions traveling to and from school. Each journey added to the richness of life. Old 63 was gradually replaced by a new four-lane highway, which opened during my junior year in college. It provided a safer, more direct route to Terre Haute and relieved much of the strain from U.S. 41. Old 63 was left to the locals and motorists not hurried in their travels.

As much as I welcomed progress, the new roadway lacked the character and charm offered by Old 63. I continued my travels using the new highway, thankful for its convenience, but like the traveler in Frost's poem, I occasionally returned to "the one less traveled by, and that has made all the difference."

Somethin' About This Time of Year

Every year about this time, he recalls when the magic began. Though the date is not noted prominently on any calendar, September 24 is special. In fact, until 1960 it was just another ordinary early autumn day. Then all that changed. The day dawned disguised as summer, offering warm abundant sunshine, wispy white clouds, azure skies, and a benevolent breeze that coaxed verdant leaves through a light workout. Without question, this late September Saturday was a picture-perfect, top-down, radio-blasting, good-time day.

In 1960, he was 19, starting his third year of apprenticeship in the steel mill. Apprentices were usually scheduled to work Saturdays—either days or 4:00 to 12:00. That Saturday, however, he wasn't scheduled. Now he can't recall what particular ploy he used to get off; even he'd lost track.

A few days earlier, he'd been summoned to the foreman's office to explain how his grandmother had died on three different occasions—all Saturdays! He fumbled through a story about having three sickly grandmothers, trying to convince his boss. But by now his supervisors were well aware of his aversion to working on Saturday. Once in a while he'd work a day shift, but 4:00 to 12:00? Never! His philosophy about working Saturday was quite simple: He'd only be 19 once, and intended to enjoy as much of it as he could, especially weekends.

What encouraged this free-spirited attitude was the acquisition of a new car. Late in June, he had purchased a 1960 Oldsmobile 98 convertible, ebony with a white top. Thereafter, at every opportunity, he'd go cruisin' with the top down and the radio's volume up!

It became his regular routine to meet the guys after work and make the rounds of local drive-in restaurants, checking out the street sleds, carhops, and occasionally, the menu. One particular teenage oasis, the Pow-Wow in Hessville, Indiana, caught his favor. Besides enjoying the best-tasting tomato burgers in the Calumet Region, he also took a liking to one of the carhops. Each time he arrived, he'd circle around and park in her assigned section. There he waited for her to take his order, while bands of flashing pink neon light danced upon the mirror-like ebony of the ragtop. Entertainment was courtesy of Top 40 radio. All these years later,

352

he still knows the words to "Alley-Oop," "Good Timin'," "Only The Lonely," and "Image Of A Girl."

After almost a summer of informal, across-the-serving-tray small talk, he finally found the courage and asked her out. By now he knew she was a senior at Morton High School, had met some of her friends, shared family stories, and generally enjoyed each other's company. Their "date" was actually an agreement to meet at Morton's homecoming football game and watch the game together. She was one of the Homecoming Queen Attendants, and would ride to the game on one of the floats. He was skeptical about the arrangement, but agreed to meet at the field.

On Saturday, September 24, 1960, Hammond Morton hosted Fort Wayne South Side at Hammond High's football field. True to her word, she was there. They watched the game, talked, and shared popcorn and Coca-Cola. Mostly they looked at each other. Afterwards, they feasted on cheeseburgers and fries from Fat Boy Drive-In. (He still contends Fat Boy had the greatest cheeseburgers and cole-slaw on earth.) They rode around, stopping at the Pow-Wow so she could exchange girl-talk and gossip about the game. Two Pepsis later, they went for another drive and simply talked.

As background to their conversation, Elvis sang "It's Now Or Never." When the King finished, the Drifters asked to "Save The Last Dance For Me," and Ron Holden rounded out the set with "Love You So." They drove through neighbor-hood streets—destination or direction wasn't important. They laughed and talked, and enjoyed the moment. All too soon, it was time to take her home. When the evening ended, he asked if he could see her again. She said yes. Their courtship lasted more than four years. Later, when he asked if he could see her forever, she again said yes. Married more than 40 years ago, the magic continues.

I know this couple very well; they've been through quite a lot together. As a token of friendship, the carhop later gave me her official Pow-Wow menu (S9) and the program from that 1960 homecoming game. Most of all, she gave me her heart, and that's made all the difference in my life.

So go ahead and mark your calendar—September 24. There's somethin' about this time of year. It's when the magic began.

The Final Pow-Wow

Sometimes progress isn't all it's cracked up to be. The other day while on an errand in Hessville, I noticed the Pow-Wow Drive-In had been torn down and replaced by a Kentucky Fried Chicken. During the early '60s, the Pow-Wow was a favorite adolescent oasis where greasers could showcase their street sleds and check out the chicks.

Strategically placed on the property, the white rectangular masonry building afforded young customers the opportunity to circle around before selecting a favorite parking space. Multiple bands of flashing pink neon at the roofline beckoned patrons. Carhops took orders for burgers, soft drinks, and fries, while an overworked jukebox serenaded the Clearasil crowd with the latest hits, providing the soundtrack for what they hoped was an endless summer.

I liked the Pow-Wow. They had the world's best-tasting tomato burger. Countless times after working 4:00 to 12:00 in the steel mill, I'd drive Kennedy Avenue to 169th Street and take a right, homing in on the sight and sound of pink neon and music. Those post-midnight pow-wows still bring fond memories after more than 40 years. Now it's all gone. Progress.

It's difficult to explain, but when I saw that the Pow-Wow was gone, I had the same melancholy ache that I felt when my high school was modernized. It looked good and the exterior fundamentally remained the same, but it's not the school stored in my memory. I remember varnished oak doors, mechanical transoms, tiled hallways, creaky floors, well-worn stairs, traditional classrooms, timeworn desks, familiar faces—everything that was part of my life once-upon-a-time was now changed, gone. Progress.

It's like walking along the main street of your hometown. You look at buildings and remember when so-and-so's drugstore was there or the clothing store where you bought your first suit. An empty lot is all that remains of the barbershop you went to as a kid. Store windows that once showcased televisions and sporting goods now feature items for a new generation. The old teen hangout, home to pinball machines and snooker tables, is now a beauty parlor. Driving down streets where you once lived, remembering people, events, moments.

Gone. Time to move on. Progress. Maybe Tom Wolfe is right: You can't go home again.

Sometimes, I wish it were possible to keep special moments suspended in time and savor them again whenever the mood strikes. So far, in spite of all our technological breakthroughs, we're only able to do that using our heart.

As unsettling as change can be, I suspect it is necessary. We need change in order to have something to look back on. Still, I'm not too sure I like that arrangement. Time passes so quickly and change occurs so fast that one feels left out, unimportant—as if one doesn't belong. You're still in the parade, but out of step.

Like memories, we look to landmarks to reinforce a tangible connection to events that shaped who and what we are. When one of those personal benchmarks is changed or taken away, we feel a loss. One more part of once-upon-a-time is gone. Reluctantly, we adjust and accept change, not quite understanding the melancholy ache visiting the heart.

There is another reason why I will miss the Pow-Wow. It was there, in September 1960, that I met the love of my life. Five years later, the former carhop and steelworker promised to love and honor each other, and live together happily ever after. That was over 40 years ago—so far, so good.

Today when I ride by that hallowed location, I see the familiar KFC logo and color scheme. Colonel Cluck-Cluck doesn't use neon; he has his recipe of secret herbs and spices to entice customers. And everyone knows the kinds of chicks found on the premises so there's no need to circle around and check 'em out. Regular or crispy? I was never asked *that* at the Pow-Wow.

I wonder about the youngsters who are in such a hurry to grow up. Will they have benchmarks memories and moments to remember? Someday they'll be driving around and notice their old school has been torn down, or that the house they lived in as a child is now an insurance office, or that the park where they enjoyed nature is now filled with equipment made from recycled plastic bottles and paved over with shredded rubber tires.

One day, when a new generation is firmly in command, they'll stroll down the main street of their hometown and see unfamiliar faces. Progress. One wonders if they will find treasure in remembering once-upon-a-time moments.

My Favorite Valentine

February is the year's designated love pump. Because of Valentine's Day, the second page of the calendar is typecast. Everything is heart-oriented and Cupid-driven. For a month slighted in days, February packs more opportunity to celebrate affection than all other months combined.

February knows romance. Love-agent Cupid, armed and ready, sits smack-dab-in-the-middle. Like a delicious, intoxicating elixir, Valentine's Day mellows human DNA, encouraging both sexes to demonstrate endearment and love to special someones. Magically, Cupid's spell is more discombobulating than Love Potion No. 9!

Across the country, card and candy shops do land-office business. Jewelry stores and florists deplete inventories as matters of the heart take center stage. Deputized Cupids search out, gift-wrap, and present their expressions of "Be my valentine."

Valentine's Day is official license for burly he-man types to offer tender and heartfelt words without diminished ego or image. For 24 hours, chocolate and sweetness unabashedly ooze.

In grade school, valentines were simple and direct. Cards had silly puns or innocuous phrases, and were casually exchanged among classmates. In high school, valentines took on added importance. Entwined with class rings and going steady, Cupid-dazed couples shared adolescent affection.

Then in what seemed like a moment, Valentine's Day became serious. Here was a day set aside to honor sweethearts, soulmates, and be-mine-forever-afters. Cards, candy, flowers, gifts, kind words, thoughtful deeds, and romantic surprises are showered upon the love of one's life.

I met my favorite valentine more than 45 years ago in September 1960. We've been happily married for over four decades now. What single word best describes my lifelong valentine? Adorable! This past Valentine's Day, our local newspaper, *The Times*, offered to print "Valentine's Day Love Lines" as a way to share senti-

ments with someone special. They were published on February 14. My contribution was as follows:

Suzanne:
More than 45 years ago, I looked into
Your eyes and saw the rest of my life.
Thanks for teaching me how to see
With my heart, and for putting magic
In all my days.
Love,
Al

Love

Of all the words available to convey heartfelt thoughts and feelings, no word is employed more extensively than the word "love." It takes on universal importance, as people everywhere express endearment, affection, and thoughtfulness. This single word contains a treasury of emotional meanings. Available in both genuine and generic forms, love is the equalizer, the conqueror—the essence of who we are. Love nourishes the mind, softens the heart, and enlightens the soul. The amount of love we give to others defines our character. The quantity of love we receive validates our importance to one another. Love is the standard by which life's worth is measured.

Each life is a gift of supreme love. Like a fragile exotic flower, love must be nurtured, cultivated, and cared for. If love is shared, it blossoms into bouquets, embellishing all who give and receive.

Love is both question and answer. Love is truth. It is the subject of stories and songs. Thoughts and topics about love fill television and movie screens, books, publications, photographs, and paintings. Love's appeal is worldwide, affecting one and all. More ancient than Ecclesiastes, as modern as today, love is an equal opportunity employer. One size fits all. As lyrics from a popular tune states, "Love Is All We Need." However, a follow-up question might be "What is love?" Relax, this is a take-home exam—and the answers are many.

Love is happiness—inside, outside, and all around. Love is warm summer days and crystal cold winters. Love is songbirds celebrating spring. Love is a harvest moon and cool autumn nights. Love is holding hands and joining hearts. Love is laughter and friendship. Love is "Welcome" and "Thank You" and all words in between. Love is a hug from someone special. Love is a cozy fire, a gentle rain, and the quiet of early morning. Love is commitment, honor, and trust—shared together as one—in a happily-ever-after-marriage.

Love is caring for the afflicted. Love is overlooking imperfections and flaws in others. Love is forgiveness. Love is laughter and tears, good times and not-so-good times. Love is valentines drawn by a child. Love is saying bedtime prayers with your children and then kissing them goodnight.

Love is worshiping on Sunday, Saturday, or any day of the week. Love is helping those who are in need. Love is kind words attached to a smile. Love is teaching and helping others to become. Love is being honest, dependable, consistent, and fair. Love is without pretense—a cup of human kindness served willingly at anytime. Love is family. Love is remembering loved ones and friends who have passed on. Love is goodness, decency, and understanding. Love is being given another chance to do better. Love is making amends. Love is healing.

Love is thanksgiving for favors great and small. Love is remembrance of those who touched your life in a special way. Love is keeping one's word—no matter what! Love is sacrifice, hard work, and dedication to duty. Love is a night sky sprinkled with stars. Love is making others feel important. Love is helping children grow, learn, and live. Love is faith in each other.

Love is something to fall in and out of. Love is something to live and die for. Love is justification for doing some pretty stupid things. Love is the reason to act romantic without being embarrassed. Love is the heart's welcome mat. Love is Christmas and presents under the tree. Love is what warms the keepsakes of life. Love is home. Love is melancholy and memories of days gone by. Love is having someone believe in you.

Love is the laughter of children. Love is the glow of grandparents holding their grandchildren. Love is parents who put their children first, and work and sacrifice so their kids will have it better. Love is what keeps the devil miserable. Love comes prepackaged from heaven in all shapes and sizes. Love is exercise for the spirit. Love is a verb of life. Love is the poetry of our values, the melody of our beliefs, and the symphony of our soul. Love is moments to remember. Love is God, and God is Love—all in all, a pretty good deal. Love is something you never want to be out of. Love is the gift that keeps on giving. Love is part of everyone's favorite triangle: I Love You!

978-0-595-39788-4
0-595-39788-3